SUPPORTING TUNNELLING OPERATIONS
IN THE GREAT WAR

SUPPORTING TUNNELLING OPERATIONS
IN THE GREAT WAR

THE ALPHABET COMPANY

DAMIEN FINLAYSON

Pen & Sword
MILITARY

AN IMPRINT OF PEN & SWORD BOOKS LTD.
YORKSHIRE – PHILADELPHIA

First published in Australia in 2017 by Big Sky Publishing Pty Ltd as *The Lightning Keepers: The AIF's Alphabet Company in the Great War*

First published in Great Britain in 2018 by

Pen & Sword Military

An imprint of

Pen & Sword Books Ltd

Yorkshire - Philadelphia

ISBN 978 1 52674 018 2

A CIP catalogue record for this book is available from the British Library.

Printed and bound in England by CPI Group Ltd, Croydon, CR0 4YY

Pen & Sword Books Ltd incorporates the Imprints of Pen & Sword Books Archaeology, Atlas, Aviation, Battleground, Discovery, Family History, History, Maritime, Military, Naval, Politics, Railways, Select, Transport, True Crime, Fiction, Frontline Books, Leo Cooper, Praetorian Press, Seaforth Publishing, Wharncliffe and White Owl.

For a complete list of Pen & Sword titles please contact

PEN & SWORD BOOKS LIMITED

47 Church Street, Barnsley, South Yorkshire, S70 2AS, England

E-mail: enquiries@pen-and-sword.co.uk

Website: www.pen-and-sword.co.uk

or

PEN AND SWORD BOOKS

1950 Lawrence Rd, Havertown, PA 19083, USA

E-mail: Uspen-and-sword@casematepublishers.com

Website: www.penandswordbooks.com

CONTENTS

ACKNOWLEDGEMENTS

As this book is the collective product of many hands and minds, I find the acknowledgements section the most difficult to write. Where do I start? Can I be sure I haven't omitted an individual whose material or psychological support is, like that of many others, woven into the background throughout these pages? I hope I acknowledge everyone but, if I leave anyone out, *mea culpa*, please forgive me!

I must start with my wonderful life partner Sacha, who suffered my first book with grit and determination at a time when babies began appearing and houses and careers were being simultaneously consolidated. I did say back then that I would try not to write another one. It's now obvious that my efforts in that respect failed. However, Sacha has stuck by me and endured lonely hours as I have written this book and, for that dedication and understanding, she has my eternal gratitude.

Once again I'm so very grateful to the team at the Australian Army History Unit and Dr Andrew Richardson in particular. Andrew accepted the manuscript for this book in blind faith having taken an earlier, more daring leap with *Crumps & Camouflets*. Thank you also to Denny Neave and the team at Big Sky Publishing who took it from Andrew, polished it, wrapped a sturdy cover around it and set it free. Cathy McCullagh, my wonderful editor on *Crumps*, once again took a shoddy manuscript and did most of the hard work chipping, nay hacking, the rough edges from every chapter. My thanks to Cathy for taking on and completing another monumental task.

It goes without saying that this book would not have seen the light of day if not for the sheer tenacity and drive of Ian Morse, the grandson of the Alphabet Company's commanding officer, Richard (Victor) Morse, DSO. The Alphabet Company's unique difficulty was that its war diary, the detailed record of a unit's service in the field of conflict, was destroyed at the very end of the war. Ian not only handed over the makeshift war diary, written from memory by his grandfather prior to his repatriation to Australia, but also provided a wealth of personal photos and, most importantly, a copy of all the letters his grandfather wrote to his grandmother during the time Victor was in France. A number of quotes from the letters populate this book and it was only through the letters that glimpses of daily life in the unit were revealed. They made all the difference and breathed humanity into what had previously been an aspirational idea. I hope Ian considers that his trust in my using such personal information was justified.

There have been numerous people spread across various archival institutions whose assistance has facilitated the production of this book. They include but are not limited to: Lisa Olrihs (Imperial War Museum), Gord Beck (Mills Library, McMaster University), Andrew Currey and Alyssa Phabmixay (Australian War Memorial), Peter Donnelly (King's Own Royal Regiment Museum) and the team at the Australian National Archives.

Mike Jackson, a fellow member of the Western Front Association, who had no vested interest in this book, spent many hours in the British National Archives on my behalf photographing what will have seemed endless pages from a folder containing hand-drawn and coloured geological borehole logs. Words cannot convey my gratitude for this extraordinary act of kindness and I would like to acknowledge the valuable support that Mike's selfless dedication provided. I would also like to acknowledge Phillip Robinson and the team in the Durand Group who have a mutual interest in tunnelling activities in and around Loos and Vimy Ridge. We have assisted each other where we can and the Durand Group's generous contributions have made their way into this book. John Reading from the Australian Tunnellers Research website also provided images and input into the nominal roll which appears as the appendix. My thanks to these people and the members who support their organisations because, without them, the task of researchers and writers would be immeasurably more difficult and time consuming.

Damien Finlayson

PREFACE

My dear Morse,

This is only a line to congratulate you and your Company very heartily upon the special mention which has been made of the good work in the C-in-C's Order of the Day of 4ᵗʰ December. You must, I'm sure be extremely proud of this, for as far as I can remember it is one of the very few occasions upon which a Company has been specially selected for such a distinction ...

These simple lines, from a letter dated 11 December 1918, belie the significance of the achievements to which they allude and the three men at their centre. The letter was penned by Lieutenant General Sir William Birdwood, KCB, KCSI, KCMG, KBE, CIE, DSO, former General Officer Commanding I Anzac Corps and a man who endeared himself to many Australian soldiers in the First World War. At the time of writing, Birdwood had just relinquished command of the British Fifth Army on the Western Front.

The abbreviated form 'C-in-C' refers to the Commander-in-Chief, Field Marshal Sir Douglas Haig, KT, GCB, GCVO, KCIE, who commanded all British forces on the Western Front, at that time just under two million men. The letter's recipient was Major Richard Victor Morse, DSO, known to all as Victor, and the commanding officer of the Australian Electrical and Mechanical Mining and Boring Company. The number of men under his command at the time amounted to some 260.

During World War I, Field Marshal Haig's Special Orders of the Day were roughly equivalent to the posting of blogs on social media internet sites today. They represented a means of publically communicating important messages to a large number of people through a single portal. On 4 December 1918, less than a month after the cessation of hostilities that marked the end of the First World War, Haig published a Special Order in which he expressed his thanks to all the men associated with the work of the tunnelling companies for their contribution to the Allied victory. By war's end, a total of 25 British, three Canadian, one New Zealand and three Australian tunnelling companies had served across the entire Western Front. At full strength, each company boasted on average around 600 men, the total number of tunnellers in the British Expeditionary Force (BEF) amounting to just over 19,000. There were also many thousands who had passed through the ranks of the companies and had been repatriated due to wounds they had suffered or illnesses contracted in the course of their duties. By 4 December 1918 several thousand more were no longer alive to hear the Special Order read to them by their commanding office. These were the men who had been killed or who had died on active service with the tunnelling companies. Of these, 340 were Australian.

Haig concludes his Special Order with the sentence: 'I should like to include in the appreciation the work done by the Army Mine Schools and by the Australian Electrical and Mechanical Mining and Boring Company.' As Birdwood remarks, what makes this declaration so memorable is the fact that individual units were rarely singled out. So why was the Australian Electrical and Mechanical Mining and Boring Company specifically mentioned? The reason is simple: it was a unique unit in the BEF. It was also a unit whose influence far exceeded the meagre size of its workforce. It was one of the quiet achievers of the Western Front, without whose efforts the living conditions of the men in front-line positions throughout the British sector would have been even more appalling than history records. Indeed the success of many of the Allied tunnelling companies on the Western Front was due, at least in part, to the crucial but largely unsung services provided by this unit.

The story of the three Australian tunnelling companies following the disbandment of the Australian Mining Corps on the Western Front in May 1916 is told in *Crumps and Camouflets*, the seminal history of Australian tunnelling and mining in the First World War. *Crumps and Camouflets* also mentions a smaller sibling unit to the tunnelling companies, likewise born of the demise of the Mining Corps. The story of this unit was lost, scattered and blurred even more comprehensively than that of the tunnellers, so much so that it was impossible to include a full description of its history in *Crumps and Camouflets*. Now, some years later, *The Lightning Keepers* sets out to redress that omission, focusing purely on the exploits and achievements of the Australian Electrical and Mechanical Mining and Boring Company, the story of the men who filled the unit's ranks, their methods, equipment and the extraordinary grit they displayed in performing some of the most unpleasant and difficult tasks in a war noted for the dreadful conditions in which it was waged.

Any history of the Australian Electrical and Mechanical Mining and Boring Company must necessarily begin with the inevitable abbreviation of the unit's unwieldy name. Australians are famously skillful at abbreviating and reinventing names and this unit presented an excellent opportunity to put such skills to the test. Even its acronym, AE&MM&B Coy, proved too cumbersome for most and, by late 1916, some bright spark, no doubt nonplussed by the jumble of letters, devised the nickname 'the Alphabetical [or Alphabet] Company' which immediately stuck, at least in unofficial circles.

The Lightning Keepers is the story of the 'Alphabeticals', the men of the Alphabet Company who, under the command of Major Victor Morse, DSO, operated and maintained pumps, generators, ventilation fans, drilling equipment and other rather more ingenious devices in extreme circumstances, many of which could never have been imagined by their manufacturers. While not formally established as the Australian Electrical and Mechanical Mining and Boring Company until October 1916, for the sake of simplicity the unit will be referred to as the Alphabet Company from the time of its arrival in France in May 1916.

It is not difficult to understand why the Alphabet Company has been overlooked for the past century. It was numerically one of the smallest Australian units of the First World War, with just some 260 souls at full strength. It was established on the battlefield and was therefore largely unknown to the military establishment in Australia and certainly to the general public. Much of the work in which it was engaged was designed to support front-line tunnelling activities, which were generally secret undertakings. Most importantly however, the vast bulk of records relating to the unit diary, which all BEF units were required to maintain, were destroyed in a fire just months before they were due to be handed to the War Office. While a unit history was hastily typed up by the company's commander, Major Victor Morse, based on his recollections and the remnants of records salvaged from the fire, the level of detail that characterises this 'history' is minimal in comparison to the amount of information that would otherwise have been available to historians. So, for all intents and purposes, the Alphabet Company and the Alphabeticals have drifted through history known only to fellow veterans of the war through first-hand contact or experience.

Yet, while small in size and not particularly well known, the Alphabet Company's area of operations in the British sector of the Western Front was enormous. It arrived in France with 13 electric generating sets, underground ventilation and water-pumping equipment, almost 40 portable drilling machines and large, steam-powered drilling machines. Given the conditions in which the troops lived and fought, this equipment was desperately needed, as were the men who operated and maintained it under the same, often horrendous conditions. As their work was increasingly prized, more and more equipment was purchased and more men trained in its operation, their workplaces frequently hot, cramped, smelly little dugouts, cellars or roughly constructed lean-tos.

Despite the critical loss of records and the passing of a century, effectively preventing a faithful and detailed account of all the works and all the places in which the unit operated during its time in France and Belgium, it is possible to describe the typical work of the unit based on the remaining records. While the emphasis of this volume is necessarily on some of the better known battlefields of the Western Front, much of what is portrayed in *The Lightning Keepers* is new to the landscape of Australian military history and will come as a revelation to many scholars of this period. In this way, this book seeks to do justice to the work of the dynamic little unit that was the Alphabet Company and the men who were the lightning keepers.

CHAPTER 1

THE AUSTRALIAN MINING CORPS

The Alphabet Company's story begins with the raising of the Australian Mining Corps, just one element of Australia's response to the outbreak of war in Europe in 1914. On 28 June, the assassination of Archduke Franz Ferdinand of Austria and his wife Sophie in Sarajevo became the catalyst for a series of events that culminated in a spectacular and catastrophic collapse in European harmony in which one of the opening acts was the invasion of Belgium by German forces. Plans for such an invasion had, in fact, been prepared years in advance by the German high command. Germany was the lead player in the Triple Alliance, an alliance between Germany, Austria-Hungary and Italy. The counter-alliance, known as the Entente, comprised the empires of Great Britain, France and Russia. The German 'Schlieffen Plan' had been carefully formulated in the dawning days of the twentieth century. In the event of a continental war, the Germans planned to overthrow France through the rapid encirclement and capture of Paris before turning their attention to the east to deal with Russia. The fundamental premise for the plan was swift, open and mobile warfare which would see German forces sweeping down through a violation of neutral Belgium and into northern France. On 31 July, Russia was the first of the Entente powers to mobilise its armies against Austria-Hungary which, three days earlier, had declared war on Serbia. Germany, as the primary supporter of Austria-Hungary, had little choice but to assist its ally and implemented the Schlieffen Plan. This sparked a domino effect and Europe suddenly found itself in the throes of a war that quickly infected other parts of the globe.

Once enacted however, the plan was only a partial success. Its Achilles' heel soon became evident in the security of supply lines and the unexpectedly dogged resistance of the Belgians, French and the hastily marshalled British Expeditionary Force (BEF). By the second week of September 1914, just one month after the declaration of war, the momentum of the initial German thrust had been lost and the advance to Paris was halted at the Battle of the Marne. The Schlieffen Plan collapsed and the war, like most wars, descended into a huge and deadly guessing game.

After a desperate northward 'race for the sea', both sides dug in, resolving to defend every inch of hard-won ground. A war of stagnation commenced and with it what became known as 'trench warfare'. This lethal stalemate was to last for the next three and a half years and plunge the lives of millions of men on both sides, and millions more civilians who remained on the fringes of the killing zones, into a nightmarish existence.

The stagnation that typified trench warfare was not the result of a lack of progress in the science of warfare — quite the reverse, in fact. The evolution of military technology in the first decade of the twentieth century was nothing short of phenomenal compared to the relative hiatus that had gripped the preceding century. British military tactics and equipment varied little between the Battle of Waterloo in 1815 and the fall of Sebastopol in the Crimean War, 40 years later. Possibly the greatest advance of the nineteenth century was the rifling of gun barrels that allowed projectiles to be fired in a straight line, dramatically improving the likelihood of actually hitting an opponent.

As the end of the nineteenth century approached, developments in science and technology stemming from the industrial revolution drove the pace of technological change. The powerful industrial countries of Western Europe relied on their technological supremacy to either advance or maintain their imperial aspirations and, as is the case today, advances in science and industry were harnessed by the superpowers of the day to maintain their military supremacy.

The power of the newly developed technology and the modern tactics of warfare were certainly in evidence in the second Boer War of 1899 to 1902, a conflict that was characterised by a marked disparity in firepower between the Boer forces and the British. By contrast, from the onset of the First World War, the lead protagonists were evenly matched in their capacity to develop and execute the latest technologies. The scale of conflict that characterised this war was utterly unprecedented in military history and only a handful of military strategists, including the British Secretary of State for War, Lord Horatio Kitchener, had any inkling of the devastating effects and the tragic consequences of the new technologies now employed by enemies of equal strength. However a mismatch remained between the architects of conflict and the technology at their disposal. As the roar of guns heralded the outbreak of the First World War, the tactics of most military planners were already anachronistic and unsuited to the deployment and use of the increasingly sophisticated resources at their disposal.

The early days of the war quickly produced a stalemate along the Western Front and, as the winter of 1914 descended, the now infamous war of attrition commenced, although its formal adoption as a military strategy was not to occur until later. Immobility, however, was to reap unexpected benefits. As the two sides settled and dug in, the stability of their lines allowed new and innovative strategies to be planned and trialled, sometimes with a high degree of effectiveness. Less successful strategies were also trialled and many proved abject failures, often leading to the waste of valuable life. Some developments were radical in the extreme: centuries of reliance on horsed cavalry ceased almost overnight, replaced by a fortified equivalent — the tank. Other developments that evolved to meet the new challenge of modern trench warfare included the use of creeping barrages of massed artillery of a wide range of calibres to shield advancing ground attacks. The ingenious use of raiding parties was tested and perfected, portable trench mortars and flame-throwers were developed, aerial bombardment was tentatively used with the arrival of fledgling air forces, and the first chemical agents (chlorine and mustard gas) made their appearance — all among a flourish of inventive techniques aimed at breaking the deadlock.

For both sides, however, the dominant factor in the new style of warfare was quickly discovered: the effective use of overwhelming artillery firepower, rapidly recognised as the key to winning the war. The arsenal of artillery that was eventually employed by both sides during the conflict was staggering and ranged in calibre from portable trench mortars to 15-inch railway-mounted naval guns. Both sides realised almost immediately that maximising the efficient use of artillery depended on the ability to view an enemy's positions and thus accurately guide the shells to their targets. This could be achieved by gaining control of the elevated ground overlooking the enemy. High ground therefore became the prized objective so fiercely disputed during the war. At the time the Western Front readied itself for a long campaign in late 1914, the German Army occupied much of the high ground, particularly in the characteristically flat landscape of northern France and Flanders, and this was to play a pivotal role in the strategic use of tunnelling and mining.

It was on the Western Front that an unseen and largely unheard war was waged underground while battles and skirmishes took place on the surface, in the trenches and across no man's land. In that 'war within a war', a dramatic panorama unfolded, largely unknown to the wider military community and to the even more remote outside world. Information passed to families at home in letters or postcards was so heavily censored that it was impossible, even for those closely connected to the hidden combatants, to understand exactly what they were doing or where they were for most of the time. The underground war was waged by British and German miners. These were the 'tunnellers' of the Western Front.

Over a brief three-year period from August 1914 to June 1917, military mining rose from an obscure and uncoordinated ad hoc operation to a sophisticated and systematic form of warfare that has remained unsurpassed since the First World War. The need for miners and mining engineers in the theatre of war was born of the single feature that was unique to the first three years of World War I — immobility.

As the stagnation of trench warfare shaped the campaign that unfolded on the Western Front, commanders and strategists quickly realised that frontal attacks launched against a well-entrenched enemy would almost always result in serious loss of life and equipment. The only reasonable alternative lay in attack from *under* the ground. In many parts of the front, the distance between the opposing trench-lines amounted to less than 100 metres with little prospect of movement on either side. These conditions were perfectly suited to the use of mining as a weapon with which to inflict enormous damage on enemy materiel and manpower and, more insidiously, to drain his morale and create a pervasive state of permanent anxiety.

'Military mining' bore little resemblance to civilian or commercial mining. The mining described in this book refers to the act of placing an explosive device — a 'mine' — below the ground with the intention of destroying enemy personnel or infrastructure. The act of tunnelling was necessary to place the destructive charge below the enemy position. This was the prime reason for the formation of the allied French, British, Australian, Canadian and even Portuguese tunnelling companies. They were formed to counter the German mining threat.

Mining was introduced almost immediately after the front lines on the Western Front crystallised in late 1914 and it was German miners who took the initiative. On 20 December 1914 the first mines of the war were detonated under the British front line outside the village of Festubert. The total charge used in that first subterranean attack was a mere 0.34 tonnes, a tiny amount compared to what would soon become the norm. In spite of the comparatively small charge, the effect on the morale of the soldiers who were the target of the explosions was shattering. The mining war on the Western Front had commenced.

A mining war also developed in other theatres of conflict. After landing on the Gallipoli peninsula in late April 1915, the Australians initiated a protracted program to counter and dominate Turkish mining efforts at Pope's, Quinn's and Courtney's posts, at the head of Monash Gully where front lines were a mere tens of metres apart. The Australian mining experience on the peninsula throughout 1915 was, however, based on ad hoc, improvised units of men selected in the field, using whatever materials they could find. This situation highlighted the need for specialists to undertake this type of military operation. As a consequence, while the latter phases of the Gallipoli campaign were unfolding, officers and men with mining experience were being selected from recruits within Australia to form specially trained and equipped tunnelling companies.

Plate 1. Brigadier General Robert 'Ducky' Napier Harvey, CB, CMG, DSO, Inspector of Mines for the BEF in France. Harvey was responsible for all tunnelling companies in the British sector of the Western Front (photo from Grieve and Newman, *Tunnellers*).

While ultimately successful, the Australian mining strategy at Gallipoli was hampered by limited access to the latest technology. By contrast, military mining on the Western Front evolved into a smoothly run and well-coordinated operation. On 1 January 1916, the War Office approved a request from General Headquarters (GHQ) for the formation of a new staff post: Inspector of Mines. This post would place supreme command and coordination of all British mining operations on the Western Front under the leadership of one man. Colonel Robert Napier Harvey of the Royal Engineers and formerly the aide to Brigadier

General George Fowke, the then Commander of the Royal Engineers in France, was appointed Inspector of Mines for the BEF and promoted to the rank of brigadier general, based at GHQ. Although the post was held by an officer of the Royal Engineers, his chain of command and area of responsibility were largely distinct and separate from typical engineer units.

The BEF was divided into armies. A Controller of Mines was assigned to the staff of each army headquarters and assumed direct control of mining operations within his army area. All tunnelling companies operating within an army area reported directly to its army Controller of Mines.

Both the First and Second armies established their own mine schools. The schools provided basic mining training and refresher courses for the tunnellers as well as specialist courses in mine rescue and the art of listening for enemy counter-mining. Selected officers and sappers from each of the tunnelling companies operating in those army areas were sent for initial training and follow-up revision in a range of specialist military mining skills. They were also put through an intense physical training regime. The First Army Mine School was based at Houchin, south-west of Béthune, while the Second Army Mine School was located at Proven, north-west of Ypres.

Tannatt William Edgeworth David

The formation of an operational military unit which concentrated the skills of the Australian mining fraternity was largely due to the efforts of a world-renowned professor of geology from Sydney University. Tannatt William Edgeworth David, or Edgeworth David as he was more commonly known, is considered the founding father of the Australian Mining Corps and, by association, the unit that is the subject of this story, the Australian Electrical and Mechanical Mining and Boring Company. The Australian tunnellers held Edgeworth David in the same high regard as the British tunnelling companies reserved for their legendary founder, the British engineering powerhouse John Norton-Griffiths.

Edgeworth David was born in Wales on 28 January 1858 and was, by any measure, a remarkable individual. He was an habitual adventurer and campaigner who cherished a constant desire to be in the thick of the action. He arrived in Australia in 1882 and, soon after, discovered and mapped the Maitland coalfield while working as a geological surveyor with the New South Wales (NSW) government. He was appointed Professor of Geology and Physical Geography at the University of Sydney in 1891 and, by 1896, had risen to be the President of the Royal Society of NSW. By the turn of the twentieth century he had built an enviable reputation in senior government and academic circles within Australia.

Edgeworth David was eager to use his social standing and professional profile to further the cause of science and exploration. From 1906 to 1907 he used his influence with the Australian government to raise badly needed funds for Ernest Shackleton's 1907–09 Antarctic expedition. Not content with having secured funding for the expedition, Edgeworth David — by then a sprightly 50 years old with a slight, almost frail stature — also secured himself a place on the expedition as the head of scientific staff.

Plate 2. Portrait of Major (later Lieutenant Colonel) Tannatt William Edgeworth David, CMG, taken on 16 February 1916, four days prior to his departure from Sydney aboard the HMAT *Ulysses* as Senior Technical Adviser to the Australian Mining Corps (AWM P01017.001).

Having been created a Companion of the Order of St Michael and St George in 1910 following his return to Australia, and never one for resting on his laurels, Edgeworth David soon forged ahead with his next visionary scheme.

In 1911 he became closely involved with preparations and fundraising for his young friend Douglas Mawson's epic Antarctic expedition. This time however, the hardy adventurer did not undertake the journey himself. Instead, just three years later, when Europe erupted into war, Edgeworth David prepared himself for a journey of a different kind. The First World War adventure would prove too tempting for the seasoned campaigner to resist.

In spite of his age, Edgeworth David was determined to be actively involved in the war and was also fervent in his support for Australia's commitment to the conflict. At the outbreak of war he held the position of NSW Branch President of the Universal Service League. The League was an influential body and listed a number of powerful Australians among its more prominent members, including the Anglican Archbishop of Sydney, Dr John Wright, and the former Premier of NSW, Sir Joseph Carruthers. One of the society's prime objectives was to:

> … advocate the adoption for the period of the present war, the principle of universal compulsory war service, whether at home or abroad; and to support the Government in producing at the earliest possible moment such organisation as is necessary to secure wise and just application of this principle.[1]

While still a fledgling nation in 1914, Australia had already profited from over 60 years of large-scale mining operations equal to anywhere else in the world; indeed mining had provided significant ballast for the young country's economy. Australia was rich in both minerals and the men experienced in extracting these precious resources. By 1915, reports describing the critical role of tunnelling on the Gallipoli peninsula and the mining operations undertaken by both sides in France were being carefully studied in Australia. Such reports set the formidable minds of Edgeworth David and his counterpart at the University of Melbourne, Professor Ernest Skeats, to work.[2] It was not a vast leap of imagination for men well versed in the sciences of geology and mining to recognise the value of applying such skills to an Australian contribution to the war. Given the spirit of patriotism that gripped Australia in the months immediately following the Gallipoli landing, the proposal that Australia provide its own military mining companies was quickly appreciated and encouraged.

In August 1915 the professors made a submission to the Minister for Defence, Senator George Pearce, proposing the formation of a unit whose specific purpose would be military mining and tunnelling. The proposal was duly accepted and, on 9 September 1915, Senator Pearce sent a cable to the

British Secretary of State for the Colonies, Andrew Bonar Law, offering the services of an Australian Mining Corps:

> In view of the Commonwealth's exceptional resources in expert miners, mining engineers and machinery this government is prepared to organize at once and dispatch at an early date a Mining Corps numbering up to 1,000 for service in the Dardanelles or elsewhere, such Corps to consist of miners skilled in the handling of mining machinery and plant for rapid tunnelling, whether with or without explosives, experienced mining engineers and geologists and fully equipped with all necessary machinery and appliances.[3]

The offer was duly accepted and, although requested to provide units of around 300 men, the size of the tunnelling companies then being formed in Britain, a mining corps comprising three tunnelling companies was envisaged, totalling a slightly larger number of men than specified in the original cable. By the middle of October 1915 details of the proposed Mining Corps had become official and recruitment began in earnest.[4] The Mining Corps officers would comprise mining engineers and surveyors with underground experience, while its non-commissioned officers (NCOs) and sappers would be men experienced in underground work. Due to the specific nature of the work, a number of special conditions applied to the recruitment of miners to fill the ranks of the corps. The age limit was extended from 45 (the age usually applied to the Australian Imperial Force — AIF) to 50 years and soldiers with the desired skills who had already enlisted in the AIF could now transfer to the new unit.

The formation of a Mining Corps afforded Edgeworth David a golden opportunity to put into practice the founding principle of the Universal Service League. Characteristically, he was the driving force behind the recruitment and organisation of the corps and, reminiscent of the Shackleton Expedition, he used his involvement as a means to join the team. On 25 October 1915, at the age of 57, he was commissioned into the corps with the rank of major as the Officer in Charge of the Technical Headquarters Staff.

The corps was effectively established as 'an experiment to overcome exceptional conditions arising from trench warfare on the Western Front'.[5] A committee was formed in each state and nominated officers were authorised to select recruits from miners already enlisted. Miners were formally enlisted at local enlistment stations and, from there, the men were sent to local training camps which also acted as staging camps.

Those recruits with mining engineering qualifications were originally enlisted as reinforcements for the Field Company of Engineers which was a typical engineering support unit for an infantry division. They were then transferred to the newly formed Australian Mining Corps after first attending the Officers' Training School for Engineers at Moore Park in Sydney. The training at Moore Park during those early days was a source of bemusement to many. Much of the field training was spent running, building observation masts of ever-increasing height and learning knot-tying and lashing. As a junior subaltern, Oliver Woodward reminisced that such training 'hardly seemed appropriate' and it challenged his preconceptions of the way an officer should be equipped on the eve of his embarkation for the war in Europe.[6] As junior officers were identified and transferred for service in the Mining Corps, the incongruity of their situation was amplified when they took up residence at the Sydney Cricket Ground, their dormitory under the Members' Stand and their mess in the Members' Dining Room.[7]

In December 1915, the corps was concentrated at its own training camp at Casula near Liverpool on the western outskirts of Sydney. Here candidates were tested for their fitness to undertake tunnelling work and those found unsuitable transferred out. Those who were accepted embarked on a course of training conducted between December 1915 and February 1916. The training school provided more intensive training in military drill and specialist mining work.

The Mining Corps was equipped as a unit of the Australian Corps of Engineers. The colour patch worn on the shoulder and used to signify the wearer's unit was a purple 'T', identifying the wearer as a tunneller. When the companies later separated into individual fighting units, a metal number denoting the company number was worn over the patch. Having arrived in France and before their worth had been proven, the tunnellers' colour patch would evoke ingenious suggestions from the resident troops as to the exact role of the wearer, 'tourist' proving the most popular designation and the one that justifiably attracted the most colourful retorts.

In the heady days of patriotic fervour that gripped Australia in 1915 and into 1916, a steady stream of donations found their way to military units from private individuals and companies. Not all these donations took the form of currency and, foremost among the paraphernalia that arrived at the Australian Mining Corps was the latest model Studebaker car (curiously, minus the tyres) for the use of the officers at Corps Headquarters. The Studebaker was funded by a number of private businesses in Brisbane, Sydney, Melbourne, Adelaide and Perth.

The Australian Mining Corps consisted of a headquarters and three companies and even sported its own band of professional musicians, many of whom were later absorbed into the Alphabet Company. Corps Headquarters comprised 12 officers and 29 other ranks commanded by Lieutenant Colonel Albert Fewtrell, a 30-year-old civil engineer from Drummoyne in Sydney. Prior to enlistment, Fewtrell had been employed by the NSW Railways and also held a regular commission with the Australian Field Engineers which had facilitated his elevation to the position of Commanding Officer (CO).

Plate 3. Australian Mining Corps Band. The officer seated to the left of the drum is Captain Stanley Hunter (image courtesy of R. Nilsson).

Each of the three Mining Corps tunnelling companies consisted of 14 officers and around 370 other ranks. The corps was, in fact, not much larger than a typical infantry battalion and was sometimes referred to as the 'Mining Battalion'. A typical infantry battalion at full strength comprised a headquarters and four companies totalling some 1000 officers and men. Australian tunnelling companies differed from contemporary Australian military units in almost every conceivable way — a fact that was to become a source of considerable pride to the men of the unit.

The first draft of reinforcements for the Australian Mining Corps also assembled in Sydney and consisted of two officers, Lieutenants Reginald Langdon and Hubert Carroll, along with 100 other ranks. By mid-February 1916 the Australian Mining Corps, now comprising 55 officers, 1250 other ranks and associated stores and mining equipment, was ready to depart for the war.

Plate 4. Officers of the Australian Mining Corps, Casula Camp, Sydney, January 1916. Notable officers in the context of this story are: Captain Richard Victor Morse (second row seated, second left), Captain Stanley Hunter (second row seated, fourth left), Major William Tannatt Edgeworth David (second row seated, fifth left) and Lieutenant Colonel Albert Fewtrell (Officer Commanding Australian Mining Corps Headquarters, second row seated, centre). The mascot was a bulldog named Puncher. Six officers in this photograph did not return from the war, while 22 were later decorated. Missing from this photograph are Captain James Shand and Lieutenant William Anderson who embarked with the corps in Sydney and later become members of the Alphabet Company (AWM PR87/108).

British Mining on the Western Front in 1916

By the time the Australian companies arrived in France in May 1916, the mining situation along the Western Front was well established. Mining operations had been conducted by specially formed and dedicated tunnelling companies since February 1915. In the intervening 16 months, the skills of exclusively British tunnelling companies had been employed along the length of the British front. However there were numerous mining 'hotspots' where mining and tunnelling activity had been intense since the early days of 1915. Mining was not conducted continuously along the whole front line, but usually at key strategic positions where the front lines were close and one side or the other had a point of strategic ascendancy such as elevated ground or a 'salient'.

Salients were formed where the front lines deviated from a straight line to form a projection. Where the landscape is flat, a salient provides an advantage to the troops holding the inside of that projection as machine-guns and artillery in the salient can direct a line of fire along and sometimes behind the front lines of the opposing force.

One of the largest salients on the Western Front was the Ypres salient which ran in an extended arc around and to the east of the city of Ypres in north-western Belgium. The British held the Ypres salient while the Germans held the high ground around the salient and were able to look into and across it and direct accurate fire on the British. Many salients were much smaller, extending just a few hundred metres to a kilometre or so in length. Because of the advantage they provided to opposing forces, salients were the targets of fierce fighting in attempts to wrest the advantage from the enemy. The jutting nature of many salients usually meant that the distance between the two front lines was reduced, making them an obvious target for mining activity.

The operations of the British tunnelling companies would eventually cover vast swathes of the British front line during the period of underground warfare that effectively lasted until mid-1917. Mining 'hotspots' such as Hill 60 in the Ypres salient, the Mound, the Bluff (outside the village of St Eloi), the Brickstacks at Cuinchy, Hill 70 outside Lens, and the Hohenzollern Redoubt near Auchy-les-Mines were the first targets for the fledgling tunnelling companies. Over the course of the next two years, those names would become etched in the collective psyche of a multitude of men — tunnellers and infantrymen alike. As more British divisions arrived and occupied more of the Western Front trench lines, the frontage covered by mining operations increased accordingly. Eventually, the full extent of the British sector was covered by the tunnelling companies, from Nieuport Bains (Nieuwpoort Bad) on the Belgian coast to the Somme River in Picardy, France.

To the uninitiated, tunnelling represents the simple act of digging a narrow hole in the ground, often to allow others to crawl through. In reality, however, there was nothing simple about tunnelling. What the tunnellers created in their assigned sectors were complex and elaborate underground systems of connected shafts, inclines, tunnels, drives, chambers, dugouts, subways and posts. The tunnel systems contained medical dressing stations, fully equipped and manned mine rescue stations, dugouts (underground rooms where men could rest and shelter from shellfire), command posts and even infantry subways similar to train subways that allowed large numbers of men to walk below ground in safety, equipped with electric lighting, water-pumping apparatus and ventilation systems.

Where the water table permitted, the mining systems were worked on a number of levels simultaneously. The first level — termed the 'shallow' system — usually lay just below root level, at a depth of three to six metres. The second system occurred at around 15 metres and was usually referred to as the 'fighting' or 'intermediate' system. The deep systems were often sunk to around 30 to 35 metres in depth. Fighting between opposing miners in the multi-level systems usually occurred in the intermediate level where listening was concentrated and camouflets were fired. The deep systems were sunk for the laying of massive quantities of explosives. Most excavations were fully supported and lined with wood, typically Oregon pine, which was supplied in standardised 'sets'. In the chalkier subsoil of the Picardy region around the Somme and up as far as the Béthune coalfields, there was less need to fully line the tunnels and chambers with wood, chalk being less susceptible to collapse than the clay and sand-rich substrata of Flanders.

A number of factors directly influenced the success of military tunnelling and mining operations and, consequently, whether the miners would live or die. It was crucial for the miners to possess a good understanding of the strata through which they were expected to tunnel and a very accurate surveying capability. They needed equipment to allow them to hear through solid earth and, at the same time, decipher the sounds that could be heard. It was also essential that they could work in absolute silence as it was secrecy that comprised the fundamental and overriding principle behind the success of this method of warfare. The need to maintain secrecy led to the adoption of extraordinary *modus operandi* and dominated the manner in which the work of the tunnellers was conducted.

The men worked continuously in shifts underground — in some areas for years on end — and, until mid-1917, always in silence, trying to make as little noise as possible to avoid signalling their position to the enemy. The miners tapped, picked, shovelled and listened, fully aware that the enemy was doing the same somewhere in the morass of earth in front, above or below them. The men working below ground were intensely aware that, at any given moment, their lives could be extinguished without warning or they could be suddenly cut off from their comrades by hundreds of tonnes of collapsed earth and debris, to die slowly and alone in the dark. They existed as players in a deadly game of cat and mouse, caught in two wars simultaneously. Above ground was the regular war fought by the infantry soldier. The tunnellers lived that war during their time of rest between shifts and were exposed to the same risks of wounding or death as their fellow soldiers. Like their brothers in the infantry, many tunnellers were killed above ground by shell and gunfire. Returning to their work underground, the tunnellers descended from the regular to the unseen war — the war that only they knew, the terrors of which only they were conscious. Many tunnellers on both sides of the conflict died in that subterranean war.[8]

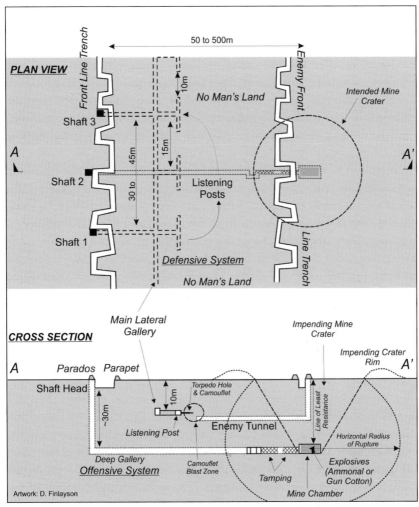

Diagram 1. Schematic diagrams illustrating the basic differences between offensive and defensive mining.

It is difficult to imagine how anyone could endure such an existence without severe psychological trauma. The men spent up to eight hours a day, every day, in a dimly lit, cramped, damp, isolated and silent environment with the constant spectre of a sudden, violent death. Yet, endure it they did.

The objective of military mining was essentially to dig to a selected location below the enemy's position without being detected and then destroy that position. With two opposing groups of miners facing each other, one force would often attack while the other defended, although on occasions both forces simultaneously attacked and, at other times, simultaneously defended. For each scenario, a different method of mining was employed.

Defensive mining was undertaken solely in response to the actions of enemy miners. The main defensive mining structure was a 'lateral gallery', a tunnel running below no man's land in front of and parallel to the trench system or other strategically important points being defended. The standard mine gallery measured a claustrophobic 1.3 metres high by 0.7 metres wide. Movement along these galleries could never be described as either easy or rapid.

The galleries were sunk sufficiently in advance of the front-line trenches to ensure that, if an enemy mine was detonated, it would not damage the front-line positions. The lateral gallery was initially constructed by digging a vertical shaft from a dugout in a front-line trench or an angled shaft from a communication trench located some distance behind the front line. A number of shafts were dug along the front to be defended, spaced at intervals of around 35 and 70 metres. Once the shafts were dug and stabilised to a predetermined depth, a 'drive' would be constructed. A drive was effectively a straight tunnel directed towards the enemy trenches. Drives would be excavated to a fixed length and, when they reached that length, 'cross cuts' or tunnels at right angles to the head of the drive, would be dug. When the cross cuts from each shaft joined, they formed the lateral gallery, equivalent to an underground front-line trench.

Listening posts were excavated at intervals of around 15 metres along the face of the lateral gallery closest to the Germans. These posts took the form of short tunnels, again driven directly towards the enemy trenches, extending out below no man's land. Once they were sufficiently distant from the front-line trenches to ensure that an enemy mine could not damage those trench lines, two short dugouts were constructed to form a 'T' at the head of the drives. These dugouts formed the listening post, with each branch of the 'T' facing another from the neighbouring listening posts. In this way it was possible to detect a sound through the earth from more than one point and thus 'triangulate' the position, or fix a bearing on it in three-dimensional space. The source of the noise could then be pinpointed and, if the listener determined that it came from an enemy miner moving towards the workings either in front, above or below, the sounds could be tracked and followed until defensive counter-measures were deemed necessary. When a critical distance was reached, a defensive measure was taken — either a camouflet or, if a more powerful charge was required, a mine.

DISCOVER MORE ABOUT MILITARY HISTORY

Pen & Sword Books have over 4000 books currently available, our imprints include; Aviation, Naval, Military, Archaeology, Transport, Frontline, Seaforth and the Battleground series, and we cover all periods of history on land, sea and air.

Keep up to date with our new releases by completing and returning the form below (no stamp required if posting in the UK).

Alternatively, if you have access to the internet, please complete your details online via our website at **www.pen-and-sword.co.uk.**

All those subscribing to our mailing list via our website will receive a free e-book, *Mosquito Missions* by Martin W Bowman. Please enter code number ACC1 when subscribing to receive your free e-book.

Mr/Mrs/Ms ....

Address...

Postcode.......................... Email address...

Website: www.pen-and-sword.co.uk Email: enquiries@pen-and-sword.co.uk
Telephone: 01226 734555   Fax: 01226 734438
Stay in touch: facebook.com/penandswordbooks or follow us on Twitter @penswordbooks

Mines and Camouflets — the Tunnellers' Weapons

Offensive mining involved tunnelling from the shafts in the most direct route possible to predetermined locations below strategically important enemy positions. Once a particular location was reached, a chamber was excavated, charged with a calculated amount of high explosive, wired up and tamped. The objective of offensive mining was usually to destroy enemy positions on the surface. The deeper the mine was laid, the greater the payload required for the explosion to break the surface of the earth. The craters formed by the deeper mines were vast, a clear consequence of the enormous charge that had been laid.

Many of the shallow mines resulted in craters not significantly bigger than would be formed by a large calibre artillery shell. In the case of mines laid for the Somme offensive in July 1916, the mines were deliberately over-charged to produce craters with lips as high as three and a half metres. Huge craters resulted, many of which are still evident today, including the Lochnagar Crater outside the village of La Boisselle. The forward lips of the craters were to act as ready-made parapets for the attacking British infantry who would consolidate the crater lips and establish machine-gun emplacements as a defence against counter-attacks. Generally, however, this plan was not realised. Indeed, in many cases, it was the enemy who consolidated the craters. The Germans proved time and again that they were particularly adept at capturing mine craters and making the best use of the protection that these craters afforded.

The tunnellers referred to underground explosions as 'blows', and these were categorised in two types. The first was a 'mine' — a charge of explosives of a calculated size which penetrated the surface of the ground and caused damage to whatever lay within the blast zone above the charge. The second was a 'camouflet' — a smaller charge designed not to break the ground surface, but rather to destroy enemy tunnels and mines. The camouflet was the tunneller's equivalent to a duelling pistol. British and German tunnellers spent most of their time attempting to locate one another below ground, second-guess their adversary's moves and destroy enemy workings before these could be used to kill friendly troops or damage the front line they were engaged to protect.

By the time the Australians arrived in early 1916, the science of mining in the clay of Flanders and the chalk of northern France was well advanced. Not only were there advances in the type of explosives being used, the sheer size of the mines being deployed on a day-to-day basis was vastly greater than those first used by the Germans at Festubert in December 1914. Mines with explosive charges of around four and a half tonnes and camouflets of around half a tonne were routinely used. But even these charges would eventually be dwarfed in size by the mines used at the climax of mining on 7 June 1917.

Prior to July 1915, gunpowder, or 'black powder' as it was sometimes called, and guncotton were the tunnellers' explosives of choice. Gunpowder was a simple explosive compound that could be ignited easily with a lit fuse. Guncotton was a more stable compound with two and a half times the explosive force of gunpowder. The most advanced explosive compound was ammonal, developed before the war, but not widely known and not immediately used. Ammonal comprised a mixture of ammonium nitrate, trinitrotoluene (TNT), aluminium shavings and charcoal. It proved such an effective compound that, following a hastily arranged trial under battle conditions, ammonal became the explosive mainstay of the tunnelling war. The great advantage of both guncotton and ammonal was their stability, allowing ease of transport and handling — ammonal could generally be stacked safely in 20-kilogram boxes. In terms of sheer weight of firepower, however, it was ammonal that proved its deadly edge. It had almost four times the explosive power of normal gunpowder and almost twice that of guncotton.

Ammonal was sufficiently stable to be transported to the front in battle conditions without exploding if struck by a stray bullet or fragment of shrapnel. Most importantly, in the quagmire that was the Western Front, it was waterproof. Both guncotton and ammonal required the use of a detonator to ignite. Detonators were small explosive charges, usually electrically fired. When a large mine was laid, often involving many hundreds or, in some cases, thousands of boxes of ammonal, the detonators were laid inside a number of these boxes. These were known as the priming charges. The priming charges, when detonated, acted as a catalyst to ignite the remainder of the ammonal charge.

The mines used on the Western Front employed enormous explosive charges —and there was a reason for their size. In order to outwit the German miners, the Allied tunnelling companies attempted to mine to a greater depth than their opponents. The deeper the mines were buried, the more sizeable the charge required to effect the desired outcome. The experience gained by the firing of innumerable mines and camouflets by the British tunnellers meant that, by the time the Australian tunnelling companies arrived, there were precise mathematical equations developed for predicting the size of a mine crater when a mine of a given charge was detonated at any depth below ground in any given geological strata. This was the clearest indication of the advances in mining science on the Western Front.

The shortest distance between the centre of a mine charge and the ground surface was known as the line of least resistance. The distance from a mine charge to the limit of the underground effect of an explosion was known as the horizontal radius of rupture. Knowledge of the likely horizontal radius of rupture prior to the detonation of a mine was critical for two reasons. Once approaching enemy workings were detected or the miners suspected that a charge was being prepared, the distance of the work was determined either by listening or estimation. A camouflet was the most common means of destroying or disrupting nearby enemy workings without causing too much peripheral damage. When preparing charges for a camouflet, the miners had to be sure that the charge was of sufficient magnitude to destroy the enemy workings through the ground beyond the charge, otherwise the camouflet would prove totally useless. In addition, the miners had to estimate the likely effect of an explosion on their own nearby workings. If a camouflet was required to intercept an approaching enemy mine gallery, the miners would place the charge in the optimum location to destroy the approaching works while, at the same time, minimising any damage to their own workings.

Knowledge of distances and depths was therefore crucial to the operations of the tunnelling companies and surveying was used to overcome the inexactness of guesswork. Systematic surveying of the mining systems was conducted using theodolites, usually on a weekly basis with assistance from the British field survey companies of the Royal Engineers. The survey results were plotted on a coordinate system that was overlaid with aerial photographs showing the British and German trench systems. Daily progress of work was plotted on the coordinate overlays, and tracings of the updated mine system were made and forwarded to the relevant Army Controller of Mines at the end of each week.

The task of surveying the mines was simplified by the fact that mine galleries were usually driven in a direct line because soil removed from under the ground had to be disposed of above the ground. Soil disposal was a major problem that plagued all tunnelling operations. The straighter the tunnels, the smaller the quantity of soil produced for disposal. It was soil disposal, rather than the size of the tunnellers themselves, that was a major factor in dictating the dimensions of the tunnels and ensuring they remained necessarily small.

Allied mining in northern France and Flanders was conducted in two distinct geological environments: clay and chalk. Each environment required a different approach to mining. On the Western Front, the boundary between the two different geological areas lay in the vicinity of the La Bassée Canal between Lens and Armentières. The geology of Flanders, in the northern, Belgian sector of the

Western Front, is characteristically clay and, apart from a strategically important but low-lying ridge that arcs around the south and east of Ypres, the landscape is relatively flat. The combined effect of clay soil and flat topography spells poor natural drainage in the Flanders region. Centuries of cultivation have overcome this through heavy modification of the landscape with the construction of a network of drains and ditches to rid the land of water during wet periods. The flat topography and the inability of rainwater to quickly drain through the ground also ensure that groundwater lies close to the surface of the earth. When the carefully laid network of man-made drainage was damaged or destroyed, as it was along much of the front during the war, the result was the infamous waterlogging and mud of the Flanders fields.

Unlike Flanders and the northern sector, the southern geological zone of the Artois and Picardy is characterised by chalk and, although not mountainous, the countryside is generally more undulating than Flanders and gives rise to a number of important rivers including the Somme, Scarpe and Escaut, many of which have had their flow modified through the construction of interconnected canals.

Disposal of soil proved one of the greatest threats to maintaining secrecy since the soil being removed from below the ground was usually a different colour to that of the surface. Simply dumping the mined soil behind the mine shafts would have clearly advertised the location of the mines on German aerial photographs. Not only would the position of the soil indicate that tunnelling was actively occurring, it would also point to the precise location of the mine entrances. This problem was particularly evident in the mining systems south of the La Bassée Canal near Béthune, where the underground strata changed from the clay and sand of the north to the chalk of the south. The startling white of the chalk waste rock was easily recognisable from a distance. Great care was taken to remove the mine waste and either disperse it so that it blended into the surface soil, or move it to dumps well behind the front lines. Sometimes it was necessary to cover the waste with camouflage netting.

A mine explosion was a terrifying experience for those who survived and an awe-inspiring spectacle for those who witnessed the blow, even from a safe distance. When a large mine was detonated there was no immediate explosive boom, just a deep, almost inaudible rumble, followed by a pause. Sometimes even the officers detonating a mine, particularly a deep mine, would be uncertain as to whether the mine had exploded. Seconds later, however, all doubt would be dispelled as the earth above the charge literally stood up, the pressure of expanding gases from the mine chamber pushing all above it upwards and outwards. In such an explosion, as the earth is pushed up, the restrictive pressure on the super-heated and confined gases diminishes, allowing the gas to expand, accelerating upwards and outwards. The fractured earth increasingly expands, pushed out by the rapidly expanding gas. A dome of earth forms and, as it grows, it starts to dissolve — almost gracefully — into a massive, three-dimensional jigsaw puzzle. The gas and vapour at the core is suddenly free to escape through the myriad expanding cracks. As it does, it reacts with oxygen and ignites. The inside of the dome appears to explode for a second time as flames blast through the cracks and the monstrous apparition booms. Jets of white and red-hot flame and vapour shoot through the sides and top of the dome, further propelling the earth in all directions. With the release of pressure from its centre, the mass of earth collapses back on itself in a chaotic jumble and the dome subsides. Much of the soil does not fall back to where it originated, but lands out to the side of the centre of the explosion. Consequently a crater is formed and a crater lip, a mound encircling the crater which is highest at the edge of the hole, drops away until the original level of the ground is reached.

Mine blasts did not discriminate: everything within the immediate blast zone was destroyed. At the edge of the blast zone, thousands of tonnes of airborne soil and detritus descended, burying everything below. Those fortunate enough not to be carried skyward in an initial mine blast could still be buried alive by the fallout in the nearby trenches or killed by the concussion of the shock wave. Once-familiar stretches of trench could disappear in an instant, along with any listening posts, machine-gun pits or dugouts that could contain a score of sheltering men. For days following a mine explosion, poisonous gases, namely odourless carbon dioxide and carbon monoxide, would seep up through the shattered earth and, unless dispersed by the wind, form invisible and deadly pools at the bottom of the mine craters.

Mines were very powerful weapons, not only for their physical destructive power, but also for their demoralising psychological effect on survivors and witnesses. Once mining was a reality on the Western Front, infantry soldiers in strategic front-line trenches were subjected to intense psychological pressure. Battlefield stress in soldiers is often alleviated by the soldier's belief that he has a chance to defend himself against an assault, even if the odds of surviving are overwhelmingly low. Infantrymen could see attacking enemy infantry running, stumbling or falling towards their positions; they could endure the onslaught of intense artillery bombardments by seeking shelter in deep dugouts; but, unaided, they were completely powerless to defend themselves from an attack through the earth from below. They could not hear when a tunnel was being dug towards them; they could not tell whether a huge payload of high explosive was being placed below them and there was no way of knowing when such a payload was scheduled to ignite. Once the infantry was able to see the effects of an enemy mine attack, the morale of the troops in front-line trenches was significantly compromised. Without the protection of their own tunnellers, men in front-line trenches and dugouts lived in a constant state of stress:

> The knowledge that dirty work was going on underground gave new meaning to sounds. The tread of an unseen man pacing up and down for warmth on the bricked or duck-boarded trench, the tap of a foot beating time to a tune running in someone's head, the drip of water, any repeated sound of that sort was apt to be hair-raising — especially in the small hours when vitality is low and we are active to fancy's prompting.[9]

During the early months of the British tunnelling companies' operations in Flanders and France, a love-hate relationship developed between the infantry and the tunnellers, particularly between the senior officers in the infantry and the tunnelling companies in their sector. It was a great comfort and morale boost to the infantry holding a stretch of line to know that tunnellers were operating below them as they knew that the tunnellers were providing protection from enemy mine attack. The presence of tunnellers was, however, a double-edged sword, as it meant also that there were enemy tunnellers in large numbers opposite. More importantly, it drew unwanted attention from the enemy who actively sought to locate and destroy the mine shafts. Tunnelling thus attracted the attention of artillery and raiding parties:

> The tactical advantages of a mine successfully blown caused daily activity in sapping and wiring; and small arms, bomb, trench-mortar and artillery covered or hindered the work.[10]

Gas — the Silent Killer

Tunnelling, by its very nature, is an intrinsically dangerous occupation. In war, the dangers are wholly magnified. On the Western Front, death or injury resulting from tunnel galleries being crushed by mine or camouflet explosions was an obvious and ever-present danger. An equally deadly but far more insidious danger to the tunnellers was suffocation by carbon monoxide poisoning.

Carbon monoxide is a colourless, odourless and tasteless gas, a by-product of the combustion of oxygen and a fuel. In the case of underground mining, the fuel comprised high explosive compounds. Other gases, hydrogen, methane and nitrogen monoxide, also resulted from the detonation of the ammonium-nitrate explosive compounds used extensively in mining on the Western Front. In favourable conditions, hydrogen and methane are explosive gases in their own right. However, it was carbon monoxide that posed the greatest threat to the tunnellers. Carbon monoxide is a gas absorbed through the lungs in preference to oxygen but, unlike oxygen, it cannot provide respiration. If it is present in sufficient quantities, the body will absorb it while the breather remains unaware that he is actually starving his body of oxygen. If carbon monoxide comprises as little as 10% of inhaled air, the inhaler can lapse into unconsciousness. Once the realisation dawns — if it does at all — it is usually too late to take evasive action. Unless oxygen can be provided, death will quickly follow.

A contemporary wartime description of the effects of carbon monoxide told of:

> Headache of a peculiar throbbing character is complained of by nearly all who have been gassed. Pain in the pit of the stomach, and vomiting and fluttering and palpitation of the heart, with breathlessness on the least exertion, are also complained of. Trembling is frequently seen. The patient generally complains bitterly of cold. Convulsions may be met with. On recovering consciousness men are frequently dazed, confused, and stupid looking. Other men become delirious, struggle and fight, talking in an incoherent manner, shouting, laughing or crying. Care should be taken that these men do themselves no harm when they are being removed on the stretcher. Others again become very drowsy, great difficulty being experienced in rousing them.[11]

In *War Underground*, Alexander Barrie describes the effects of gas poisoning:

> In small amounts it caused giddiness, breathlessness and headaches followed quickly by painful vomiting and retching. Often victims struggling up an escape shaft were suddenly hit with muscular paralysis and in some cases fell to the bottom as a result. There they almost invariably died. Ironically, due to the action of the gas on the blood, victims always looked in rosy good health.[12]

Above the ground, when artillery shells detonated, the residual gases resulting from the combustion of the explosive compounds were usually quickly diluted in the open air and their poisonous effects dissipated. Even after large mines were detonated and the craters quickly occupied by men intent on using them as ready-made defensive positions, residual gas within the broken ground could dissipate with little effect on the occupiers, although this was not always the case. Atmospheric conditions played a crucial role in the effective dispersal of explosive gases.

The amount of carbon monoxide resulting from the detonation of a mine or camouflet was a function of a wide range of factors. These factors included the size of the explosive payload, the exact type of explosive used, its freshness, whether or not it was under water at the time it was detonated, and even the condition of the detonator used to explode it. When the ingredients of an explosive device are partially consumed during a detonation, more carbon monoxide is created than by an equivalent device in which the explosive fuel is completely consumed.

Underground, there was very little opportunity for carbon monoxide to become diluted. In the tunnel and gallery systems dug through the chalk that dominated the mining conditions in Artois and Picardy, the effects of carbon monoxide poisoning were generally far more dangerous than in mining systems dug into the tight Ypresian clay of Flanders. In an area in which an explosion had occurred, the softer, more porous chalk was able to retain more gas for a longer period than clay.

After a 'blow', any residual carbon monoxide in the tunnel galleries could be flushed out relatively quickly. But within the devastated ground around the detonated mine chambers and camouflets the gas would remain, held within the shattered substrata. In the older, established mining systems on the Western Front where large numbers of camouflets and mines had been detonated over time, the problem of carbon monoxide poisoning was significant. Tunnelling work had to be undertaken in ground that had become more and more impregnated with pockets of gas. The tunnellers inevitably encountered shattered ground from earlier blows which was often difficult to recognise given the pulverising action of the artillery across the entire front. The threat of carbon monoxide seeping into the tunnel where the men were working was ever-present.

Tunnelling —the Technique

The dense blue clay of Flanders was to prove too great an obstacle for the technology of that era. Flanders clay is a swelling type, made up predominantly of the clay mineral montmorillonite. The molecules that make up montmorillonite form flat sheets that absorb and release water far more effectively than other clay minerals. As water is absorbed between the microscopic clay particles, it pushes the sheets apart causing the clay to swell. Conversely, during drying, the clay shrinks, resulting in the opening of desiccation cracks in the ground. The Ypresian clay is firm and damp and, during the tunnelling process, as clay was removed to form the mine galleries, the pressure on the clay walls was released, allowing the walls to swell.

Digging new galleries or tunnels below the front lines was a risky business. In offensive mining, which saw galleries pushed out through no man's land to a position below the enemy's lines, absolute silence was paramount to the tunnellers — in short, their lives depended on it. In the clay substrata of Flanders, 'clay-kicking' was the supremely successful method for tunnelling and was adopted by the Australians wherever it could be used. The 1st Australian Tunnelling Company, in particular, used the technique extensively.

Clay-kicking involved the use of two pieces of apparatus: a clay-kicking spade and a reclined plank of wood. The angular metal spade head was 0.3 metres long with a sharpened cutting edge. It widened from the cutting edge to the rear edge of the spade, which was also 0.3 metres wide. Lugs for foot rests were placed on the rear edge either side of the spade shaft. The spade shafts were around 0.76 metres long and fitted with a cross handle that could be gripped with both hands at the top. The clay-kicker's seat was attached to a narrow plank of wood by a strap. The seat height could be quickly adjusted on the plank by sliding the seat and strap up or down. The plank itself extended from the tunnel floor to the roof, but it was angled backwards from the working face so that the sapper working the spade reclined on the seat with his back supported by the plank. The upper and lower ends of the seat-plank were placed in the small gaps between the wooden sets that made up the tunnel floors, walls and ceiling.

The clay-kicker used the strength of his legs to drive the spade head into the clay face of the tunnel, using the spade handle merely to guide the spade to the next cut and to level the spade shaft. Successive cuts to the face were made from bottom to top in steps of around 0.25 metres. The spade head was 'kicked' into the clay, then prised down, peeling slabs of clay. Not only was this a rapid way to dig solid clay, it was virtually silent. There was space for men to kneel either side of the plank-seat and remove the worked clay from the face as it was cut, passing it carefully behind them. Each cut would push the gallery forward by around half a metre. The technique involved four men at the tunnel face for digging and removing the fallen soil. As each cut was completed to the correct tunnel dimensions, two or three 'sets' of timber would be placed in the new cut. The clay-kicking apparatus would then be moved forward and the sequence would begin again. In this way, a gallery in the good, 'blue' clay the tunnellers sought, could progress at an average rate of around 21 metres a week.

Diagram 2. The clay-kicking technique used by British and Commonwealth tunnelling companies in the clay of Flanders and northern France.

A further eight men were usually employed behind the face-men, filling hempen bags with the clay and removing them to soil 'trucks'. These were small, rail-guided carts that resembled miniature railway trucks. They were built of wood and had a flat tray top measuring 0.35 by 0.75 metres. Each was capable of holding eight to ten hempen bags of soil. The trucks were mounted on rubber wheels guided by two low wooden rails. The rails were portable and could be laid rapidly. Once loaded, the trucks were either directly hauled to the surface via an inclined shaft or moved to a vertical shaft where the bags were removed and winched up using a sling. Although they were fitted with rubber wheels, trucks could not be used close to areas where silence was critical. In this situation, the sappers filling the bags at the working face would carefully drag the full bags along the floor of the wooden gallery to the trucks. This was not the only method for removing soil from tunnels. During excavation of the massive Hythe Tunnel at Loos-en-Gohelle (commonly known simply as Loos) during 1918, the 3rd Australian Tunnelling Company used a pulley system in which a rope fitted with hooks removed 500 bags of soil every hour.

Once removed from the mine system, the bags of soil would be used to protect trench parapets and cover dugouts. The 'blue' clay of deep mines discoloured the bags, making disposal much more difficult. At Hill 60, the 1st Australian Tunnelling Company often dumped soil bags in the railway cutting adjacent to the hill where they could be hidden from German observation.

Unlike mining and tunnelling, the digging and construction of infantry subways and dugouts carried no necessity for silence, and picks and shovels could be used. The infantry subway galleries were usually 1.9 metres tall by almost 1.1 metres wide and even small dugouts were 1.9 metres tall by 1.8 metres wide, allowing more men to work at the faces of these structures.[13] The increase in labour meant that progress of over 10 metres per day in the infantry subways around Hill 60 was easily achieved.[14]

Once a gallery had been pushed out to a position where a mine was to be placed, a chamber was excavated to house the charge. The size of each chamber depended on the number of boxes of explosives that had to be packed into the space. Once a chamber had been excavated and packed with the mine charge, its primers and detonators, the chamber was 'tamped'. Tamping was crucial to prevent part of the force of the mine explosion dissipating along the otherwise open mine galleries, and to push all the force of the explosion in the desired direction. Tamping also prevented entire mine systems becoming saturated with carbon dioxide and other noxious gas following an explosion.

The process of tamping saw the mine gallery leading to the mine chamber carefully and tightly backfilled with bags of soil. For small camouflets, the length of tamping ran just a few metres back from the charge. With larger mines, the tamping extended many tens of metres and used thousands of bags of soil. In more sophisticated mines such as those of the Messines Ridge, tamping consisted of a series of tamped sections separated by pockets of open gallery. As the bags were being placed, great care had to be taken not to damage the electric leads that fired the detonators in the heart of the mine charges behind the tamping. The electrical connection to the detonators at the heart of the mine charges was frequently checked to ensure that the leads were intact. If electrical connection was lost, the tamping had to be removed until the break was discovered. Once repaired, the tamping would be replaced. This was a highly labour intensive operation, as the bags would be chain-passed down the galleries to their resting places.

Once tamped, mine charges were isolated and therefore very vulnerable. There are many stories of both German and British miners breaking into their opponents' mine chambers and removing the charges. In the case of mines that had been heavily tamped, often by the time the break-in had been detected and the tamping removed, the charges were long gone and the immense effort of preparing the mines wasted. The task of the listener was thus critical.

Listening was an essential element of all mining operations and the detection of approaching German tunnelling the responsibility of a noble band of listeners. These men sat for long, lonely hours at their listening posts, a series of small chambers dug from a lateral gallery facing the enemy's mine workings. Oliver Woodward described the unacknowledged heroism of the listeners:

> The lot of the listener is a most unenviable one, and, unfortunately, as regards the general public and perhaps other arms of the service, is not truly recognised. It was a branch of duty which entailed constant faithful service without the glamour attached to the other branches of the service. A listener might be posted hundreds of feet behind enemy lines, keeping his lonely vigil, his only means of escape being a gallery 4 ft. 3 in. high and 2 ft. 3 in. wide. Once per tour of duty he was visited by his N.C.O. and the officer on duty. His tour of duty was 6 hours listening, 6 hours rest (in which he obtains his meals), and then back at duty again. The history of the company[15] shows many acts of heroism performed by those trusty soldiers, to whose efforts has to be placed the successful guarding of Hill 60 through months of dangerous and anxious duty.[16]

The most widely employed listening device was the geophone. This was a palm-sized, mercury-filled wooden disc with two nipples to which a stethoscope was attached. At his listening post, the listener cut a flat bench into the clay wall that faced the German lines. He placed his geophone on this bench of soil and, after making himself as comfortable as possible, commenced listening. With a candle as a source of light and warmth, he wrote down sounds, his interpretation of them and the times they occurred in a small notebook.

Any sound determined to be that of enemy movement was then tracked using two geophones with each stethoscope lead attached to a geophone. This provided stereophonic sound to the listener. A well-trained listener could position the two geophones on the soil bench or wall in front of him so that the sound coming through the earth seemed to be coming directly towards him. A compass bearing was then taken from the position of the line of the geophones to the direction of the sound. From time to time the sound would be monitored and its progress tracked. The distance and direction of the sounds could be accurately followed using the bearings noted by two or more listeners in adjoining listening posts.

The listeners were specially trained sappers who attended a training course at an army mine school before taking on listening tasks at the front line. These courses usually lasted around 10 days and involved days of practice in mock mine galleries that had been purpose-dug at the schools for listening and mine-rescue training exercises.

A large-scale plan of listening posts in the mine system was sometimes maintained in the company headquarters and daily reports from each listening post were tabulated. These reports allowed the progress and direction of the German workings to be tracked. When German workings were considered to be too close for comfort, action was taken, usually in the form of a camouflet. At Hill 60, where the 1st Australian Tunnelling Company operated between November 1916 and July 1917, there were 26 listening posts — not an unusual number in the larger mine systems.

Electric listening devices consisting of microphones connected to a telephone earpiece were also used. A series of these would be placed along a main lateral in a mining system and linked back to a central listening station. At the station, one listener would connect to each microphone in turn, in similar fashion to an operator on an old-fashioned telephone exchange. While these systems saved labour and freed men from an otherwise potentially dangerous task, the geophones were far superior for clarity of sound and the continual monitoring of noises that were frequently sporadic and therefore likely to be missed by the listener in an electronic listening station.

One quick and commonly used alternative method for destroying enemy mine workings was the 'torpedo'. A small hole was drilled through the wall of an underground gallery or listening post towards a target. The portable 'Wombat' borer, an innovative piece of equipment brought to the front by the Alphabet Company, was capable of drilling a horizontal auger hole and was normally used for boring these holes. Once the hole was drilled to the desired length, usually just short of where the enemy was estimated to be at work, an explosive charge was pushed to the end of the hole and detonated. This method had several advantages over the placement of a camouflet. The most obvious advantage was minimising damage to friendly mine workings. Since torpedo charges could be placed close to their intended target, they were significantly smaller than an equivalent camouflet charge. This not only placed the source of the explosion away from the workings, but also concentrated the explosion in a smaller area.

Sergeant Henry Somerset, a drilling contractor in his civilian life and a wartime driller with the Alphabet Company, described the method used to fit a charge in a torpedo hole. On this occasion, a torpedo hole had been pushed out 42 metres towards the German lines from a deep gallery in the Seaforth Mine System at Hill 70, Loos, in April 1917. The last 20 metres of the torpedo hole were charged with just over a quarter of a tonne of the high explosive compound ammonal:

> Insert 1 charged nose cap tube, follow with 5 ordinary tubes, then one red band tube. Each tube fits by inset joints into the one in front of it, the red band tube having an inverted cone sealed in end. Into this now insert cone or section shoe and push the seven sections (now completely joined) steadily to end of borehole (these seven comprise a section). No more than sections of seven should be pushed home at one time. After the first section has been pushed home every following section should be commenced with a section starter (the tube with a fixed long cone end to it) and finished with a red band cone into which an inverted loose cone has been sealed. Each section will slide up and into the end of the previous section and thus form one complete join of sections. Any length of torpedo can thus be obtained. Great care should be taken in waterproofing all tubes with the mixture supplied.[17]

Other Tunnelling Activities

Above ground, one of the many dangerous roles of the tunnelling companies in the front line was to accompany the infantry on trench-raiding parties in the areas where the companies were stationed. In such areas there were corresponding German mining operations below no man's land and the raids afforded an opportunity to locate and damage or destroy the German shafts. Indeed, many raids were planned with the expressed objective of locating and destroying enemy shafts or sap (tunnel) heads. Once the shafts were located, a 'mobile charge' consisting of about 20 kilograms of high explosive was dropped down or placed in the shaft and detonated with a delayed fuse.

The Germans went to considerable lengths to conceal the whereabouts of their shafts and locating them was not easy. Pinpointing enemy tunnels was made all the more difficult by the fact that many raids took place in darkness under the confusion of artillery and machine-gun fire. A tunnelling officer was usually required on such raids as these men were the best trained and experienced in identifying the tell-tale evidence of mining operations. They were also capable of distinguishing between the entrance to an underground dugout and a mine shaft. Given the extraordinary difficulty of these raids, it is not surprising that they were not always successful.

Tunnelling companies excelled in the construction of a wide range of underground structures varying in complexity from the small and simple to the large and elaborate. These structures ranged from mine chambers, sleeping quarters, company, divisional and even corps headquarters, regimental aid posts, cookhouses, engine rooms, artillery observation posts and machine-gun and trench mortar emplacements. In addition to the many tens of kilometres of tunnels, around a thousand of these structures were built by the Australian tunnelling companies below root level in a zone extending the entire length of the British sector of the Western Front from the North Sea coast at Nieuport Bains in Belgium, the Ypres salient, Ploegsteert, Armentières, Fromelles, Loos, Cambrai and along the Somme Valley from Amiens to the Hindenburg Line at Bullecourt.

One of the largest dugout complexes constructed by the Australians was 'The Rampart' dugouts built by the 2nd Australian Tunnelling Company within the south-western rampart wall at Ypres which could accommodate up to 1200 men. A similarly large dugout complex was 'The Catacombs', completed by the 1st Australian Tunnelling Company beneath Hill 63 in Ploegsteert Wood. Both dugout systems were ventilated and lit by the Alphabet Company, which was to carve its own unique niche on the Western Front.

CHAPTER 2

DESTINATION HAZEBROUCK

On 19 February 1916, the Australian Mining Corps and its first draft of reinforcements left Casula Camp and marched down The Domain in central Sydney with a company of Shropshire Light Infantry and a second company from a local rifle club. The parade was reviewed by the Military Commandant of NSW, Colonel Gustave Ramaciotti, and other distinguished guests. The corps then assembled at the Royal Agricultural Showgrounds for its final night in Sydney.

Next morning the men moved to Quay No. 1 at Woolloomooloo and boarded the troop transport HMAT *Ulysses*, a 14,500-ton converted merchant vessel. As the ship cleared the heads of Sydney Harbour en route for Melbourne, it was farewelled by the South Head Signal Station, which flashed the message, 'Goodbye, good luck, God speed to the Mining Corps'.

Two days later, the ship berthed in Melbourne. Once again, the men were required to parade in an official ceremony before state dignitaries. They disembarked and marched past the Victorian Parliament and the Governor-General, Sir Ronald Munro Ferguson.

Plates 5 (opposite) and 6 (above). Photographs taken by Captain Victor Morse of HMAT *Ulysses* at the time of the corps' embarkation from Melbourne on 1 March 1916. Above Morse's wife and children are in the centre of the scene (Victor Morse collection).

Afterwards, the corps boarded a troop train to travel the short distance to Broadmeadows Army Camp on the northern outskirts of Melbourne. Broadmeadows was one of the major Australian military staging camps at that time and presented a vast expanse of neatly rowed canvas. The men were provided with a veritable cornucopia of goods from a Melbourne Red Cross society fund, including 1000 sheepskin vests, 400 mittens, 300 pairs of sandshoes and 600 pairs of socks.[1]

On 1 March the corps reboarded HMAT *Ulysses*. The ship cleared the heads of Port Phillip Bay at 3.30 that afternoon and turned west towards the Great Australian Bight in clear weather along the route to Fremantle. On 7 March, after six smooth and uneventful days of sailing, the vessel rounded the south-western coastline of Western Australia and arrived in the port of Fremantle.

The following day, Wednesday 8 March, the men marched through the city of Fremantle in columns of four, led by the corps band. The Mayor of Kalgoorlie presented the corps with a flag and speeches were made by local politicians. Victor Morse, who made the short train journey back to Perth after the presentation, wrote later:

Coming back from Perth a crowd of small school children were on the station and rushed the carriages where any khaki existed shaking hands and giving us little notes. Hunter and I got about 20 each. It was so nice.

My Word! The rest of Australia can come to W.A. and learn how to give send offs and spontaneous receptions, every kid in the country seems to be beside the Railway line cheering and waving anytime anywhere we move, and the parents hanging out of the cottages all along the line.[2]

Late that evening, the *Ulysses* slipped from her moorings at Victoria Quay, Fremantle, en route for France and the conflict then devastating the western European countryside. The ship's decks were crammed with khaki-clad men waving, whistling and shouting their farewells to the crowds of well-wishers and loved ones ashore, a colourful melee intent on despatching the men in style. The *Ulysses* was crowded with the paraphernalia of war, including the men, machines and stores of the Australian Mining Corps. This was the first draft of 1300 officers and men of what would become the operational units of the 1st, 2nd and 3rd Australian tunnelling companies. Among them was a small group who would form the nucleus of the Alphabet Company, a unit that did not exist, even as a fanciful idea, as the *Ulysses* prepared to make her stately way across the harbour. The men of the Mining Corps were on their way to France to assume a highly specialised role in the great conflagration that had ensnared the major powers of the Western world: the First World War.

The men on board the *Ulysses* that day found themselves caught up in a heady mix of excitement and anticipation as the ship prepared to depart. For many, it was the first time they had faced the prospect of actually venturing beyond the Australian continent. The dwindling sight of Fremantle falling below the horizon was to be the last lingering memory of their country as they headed towards an uncertain future. There were also many men on board who could recall earlier memories of watching the country of their birth disappear over the stern rails of a ship. They were the men whose birthplaces lay on the other side of the globe, close to the intended destination of the ship on whose decks they now stood. English, Scottish, Irish, Italian, Welsh, Russian, American, Canadian, Finnish and Swedish sappers had joined their Australian-born brothers in the great adventure that was the war. Like others who had rushed to answer the call to arms, these men represented an enormous cross-section of Australian society. Stockmen, labourers, bank managers, engineers, teachers, timber-cutters, dentists, policemen, kangaroo shooters and university academics — the diversity of civilian professions was extraordinary, as was the fact that these professions had been left in abeyance while a new and potentially deadly mission occupied the national consciousness.

The ship was cast free of the dock at 6.00 pm and steamed slowly towards the mouth of the Swan River. Once clear of the heads, she was to await the arrival of a tug containing a small picquet of NCOs given the job of rounding up the inevitable stragglers who had managed to slink off quietly to a dockside pub for a final ale or two only to lose all track of time. On board, those men whose loved ones were already far away in the eastern states turned from the railings to settle into groups of newly formed mates and play cards, perhaps light a cigarette or fill a pipe and talk.

As the *Ulysses* cleared the heads, following the established shipping lane towards the open sea, another troopship, the SS *Indarra*, was steaming into the port. The *Ulysses* was forced to deviate from its course to allow the incoming ship to pass. As it completed this manoeuvre, a mere 100 metres outside the heads, there was an ominous shudder and the ship ground to a halt. The *Ulysses* had struck an uncharted rocky prominence on the seabed at the edge of the shipping lane. A quick inspection below decks soon revealed damage to the hull and, in spite of the furious action of the ship's pumps, the forward hold slowly filled with over two metres of water. Cases of Red Cross clothing that had been stored in this section of the ship were saturated and, in the days that followed, added a rancid smell to the odours that generally permeated a ship at sea.

To the bemusement of most of her passengers, the *Ulysses* sat fast, wallowing in the surf as the ship's crew and engineers worked frantically below decks. A little later, at 8.00 pm, the tug containing the picquet and its small catch of drunken sappers bumped against the side of the now stationary ship, providing some distraction for the idle onlookers. The tug pitched in seas six metres below the deck of the *Ulysses* and its passengers swore loudly as they clambered up the swinging rope ladders that dangled over the side of the ship. Those too intoxicated to negotiate the ladders were winched aboard with a bowline slung around their chests, much to the amusement of the men who gathered at the rails to watch the spectacle. With the last of the stragglers finally aboard, the ship remained where she was, rocked uneasily by the ocean's swell. By this time a rumour had begun to circulate: the *Ulysses* had run aground.

This soon proved to be no idle rumour and the damage assessment was sobering. Plates in the hull had been strained, rivets popped and joints parted. The men remained aboard that night, the ship's captain hopeful that the ship could be refloated and the damage repaired without too much further delay. Two tugs were called and the ship's engines strained in their attempt to thrust the ship hard astern and free it from the rocky grip of the shore. But by the following morning it was clear that this was not to be. It had become obvious to the ship's engineers that major repairs were necessary. In a final act of defiance, a portent perhaps that the attempts to free the ship were doomed, a tug's hawser became fouled in the ship's propellers requiring divers to cut and clear the thick rope.

Plans were hastily formulated for the men to be relocated to a camp onshore while the *Ulysses* was freed and docked for temporary repair. With the large-scale transport of Australian men and supplies for the war in full swing, it was no simple matter to locate another vessel at short notice. There was some small hope that a sister ship, HMAT *Nestor*, which was returning to Melbourne with wounded troops from the Middle East, would hurry back and pick them up, but this plan came to naught. All available troopships had been earmarked for other troop contingents embarking for war service from various ports around the country. HMAT *Ulysses* had been assigned to transport the Australian Mining Corps and, short of the ship slipping beneath the waves, she would complete her assigned task.

At 4.00 pm the following afternoon, the soldier passengers collected their kit and, with the assistance of a fleet of tugs, all disembarked. The damage to the ship's hull was eventually repaired with a temporary plug of concrete, the brainchild of Lieutenant Alexander Sanderson, an engineer and Mining Corps officer, and the repair was deemed adequate for the ship to make the voyage across the Indian Ocean. While these not insignificant repairs were being effected, the unit was sent to Blackboy Hill, the main military training camp in Western Australia.

Blackboy Hill was 25 kilometres inland on what was then a hot, sand-blown hill in the Darling Range on the western outskirts of the city of Perth. The last of the men from the *Ulysses* did not arrive at the camp until after midnight, completing what had been a long and disappointing day. The first night at Blackboy Camp proved far from a boost for flagging spirits. Victor Morse penned his first impressions of the camp on his arrival:

> Tis a fearful hole, it blows hard each night like our southerly, well! Last night, our first night it blew to its reputation, the Parson and Doctor's tent blew down and ours nearly did. This morning none of us could be recognized for dirt. Our faces absolutely black and our clothes covered in dirt.[3]

However this meteorological setback was soon recognised as a temporary aberration and, within days, his view of the place had altered: 'The climate here is perfect, cold night even after the hottest of days, although it doesn't produce an abundance of pretty girls, it produces kids.'[4]

The men quickly settled in and time ashore permitted them an opportunity to visit Perth where the officers wined, dined and rubbed shoulders with the city's glitterati. A patriotic local newspaper heaped praise on the presentation and bearing of the officers, its report a thinly cloaked piece of guilt-mongering propaganda:

> The officers of our recent guests the Miners' Corps are the 'swankiest of the swankiest' and judging from appearances have made a deep impression on many of the local girls. But their advent in Perth has aroused the green-eyed dander of some of our gilded shirkers, who are now reconsidering 'that unfortunate' physical defect (which exists only in their imagination) and are mad to don khaki. Many of them have received some well-deserved snubs from the fickle 'fair ones' of late.[5]

While the rank and file of the Mining Corps also had leave to visit Perth, rumblings of discontent rippled through their number. In spite of the fact that they were ensconced in Blackboy Camp, they remained subject to a number of the embarkation regulations that had applied to them while on board the ship. The most irksome issue concerned pay. Prior to embarkation, sappers had been receiving five shillings per day. Embarkation regulations, however, had reduced their daily pay to just one shilling.[6] To make matters worse, they were expected to remain in camp for longer than usual, which drastically reduced their leave. To the miners, this was clearly a double injustice. What they could not have known was that the retention of embarkation pay was more an act of kindness, since the men's pay was insufficient for them to fully enjoy themselves in the pubs and clubs of the city.

The extra time spent on Australian shores was not wasted however, as an order was placed with the local railways department for 19 water pumps. The pumps were packed in crates and added to the mass of hardware that eventually accompanied the unit to France.

The grounding of the *Ulysses* in Fremantle harbour was not the only event that threatened to derail the plans of the Australian Mining Corps. In early 1916, in the aftermath of the Gallipoli campaign, Lieutenant General Sir William Birdwood, Commander of the AIF, expressed his intention to form four pioneer battalions to accompany the four new Australian infantry divisions being equipped and trained in Egypt. Pioneer battalions were units attached to infantry divisions in the same way artillery brigades, machine-gun companies, field engineers and medical units were attached as support units to their parent infantry division. The pioneers provided basic engineering support for their attached infantry units such as trench-digging and road-building. They also provided crucial assistance to the infantry in many major battles, performing the highly dangerous task of taping out the jumping-off positions for an attack.

General Birdwood was quick to recognise that the valuable engineering skills being concentrated in the fledgling Australian Mining Corps were ready-made for his pioneer battalions. He proposed that the corps be broken up to form the technical nucleus of the new battalions. Fortunately, this proposal was strenuously opposed by the Australian Minister for Defence, Senator George Pearce, who emphasised that the Australian Mining Corps had been created for a highly specialised role and that the skills of the men in the corps were irreplaceable in that role. In a cable to the War Office in London, he outlined his opposition to Birdwood's proposal 'in view of the expense and ingenuity which created [the Mining Corps] for a particular purpose'.[7] The War Office agreed, having by that time recognised the extraordinary value of 25 of its own tunnelling companies on the Western Front.

Blissfully ignorant of the tussle occurring across the desks between Ismailia, Melbourne and London, the Australian Mining Corps continued its preparations to leave Australia. By the time the men reached Blackboy Hill, however, their morale was beginning to suffer. Experience as recruits in training camps was neither comfortable nor enjoyable, particularly during the height of an Australian summer. There had already been a mutiny at the Casula Camp and, while the miners had not participated, the seeds of discontent had been sown.

It was inevitable that the physical discomfort, perceptions of inexperience in the ranks of their officers and a natural reluctance to adhere to military discipline would compound and, over the brief period of the corps' existence, begin to erode morale. Lieutenant Colonel Fewtrell, whose task it was to address this, took his position as the unit's commander extremely seriously. He was, however, regarded as a pedant and was not an individual who tolerated 'slackness' or what he viewed as dereliction of duty. His rigid and uncompromising approach to discipline was not warmly welcomed by men unaccustomed to such discipline. Likewise, his adherence to formality was poorly received by those who clearly recalled that, until recently, he had been just a civilian, like his men. In their eyes, he had yet to earn their respect. By the time the corps reached Fremantle, the lower ranks had taken to referring to their CO as 'Colonel Futile'. Likewise, after the grounding in Fremantle harbour, the HMAT *Ulysses* was renamed the 'Useless'.[8]

Finally, on the morning of 1 April 1916, having listened to an address by the Commandant of Blackboy Camp, Lieutenant Colonel Charles Battye, and been solemnly blessed by the Anglican Archbishop of Perth, the corps bid a fond farewell to the camp and returned to the newly patched *Ulysses*. Once again, a large crowd of onlookers and well-wishers packed the wharf to witness the send-off. Streamers festooned the decks and formed a colourful paper web that flowed so densely from the side of the ship that it was difficult to see beyond 30 metres in either direction along the wharf.

At 6.00 pm the ship moved off, this time sailing through the heads unscathed and anchoring off the coast to await the morning tide. The departure was marred by a further incident, this time of more interest than import. Just as the ship cleared the mouth of Fremantle harbour, four teenage stowaways, one of them female, were discovered.[9] Finally, at 9.00 am on 2 April, *Ulysses* began her long-delayed voyage, bound for Egypt en route to France.

The voyage across the Indian Ocean proceeded smoothly and the men quickly adapted to the routine drills imposed on all troops at sea, found time to relax and formed long-lasting friendships. The miners were kept occupied with a series of concerts, a daily physical exercise regime and endless lectures by senior officers. The daily routine was quickly established. Bugle call at 6.00 am was followed by breakfast at 8.30 am, parade at 10.00 am and then a lecture or training until lunch at 1.00 pm. More training ensued after lunch before a parade at 4.00 pm and games such as cricket or emergency drill. At 6.00 pm the bugler sounded the ceremonial 'Retreat', all activity immediately ceased and the men stood to attention as a mark of respect for the fallen. They resumed their tasks once the last notes had faded and worked until 7.00 pm when dinner was served. The evening was devoted to a concert or a lecture, usually given by an officer, before the men trooped off to bed.

On board the *Ulysses* were five Australian nursing sisters including Constance Keys who had tended Australian wounded at the 1st Australian General Hospital at Heliopolis during the Gallipoli campaign. She had accompanied wounded Australians who were being repatriated on the transport ship HMAT *Themistocles*. She and four fellow nurses[10] were now bound for the Western Front, once again offering their services to tend the wounded.[11] The nurses were treated with the greatest respect and usually dined with the officers, often at the Captain's table.

After a voyage lasting almost three weeks, the ship arrived safely in the Gulf of Suez on 22 April. As the *Ulysses* sailed through the famous canal, wide-eyed 22-year-old Sapper Bert Cleary of No. 2 Company of the Mining Corps observed:

The canal is very narrow about 200 yards wide. We past [sic] a few military camps; a few stray soldiers fishing on the side and lots of Egyptians on the bank. They look very dirty. Nothing as far as the eye can see but sandy desert. Towards dark there was few trees here and there and patches of vegetation.[12]

Large military camps were also sprawled along the canal, providing some relief from the monotony of the sandy banks that reached to the water's edge. As shipping was concentrated along the canal, movement was slow and cautious, the ship's progress limited almost to walking pace. As the *Ulysses* steamed slowly up the canal, conversations broke out between the ship and the shore. The arrival of a northward-steaming ship provoked curious exchanges from the troops who gathered along the banks to watch its passing. Shouted conversations were common, frequently encompassing a search for a mate:

'Who are you?'
'Australians' would come the reply from terra firma.
'Any from Sydney?'
'Yes.'
'Is [so and so] there?'
'No, he went with the [such and such].'
'Goodbye, good luck.'

On one occasion one such conversation took place in the dark. In the middle of the exchange, a question wafted across the water to the *Ulysses* from the shore: 'Is Sergeant Birnie aboard?' 'Yes' came the reply from the decks and men shot off in all directions, officers included, to track down the unsuspecting sergeant. As the search was proceeding, the ship's hull engaged briefly with the sandy bottom of the canal, forcing a negotiation back to the middle of the channel. During this slight delay in forward motion, the missing sergeant was found and, for a precious 10 minutes while the ship's officers solved the problem, he held a hurried conversation with his brother, somewhere in the darkness on the shore of a foreign land.[13]

Without further mishap, the *Ulysses* made her way to Port Said and it was here, where the Suez Canal discharged into the Mediterranean Sea, that ships were at their most vulnerable, corralled at a single point, making them easy targets for lurking enemy bombers or submarines. Under cover of darkness, the *Ulysses* made her run for the Mediterranean. All lights above the engine room were extinguished, even smoking on deck was forbidden and from this point of the journey on, passengers and crew were required to wear life vests at all times. The ship turned west and, shadowed by a British destroyer which probed the darkness like a fleeting barracuda, made the 150-kilometre voyage along the Egyptian coast to the bustling port of Alexandria. She berthed on the morning of 25 April on the first anniversary of the Allied landings on the Gallipoli peninsula. Alexandria harbour was packed with all the ships of war: transports, warship escorts, supply ships and hospital ships.

After more than three weeks confined in the cramped quarters of a ship at sea, the arrival of the *Ulysses* at Alexandria was the catalyst for an event that was colourfully described by Edgeworth David after the war:

> … a party of some 120 out of our 1200 miners, with the wanderlust strong upon them, broke loose suddenly from our troop ship as she lay at the wharf, rushed the sentries, and went careering like a lot of released school boys up the main street of Alexandria, making for the heart of the city. Some bad sport, perhaps one should rather say, one sound disciplinarian, telephoned to the military police. And in due course the sappers were met by some charabancs driven by genial gentlemen, who offered them a lift. The offer was of course accepted, and presently the vehicle swung into a courtyard, the gates of which were promptly closed, and the sappers then realised that they were prisoners. One hundred and twenty of them were locked up in a building designed for a maximum of 60. The sappers called it the 'boob'. The night was very hot and the 'boob' threatened to become a veritable Black Hole of Calcutta. In the early dawn, an agonized SOS came from the military police to our ship to say that the sappers were tunnelling under the walls of the boob, and that it was tottering to its foundations, and would we send up a strong-armed party at once to hold and remove the prisoners.[14]

The remainder of the corps disembarked in a more orderly manner and marched through the city. Alexandria left a strong, if sullied impression on many of the men, as Bert Cleary noted in his diary:

> All the streets are as dirty as they can possibly be. The natives live in hovels. As one goes through the town natives in dirty rags shout out their names, some try to sell fruits others jewellery. For wonder they have trams. The passengers are generally Tommys with a few French and Egyptians of a lesser class. This is a great shipping place. The natives do all the work unloading and loading the ships. As soon as a boat pulls in

to the wharf the blacks are looking up at you asking for money. I can say in truth that this is the dirtiest place ever I saw. I wouldn't live here for a fortune.[15]

Once the wayward absconders had been reunited with their countrymen, they were transferred, along with the stores and luggage of the Mining Corps, to the converted transport ship, the Cunard liner HMS *Ausonia*.[16] The change in vessel had been prompted by the slab of concrete that had been used to fix the damaged plates in the hull of the *Ulysses*, keeping it afloat since Fremantle. The structural demands placed on the hull's temporary repair effort were now considered far too onerous given the type of evasive action necessary for ships to avoid enemy submarines as they crossed the Mediterranean. Allied ships were required to steam in a constant zigzag pattern and follow a tightly prescribed lane cleared by minesweepers.

The men duly boarded the *Ausonia*, her holds filled with the 200 tons of Mining Corps stores and equipment transferred from the *Ulysses* and she sailed from Alexandria on 27 April. Under naval escort, she made her way through the dangerous waters of the Mediterranean Sea, zigzagging as if her life depended on it. The restrictions on lights above deck at night continued.

Sergeant Penleigh Boyd was less than impressed with the change in travelling arrangements. He described the *Ausonia* as an 'ancient and decrepit vessel … a troopship which had been condemned before the war and then resuscitated when ships became scarce' and in whose 'murky depths' he and his companions were forced to endure the discomfort of their trans-Mediterranean sojourn.[17] 'The food on board was vile and the general filth of the ship extreme … a lot of men are growling at the tucker.'[18]

Three days later, the *Ausonia* arrived at Valetta harbour in Malta. While approaching the harbour entrance, she passed an Allied minelaying sailing ship and managed to disturb several mines which, fortunately, failed to explode. Once they had floated to the surface, they were fired on and destroyed. In port, the men disembarked for two days' shore leave. The Governor of Malta, Field Marshal Lord Methuen, then reviewed the unit as it marched past on parade.[19]

On 2 May the corps re-embarked once again before finally arriving at Marseille on the southern coast of France on the morning of 5 May 1916, 75 days after leaving Sydney. The approach to its final destination was plagued by bad weather and cool temperatures, the ship having ploughed its way through a gale the day after leaving Malta. The trip was all the more ponderous given the exaggerated course the ship was required to follow. On reaching Marseille,

Penleigh Boyd wrote, 'It was a great relief to get on land again after that filthy old boat and beastly food.'

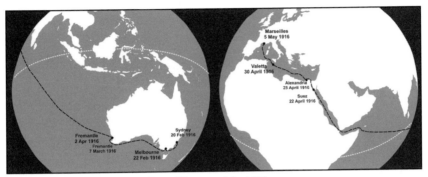

Map 1. The Voyage to the Western Front, February to May 1916.

Subsequent voyages of reinforcements for the Australian tunnelling companies did not take this route directly to France, but travelled instead via England. The route taken by those troopships followed a path across the Indian Ocean to South Africa, up the coast of West Africa and into the English Channel before entering a channel port, usually Plymouth. From Cape Town, the troopships would usually sail as part of a convoy with some form of protection, a destroyer or armed cruiser. The busy port of Freetown in Sierra Leone was a common port of call for transport convoys to meet, take on supplies and rendezvous with escort protection. As the convoys approached the English Channel their protection would increase as additional Royal Navy destroyers fell into line to accompany them for the remainder of the voyage. Once in port, the Australians were transported to training camps on the edge of Salisbury Plain before later crossing the channel to the Australian General Base Depot at Étples.

On its arrival in Marseille, the Australian Mining Corps had little time to take in the sights and sounds of the new and unfamiliar French culture. The bulk of the unit immediately entrained, bound for Hazebrouck, a major staging point for the British sector of the Western Front. Captains Morse and Anderson and Lieutenants Tooth, Smith and Phippard and 130 sappers remained in Marseille to unload the 200 tons of machinery and equipment from the ship, before following the corps two days later. Such was the quantity of stores and equipment held by the unit that 47 railway trucks and carriages were required for their movement.[20] It was the sixth time the stores had been shifted during their journey to France — the final unloading at the end of the train journey still lay ahead.

Penleigh Boyd had travelled the same route three years earlier when he had been in France with his then fiancée, Edith. The two were married in Paris and remained in France for their honeymoon. He recalled that his previous trip, in far more pleasant circumstances, had taken just 15 hours to complete; on this occasion however, the same journey took almost 50 hours. However, the men enjoyed the opportunity to gaze on the lush, green countryside, budding under the early warmth of spring, and the novel sights of the neat French villages and scattered stone farm buildings with their red-tiled rooves. They found the vista refreshing after their months at sea. For the vast majority of men this was a completely new visual experience, most having never left their native land to travel to foreign climes. The train stopped at a small siding and the men had breakfast of coffee with a ration of rum, bully beef and biscuits with butter.

Plate 7. Sergeant Theodore (Penleigh) Boyd, renowned artist and member of the Transport Section, Australian Mining Corps Headquarters, who later served with the Alphabet Company (Penleigh Boyd).

The route passed north through Lyons to Abbeville, bypassing Paris at Versailles, and continuing north to the coast at Boulogne, then Calais before turning inland again, south-east to Hazebrouck via St Omer. Back in early

March 1916 when the Australian Mining Corps had been ignominiously disembarking from its grounded troopship in Western Australia, the 1st and 2nd Australian and the New Zealand infantry divisions were preparing for their arrival in France as component divisions of I Anzac Corps. The I Anzac units had just completed reinforcement and reorganisation in Egypt in the wake of the devastating Gallipoli campaign. When the corps' first two divisions, the 1st and 2nd Australian divisions, arrived in France, they joined an Allied force of 150 divisions facing some 120 German divisions. By that time the intricate web of trenches and wire entanglements on each side, separated by a narrow and deadly strip of no man's land, had been effectively stagnant for well over 12 months. The front line of the Western Front covered some 600 kilometres and extended through Belgium and France from the North Sea coast at Nieuport Bains to the Swiss border near Fernette.

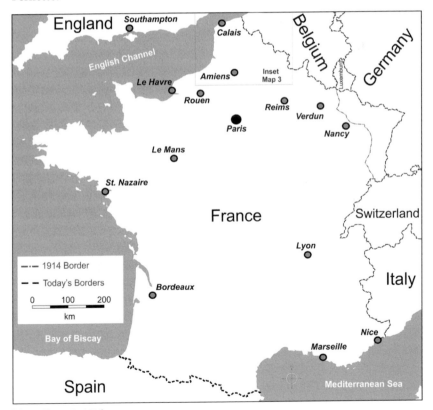

Map 2. France in 1916.

The sector of the front occupied by the BEF extended from the flat lowlands around the shattered remains of Ypres in Belgian Flanders, to the undulating chalk hills of the Somme River in Picardy, France. Belgian and French forces held the line between Ypres and the coast at Nieuport Bains.

Prior to the arrival of the Australian divisions, 44 Allied infantry and four cavalry divisions were engaged in the British-controlled sector. With the arrival of I Anzac, the strength of the BEF was boosted to just over 1.2 million men. The BEF comprised four armies which were spread along the line. In May 1916, the armies on the Western Front ran from the north with the Second Army commanded by General Sir Hubert Plumer, the First Army under General Sir Charles Munro, General Sir Edmund Allenby's Third Army and the southernmost Fourth Army under General Sir Henry Rawlinson. The Supreme British Commander in France was Field Marshal Sir Douglas Haig, who had replaced Field Marshal Sir John French in December 1915 after the disastrous Battle of Loos.

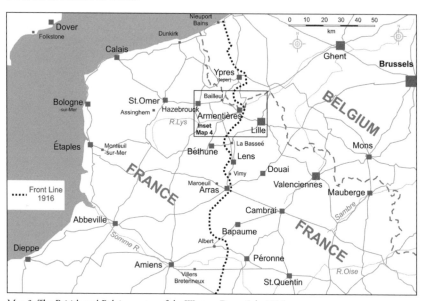

Map 3. The British and Belgian sector of the Western Front, July 1916.

Each British army generally consisted of three corps of infantry. Each infantry corps comprised three to four infantry divisions, as the need dictated. Operations within army areas were directed by an army headquarters and individual corps or divisions were transferred into and out of the army areas as required. While infantry corps were interchangeable, once in an army area, they were controlled by their relevant army headquarters which, in turn, acted on directions from GHQ where Sir Douglas Haig and his staff were based. Infantry divisions were also interchangeable between army corps; like large and complex chess pieces, they could be moved according to the threats and assaults to which GHQ responded. Each division had its own support units such as artillery, medical services, engineers etc. The support units were generally permanently attached to their parent divisions unless there was a need for additional support in special circumstances when such units could be 'borrowed' by others. Artillery units were particularly prone to being employed away from their parent divisions for major offensives.

By the end of June 1916, following the arrival of the three Australian tunnelling companies, a total of 32 Allied tunnelling companies operated along the British-held sector of the Western Front. Twenty-five of these were British and designated the 170th to 185th and 251st to 258th tunnelling companies. The empire's colonial contribution consisted of seven tunnelling companies: three Canadian, three Australian and one from New Zealand.[21] By June 1916, at the peak of mining and tunnelling activity, between 18,000 and 24,000 men were working continuously underground at any one time. During the month of June, 227 mines were detonated by British and German tunnellers on the British front alone between Ypres and the Somme River. In short, a mine exploded somewhere along the British front every three hours.[22] The Germans had a slight ascendancy over the number of British mines fired but, as history would prove, this was the Germans' peak mining period and their ascendancy would be lost as the war underground progressed.

In March 1916, the French were locked in a desperate struggle to protect the city of Verdun, 200 kilometres south-east of the British sector. In the wake of the French defeat in the Franco-Prussian War of 1870–71, a network of forts had been constructed to defend the eastern approaches to the city. Since the commencement of the onslaught against Verdun in late February 1916, the forts of Vaux, Thiaumont and Douaumont and much of the surrounding countryside had been effectively reduced to a lunar landscape. The French were looking to the British to help relieve German pressure on the battlefield that would eventually consume the lives of over 163,000 *poilus* (French infantrymen). If the stronghold of Verdun fell, the prospect of losing Paris loomed large. Plans had been made earlier in 1916 for a major offensive involving both the British and French and centring on the area of the Somme River. As more and more French divisions were drawn into the defence of Verdun, the prospect of a scaled-down offensive dominated by British divisions moved towards reality. The French campaigned desperately for the onset of the offensive which they hoped would draw German divisions away from the growing charnel house of the Verdun salient. The British high command was also keen to launch the offensive given the improvement in weather conditions with the approach of spring.

The French were granted their wish and the result was the Somme offensive. The human cost of that campaign is now infamous but, for all its errors of judgement and mismanagement, the offensive achieved its aim of diverting German reinforcements from the assault on the Verdun salient. As a result, the German assault at Verdun ultimately faltered, albeit at a massive cost to the French. The Somme offensive also inflicted serious losses on the German divisions and territorial gains were made by the British and French at a number of points along the front. Preparations for the Somme offensive required the transfer of infantry divisions and artillery from other British army areas to the Fourth Army. British tunnelling companies were keenly sought and assumed an important role in preparations for the offensive, leading to increased demand for additional tunnelling companies to fill the gaps left by the diverted British companies.

It was into this unfolding series of events that the Australian Mining Corps plunged on the morning of 8 May 1916, arriving at Hazebrouck after its lengthy rail journey. The unit established its headquarters at 80 Rue de Merville while a meat market was found to house the workshop for the mining equipment.

However, as the corps settled in, a mismatch quickly became apparent. On 10 May the Controller of Mines for the Second Army, Colonel Stevenson, in whose sector Hazebrouck lay, presented a briefing on the organisation of military mining. The newly arrived Mining Corps did not conform to the organisational and operational hierarchy of the established British tunnelling companies and clearly had no place in that organisation. A radical restructure was required and the resulting reorganisation would see the three tunnelling companies operate as separate and distinct units. This change was to be implemented forthwith as the Australian tunnellers were required at the front immediately. At the time, the mining war along the British sector of the Western Front was reaching its peak and any further training deemed necessary would simply have to be completed during operations in the front lines. In the case of the tunnellers, it was to be training at the deep end.

During the course of the lecture, the Australian officers began to appreciate the limited nature of their experience compared to that of their British counterparts. It was humbling. As Oliver Woodward recalled:

As I listened to Captain Hill[23] I could not help comparing his position to ours. Here was a man, a qualified mining engineer, who had been associated with military mining practically from its inception. He held the rank of Captain and yet in our battalion we ranged from Colonel down and we still had to see our first enemy shell burst. It was brought home very forcefully the mistakes the AIF authorities made in appointing any of us to commissioned rank. I fully realised how inefficient was my training and I felt rather apprehensive of the coming practical test in Military Mining.[24]

While 10 May 1916 marked the collective low point for the Australian tunnelling companies, it also proved a springboard for an enthusiastic band of determined technical experts with confidence in their own abilities, to exert their unique influence within a new and rapidly evolving branch of military science.

However, the corps could no longer operate under its own command structure and, more importantly, the companies that comprised the corps could not operate under an Australian chain of command. Despite this, all administrative matters relating to the companies — personnel, pay, stores etc. — would remain the responsibility of the Australian military administration. But the changes to operational responsibility meant that the Australian Mining Corps in its original form was doomed.

The brunt of the overhaul was borne by Corps Headquarters which had no obvious place in the restructure. The officers of the headquarters remained in Hazebrouck until the end of May to settle the affairs of the corps before transferring, for the most part, to other Australian units.

Mining Corps CO, Lieutenant Colonel Albert Fewtrell, was given command of the Australian 4th Pioneer Battalion.[25] Captain Norman Macrae, the Mining Corps Adjutant, was also transferred to the Australian 4th Pioneer Battalion and was later killed in action.[26] Captain James Pollock, a professor of physics from the University of Sydney, was appointed to command the Second Army Mine School at Proven, north-west of Ypres, and promoted to the rank of major. Captain Alexander Sanderson was transferred to the 3rd Australian Tunnelling Company for special duty and later became its CO following the death of Major Leslie Coulter.

At this point in May 1916 the fate of what was to become the Alphabet Company looked somewhat uncertain. With the dispersal of the overwhelming bulk of officers and men to the three Australian tunnelling companies, those officers remaining at Hazebrouck represented the remnants of the headquarters contingent: Major Edgeworth David, Captains James Shand, Victor Morse, Stanley Hunter and Captain (Chaplain) James Wilson. However this little group of men, abandoned in Hazebrouck alongside their tons of equipment, had both the expertise and equipment to meet an urgent requirement at the front at this point in the war. This was immediately recognised by the British who quickly diverted the men to a number of essential tasks. As Albert Fewtrell later remarked,

> When we reached France there were no electrification arrangements as far as the British were concerned and our arrival with thirteen generating sets was a God-send.[27]

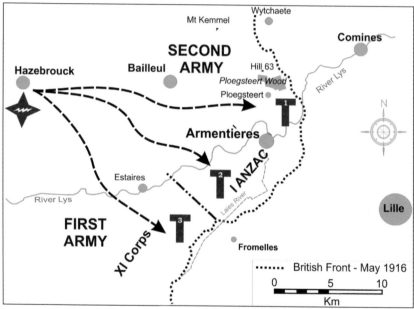

Map 4. The disbandment of the Australian Mining Corps saw the three Australian tunnelling companies move to their allotted sectors, leaving the remnants of the corps in Hazebrouck. These men formed the Australian Electrical and Mechanical Mining and Boring Company in October 1916.

The transformation of the remnants of the Australian Mining Corps headquarters into a distinctive unit with a unique set of combined skills and a footprint on the Western Front that was to be inversely proportional to its diminutive numerical strength is the remarkable story that unfolds in the pages that follow.

CHAPTER 3

HAZEBROUCK HEADQUARTERS

The dissolution of the Australian Mining Corps spawned arguably one the most influential First World War units for its size, the Australian Electrical and Mechanical Mining and Boring Company or 'Alphabet' Company, as it was more commonly known. During the months when the corps was being assembled from across the length and breadth of Australia, Edgeworth David and Stanley Hunter had the prescience to form a self-contained service unit for the Australian Mining Corps' tunnelling companies, unshackled by the restrictions of the War Office and oblivious to the hastily adopted British system of forming its tunnelling companies. This special service unit was designed to supply and maintain all the necessary mining and geological boring equipment required for successful tunnelling. In addition to the usual paraphernalia of stores, the Mining Corps left Australia with 200 tons of boring equipment, 13 petrol engines and electricity generating sets, lighting, ventilation fans, electric and hand-operated water pumps and, importantly, a clear understanding of how and where to maintain and operate the equipment. When the Australian Mining Corps boarded HMAT *Ulysses* in February 1916, the service unit was an integral part of the corps rather than a separate entity.

A small but dedicated nucleus of men, who officially became the Australian Electrical and Mechanical Mining and Boring Company under Captains Victor Morse and Stanley Hunter later in 1916, had departed Australia on the understanding that they would be supporting the Australian tunnelling companies and acting under orders from Mining Corps headquarters. On 16 May 1916 the little nucleus established its headquarters in the Hazebrouck meat market buildings and set up its first workshop in a barn. The barn was soon abandoned for a former cycle accessory factory located on the Rue de Borre.[1] Almost immediately however, its raison d'être, the Australian Mining Corps, imploded. The tunnelling components were ordered off to their various destinies and the officers of the corps headquarters were scattered throughout Flanders like chaff in the wind. The orphaned handful of men and their equipment, only recently established in Hazebrouck, were all that remained of the corps. In a parting gesture, the Australian Mining Corps band members were bequeathed and absorbed into the small group of men remaining in Hazebrouck. However, their future was quickly assured.

So it was that the month of May 1916 saw the nucleus of men for what was to become the Australian Electrical and Mechanical Mining and Boring Company commence its tour of duty on the Western Front. This was a unit unlike any other on the front, a ragtag collection of tradesmen and specialists left over from the disintegration of a proud unit eager to prove itself. The remnants were small in number, fewer than 100 men, consisting of the Australian Mining Corps bandsmen, clerks, men with specialist drilling experience who accompanied a collection of drilling gear, and electricians, plumbers and carpenters with their own collections of equipment. The officers comprised a modest group of just five: Captains Morse, Hunter, Shand (the former quartermaster of the Australian Mining Corps), Wilson (the chaplain) and the father of the unit, Major Edgeworth David.

While tunnelling and mining had been under way along the British front since the arrival of the 170th Tunnelling Company in February 1915, the rapid expansion of these operations meant that the supporting infrastructure lagged well behind. Consequently, even in May 1916, many of the British mining systems, particularly those in the clay of Flanders — the domain of the British Second Army — were poorly equipped and plagued by waterlogging, poor lighting and ventilation. Like a godsend, the small band of men from the Alphabet Company descended on the Western Front with equipment and men ready-made to resolve these problems.

General Harvey, the Inspector of Mines at GHQ, immediately recognised the potential of the small group of men and their equipment at Hazebrouck and, long before the group was formalised in name and structure, its services were in demand. The company's first task was the provision of a power generator and equipment to the Second Army Mine School at Proven, five kilometres north-west of the rest town of Poperinghe, west of Ypres. On 20 May 1916, the unit delivered and installed a 9-kilowatt electric generator and one of the company's Wombat boring machines, powered by an electric motor. This machine was used at the school to train tunnellers from the Second Army front in its use for drilling ventilation holes in underground dugouts and chambers. Two months later the same program of training was initiated at the First Army Mine school at Houchin. While these tasks were simple and relatively safe, the real work was about to begin.

In the meantime, however, the small cadre of men and officers, the remnant of a disbanded company, remained in Hazebrouck without an established unit, but in possession of tons of valuable equipment and the skills to put them to good use. The men were in a state of limbo, lacking an official title or umbrella formation. Between May and October 1916, then Captain Victor Morse wrote to his wife, advising her to address her letters to him under a variety of titles including '1st Australian Mining Corps Headquarters' or alternatively, 'Headquarters, Mining Corps, A.I.F.' In a letter dated July 1916, he suggested that the unit was, at that time, the 'Mechanical and Electrical Company'.[2] Interestingly, this title was similar to the British Electrical and Mechanical companies of which there were five in France, one attached to each of the British armies as Royal Engineers units.[3]

Fortunately, the state of limbo and uncertainty was to prove temporary. The Second Army Controller of Mines, Lieutenant Colonel Alexander Stevenson, and his CO, Inspector of Mines General Harvey, quickly recognised that, across the British First and Second Army fronts where mining operations were in full swing, the dire need for men with specialist underground skills and equipment could be met by this small group of Australians at Hazebrouck. Meanwhile, the men took the first steps towards organising a company structure, albeit one of their own design. In early July 1916, Victor Morse wrote:

> ... we are becoming a happy little family. T'will be Major David, Capt. Shand, Hunter and self, are all directly under the Inspector of Mines which is giving us a better chance.[4]

Plans were afoot to create an officially established unit which would replicate the administrative and operational chains of command of other units in the BEF and AIF. Before this could occur however, the men and officers of the group were thrown into work, divided between the First and Second British Army sectors and under the shared direction of the two armies' Controllers of Mines. While the exact number of men in the early nucleus of the unit is unclear, later in the year when describing his newly formed Alphabet Company, Victor Morse reminisced about his 'grown up being of our little 75 specialist mechanics'.[5]

So it was that during the first week of October 1916, the Australian Electrical and Mechanical Mining and Boring Company officially came into existence under the authority of AIF Order 299 (30 September 1916).[6] Its formation was gazetted by the Australian Department of Defence on 11

November 1916 under Military Order 511/1916.[7] The establishment of the new unit was specified at four officers, one warrant officer, 12 staff sergeants and sergeants and 134 other ranks. Transport for the unit was one motor car, three motorcycles, one workshop lorry, one 3-ton lorry, one water cart, one box car, two draught horses and nine bicycles.

During the period of uncertainty, a situation developed which would benefit both the Australian tunnelling companies and the soon-to-be Alphabet Company. In June 1916, a shipment of officers and men belonging to the 4th, 5th and 6th Australian tunnelling companies had left Australia, its members assuming they would be forging their own story along with the three Australian tunnelling companies already at the front. After a short stay in England, the three new companies arrived at the French port of Étaples on 28 August. Like the Mining Corps, the *esprit de corps* that had been forged in the short period since the formation of the units was about to be shattered. The men learned that the 4th Company was to be absorbed into the 1st Australian Tunnelling Company, the 5th Company into the 2nd Australian Tunnelling Company and the 6th into the 3rd Australian Tunnelling Company. These mergers occurred in the last week of September 1916 and effectively doubled the strength and capacity of the 1st, 2nd and 3rd Australian tunnelling companies.

Prior to their merger however, the Australian tunnelling companies were scoured and from their ranks men were selected whose civilian skills would be best served in a unit whose task it was to provide power to electrical machinery and drilling equipment. So it was that men from the Australian tunnelling companies with skills as mechanics, electricians, linesmen, plumbers and drilling contractors were identified and transferred to the new and improved unit. On 30 September 1916, for example, 26 men were transferred from the 1st Australian Tunnelling Company to the Alphabet Company, 15 of whom were desperately needed professional mechanics or electricians. On 25 September, Victor Morse wrote to his wife: 'Our organization is just through, so we'll change from a working mob of no-ones to a recognized unit.'

On 13 October, Captain Victor Morse was appointed CO of the now formalised Australian Electrical and Mechanical Mining and Boring Company, its ranks boosted with an influx of sappers, NCOs and, more importantly, three new, desperately needed officers.[8] The unit doubled in size and eventually totalled almost 200 men. One of the first issues Morse's men were forced to confront, however, was the unit's name. It was simply too cumbersome. As Morse told his wife: '… we cut it down to Aust Elec & Mech M Coy for address to save ink. It is such nice recognition after the struggle we've had.'[9]

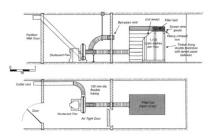

Diagram 3. The 'vivid flash' of the shoulder patch of the Alphabet Company, a lightning flash set on a purple star.

But even that first foray into nominal efficiency proved insufficient and the company was soon being referred to in writing under the acronym AE&MMB Coy, or similar variations. Verbalising the unit's name also proved far too complicated and time-consuming for the average soldier, as even its CO acknowledged: 'The new name is a corker, eh! We over here call it the Alphabetical Coy …'[10] And 'some call us the Alphabet and various and sundry names … you know 'tis some name to get around isn't it?'[11]

The men of the new company could now also proudly differentiate themselves through their unique shoulder patch. Called the Purple Flash, it consisted of a four-cornered purple star oriented to the points of the compass, overlain with a while lightning bolt at its centre.

Of the men transferred to the new unit from the tunnelling companies, several became key members in its development into an effective and highly regarded unit. One of the men transferred to the Alphabet Company from the 1st Australian Tunnelling Company was No. 388 Sergeant Arnott Moody, an electrician who became the company sergeant major, and No. 265 Sergeant Hartley Sandow, who became the unit's quartermaster sergeant. The influx of men saw the unit acquire a formal structure with assigned areas of responsibility, both in the workshops at Hazebrouck and in the various sectors of works in the forward areas of the front.

Plate 8. The Alphabet Company's electrical and mechanical workshop, Hazebrouck, 1917.

Plate 9. The Alphabet Company's plumbing workshop, Hazebrouck, 1917.

Plate 10. The Alphabet Company's blacksmith workshop, Hazebrouck, 1917.

Plate 11. The Alphabet Company's cycle repair workshop, Hazebrouck, 1917 (all images courtesy of Mr Keith Dodd).

No. 1261 Sergeant Alexander Sinclair, who had transferred from the 3rd Australian Tunnelling Company, became workshop foreman with responsibility for the men who belonged to and operated the various workshops at Hazebrouck. These men were: No. 3946 2nd Corporal John Buckie, electrical workshop; No. 4284 2nd Corporal Donald Brown, engine workshop; No. 1268 2nd Corporal Raymond Ranger, plumbing workshop; No. 3812 2nd Corporal Sydney Brown, carpentry workshop and No. 3576 2nd Corporal James Chessell, blacksmith workshop.

From the end of 1916, the Alphabet Company's establishment rarely exceeded seven officers and 260 other ranks, barely more than a third the size of a single tunnelling company. However the span of operation of this small unit along the fronts of the British First and Second armies in particular, far exceeded its numerical status.

The unit had a split personality, as it was both stationary and highly mobile at the same time. Its headquarters and main workshops were stationary and staffed by men who lived in billets close to the workshops and headquarters office where they worked. Further afield, and once engine rooms were established in the various front-line positions, a small team of men, usually comprising one or two NCOs and up to five other ranks, would maintain and operate the engine rooms and all the associated equipment supplied with power, including the laying and repair of electric cabling. These teams were also stationary, embedded with the local front-line units, and usually shared accommodation and mess facilities with the resident tunnelling company, regardless of nationality.

General Robert Harvey: 'Lord, Major, I had no idea you could do such work don't you know!'
Major Morse: ''Tis unfortunate that you've just struck us on a slack day, her! her!'

Plate 12. A sketch by Hugh Thurlow depicting conveniently frantic activity in the mechanical workshop at headquarters in Hazebrouck on the occasion of a visit by the Inspector of Mines, General Robert Harvey, on 12 November 1916. Reference to Dupont (on noticeboard at rear) is likely to be to the nearest estaminet, a place where watered-down alcohol and a simple meal could be purchased to augment army rations (AWM 3DRL/4059).

The mobile section of the company operated between headquarters and the front-line 'jobs' as they were called. This section was dominated by the officers and senior NCOs, the staff sergeants whose role it was to ensure the front-line teams were equipped to meet the demand for power supplies from the men relying on those supplies in an intensely hostile environment.

An officer was assigned responsibility for his unit's jobs in a particular army sector. Large sectors, such as that of the Second British Army, were divided between two officers. Working under their officers were the staff sergeants, who were required to monitor all the jobs across their assigned fronts. They spent time at each site and prepared a report into all aspects of those jobs, particularly equipment and supplies, the status of repairs or the need for and priority of additional supplies. On each tour, the sergeants were expected to remain in the field for several days before returning to headquarters with their reports. If an emergency repair or supply was warranted, a note would be sent from the front back to headquarters describing the emergency, and the new or replacement equipment would be despatched or collected for repair in one of the company's trucks.

The officers, on the other hand, usually made brief, daily round trips from headquarters to selected jobs as required. This was necessary to ensure communication between all the jobs was both centralised and maintained to a high level of immediacy. However this routine was particularly punishing on the officers.

Plate 13. Salvaged German mining equipment at the Alphabet Company's workshops at Hazebrouck destined for re-use by the company. Right is a small petrol engine and electric generator. Left front is an electric motor attached to a belt-driven air ventilator which in turn is attached to 150mm diameter flexible tubing, used to blow air into an underground shaft or gallery. Left rear appears to be an electric motor connected to a water pump (Victor Morse collection).

The Company Officers

The mainstay of the officer contingent for the unit was, without doubt, its CO, Major Richard (Victor) Morse, who had arrived at Hazebrouck as a captain in the headquarters section of the Australian Mining Corps. When the corps was disbanded in late May 1916 he remained with the small group of officers and men who were not assigned to Australian tunnelling companies or other commands, including Major Edgeworth David, Captain Stanley Hunter, Captain (Doctor) Rupert Heggaton, the medical officer, Captain (Chaplain) James Wilson and Captain James Shand, who had been the quartermaster of the Mining Corps.

Stanley Hunter, who was the technical expert in geological drilling, immediately took control of the drilling and boring activities of the unit and would disappear with his boring crews to manage drilling activities in the field. These were usually related to drilling water supply bores or deep geological investigation boreholes.

Major Edgeworth David was initially appointed as a roving technical adviser to the tunnelling companies. He soon became a familiar and much-loved figure in the trenches and was nicknamed 'Old Prof' or 'the old Major' by men and officers alike. Edgeworth David was operating at the forefront of the science of hydrogeology and one of his earliest undertakings was to determine the geology and stratigraphy of the substrata and the groundwater conditions of the principal mining areas along the front line. Armed with this knowledge he gave lectures to tunnelling company officers and produced detailed maps and geological cross-sections to assist the tunnellers to understand the geology of their mining sectors.

GHQ quickly recognised the value of the geological investigation and coordination program established by Edgeworth David soon after he had reached the front. Given his status as a world-renowned geologist, he soon found himself transferred to GHQ under the direct control of the Inspector of Mines, Brigadier General Harvey. As noted earlier, Harvey was also eager to safeguard the welfare of his expert after Edgeworth David had almost lost his life while being lowered down a shaft to gather information on water levels near Vimy Ridge in September 1916.

Almost from the outset, Captains James Shand and Victor Morse were responsible for all the other works with which the unit was tasked from their workshops in Hazebrouck from mid-1916. Victor Morse was given command of the electrical and mechanical sections which responded to the bulk of the technical demands.

James Shand, an accountant in civilian life, had no electrical or mechanical technical expertise and took nominal command of the unit before the Alphabet Company was officially created. The unit's formal establishment in October required the selection of a CO and James Shand was not selected due to his lack of mechanical or electrical training. He left the unit soon after to assume the position of quartermaster at the Australian General Base Depot, Étaples. Likewise, with the official formation of the Alphabet Company, Captain Heggaton left to join the 3rd Australian Tunnelling Company as its medical officer. From that point, day-to-day medical ailments and sanitation issues for the staff based at headquarters became the domain of No. 10 Lance Corporal Thomas 'Frank' Doyle.

James Wilson, the 51-year-old Methodist chaplain for the Mining Corps was also stranded in Hazebrouck following the break-up of the corps. His tenure in France was to prove brief. He fell ill with influenza a month after the break-up and was transferred to England to recover. He returned to Hazebrouck briefly before being appointed chaplain to the 2nd and 3rd Australian tunnelling companies. He then suffered a hernia, left France in January 1917 and was later repatriated to Australia.

Plate 14. The Alphabet Company officers from left to right: George Norfolk, Stanley Hunter, Victor Morse, Loftus Hills and William Logie (AWM H12781).

Four newly appointed junior officers joined the Alphabet Company towards the end of September and early October 1916. The first was Lieutenant Loftus Hills, a young geologist from the Tasmanian Geological Survey. He joined the unit from the 4th Australian Tunnelling Company and, while he was technically a member of the Alphabet Company, he spent much of his time assisting Major Edgeworth David with geological interpretation work for GHQ. His work was later recognised when he was appointed a Member of the Order of the British Empire (MBE).

Another newly appointed junior officer was 44-year-old electrician George 'Sinbad' Norfolk who transferred as No. 1274 Sergeant Norfolk from the 3rd Australian Tunnelling Company on 7 October 1916 and was commissioned as a second lieutenant a week later. Alongside his other technical duties he also assumed the role of company adjutant. After Victor Morse, George Norfolk was the longest serving officer in the unit. Promoted to lieutenant in April 1917, he remained with the unit until demobilisation in April 1919. He was awarded the Military Cross in 1917 for his role in coordinating the unit's front-line operations, in particular during the preparations for and during the Battles of Vimy Ridge and Messines.[12]

Plate 15. Lieutenant George Norfolk, MC, one of the longest serving company officers and right-hand man of the CO, Victor Morse (Victor Morse collection).

Lieutenant William Logie, a 40-year-old mechanical engineer, was the third of the new officers to join. He remained with the unit until July 1917 when his health broke down. He was admitted to hospital in England before returning to Australia where he was discharged.

The last of the October 1916 officer intake was a mining engineer, 40-year-old Lieutenant Harry Brown, from the 3rd Australian Tunnelling Company. However his transfer was temporary and he returned to the 3rd Australian Tunnelling Company in July 1917 where he remained until the end of the war.

So it was that, by the end of October 1916, the Officers' Mess consisted of Captains Morse and Hunter and Lieutenants Norfolk, Brown, Hills and Logie. Major Edgeworth David, although by now at GHQ, was regarded by Victor Morse as an *in-absentia* officer of the unit, and he would call in to greet his friends at the Hazebrouck workshops when time and commitments permitted.

The stresses and strains of the war took their toll on the officer contingent of the Alphabet Company as they did on any other unit. The early officers were generally of a more advanced age, in excess of 40, and well above the average for the AIF. The sheer demands of the work, excessively long hours of travel to and from the front lines each day and the ever-present threat of death from shells, gas or a bullet imposed a considerable strain and, as a result, men were lost though stress and exhaustion. William Logie lasted until July 1917 when fibrosis of the lungs forced his removal. Captain Stanley Hunter, at 53 and the oldest of the unit's officer contingent, managed to remain until mid-December 1917 when his body succumbed to the stresses of the job and he fell victim to gastric ulcers. Hunter was a character with a story for every occasion and his departure was keenly felt by Victor Morse, with whom he had battled through the early months in France juggling extraordinary demands for limited resources both in men and equipment. Hunter's sense of humour also buoyed Morse's spirits, particularly during late 1916 when Morse's workload was pushing him to breaking point. After leaving the unit, Stanley Hunter learned that he had been Mentioned in Despatches, and an oak leaf clasp duly adorned his British War Medal.

The next to join the roll of officers was William Thomas Anderson, a mining engineer by profession, who had originally enlisted in December 1914 as a sapper reinforcement for the 1st Field Company of Engineers.[13] After taking a course of instruction for a commission, he successfully applied for a position with the Australian Mining Corps and was assigned to the 1st Tunnelling Company. He joined the Alphabet Company in May 1917 and was awarded the Military Cross soon after for his work along the Fifth and

Second Army fronts during the latter half of 1917. He was assisted by No. 2348 Staff Sergeant Alan Denton, who had been awarded the Distinguished Conduct Medal (DCM) during the Battle of Messines for his work around the Bluff, St Eloi and the Spoilbank.

Percy Piper was the only individual in either the Australian tunnelling companies or the Alphabet Company to rise from the rank of sapper to captain. An electrician by profession, he enlisted in No. 2 Company, Australian Mining Corps, in October 1915 with the regimental number 672 and was transferred to the Alphabet Company as a 2nd corporal in September 1916. Two months later, he was promoted to staff sergeant and, by June 1917, had been awarded the DCM for conspicuous devotion to duty. He was commissioned as a second lieutenant in August 1917, promoted to full lieutenant two months later, temporary captain in September 1918 and captain in December 1918. He was extremely well regarded by both his peers as a senior NCO and as an officer. The sentiments of both parties were captured in a sketch by Sergeant Hugh Thurlow at Piper's departure from the Sergeants' Mess to join the officers.

Plate 16. 'The Passing of Piper: a Comrade Lost, a Comrade Gained' by Sergeant Hugh Thurlow, depicting the close-knit community that had developed in the company. Thurlow portrays the loss of a friend in August 1917 with the elevation of Percy Piper to officer status on the one hand and the gaining of a valued and respected professional on the other. Victor Morse is caricatured in the right-hand scene as the man with his back to the viewer and Captain Stanley Hunter is on the extreme right, with driving goggles on his cap (AWM 3DRL/4059).

Once elevated to officer status, Percy Piper, DCM, was assigned responsibility for the unit's operations in the southern half of the British Second Army's sector with his former Sergeants' Mess comrade, No. 831 Staff Sergeant Fred Whitwell, a recipient of the Meritorious Service Medal (MSM), as his assistant.

John Royle was another latecomer to the unit, arriving as a replacement for Captain Stanley Hunter, and tasked with taking charge of the unit's boring and drilling sections. After serving for 15 months with the 1st Australian Tunnelling Company, he transferred to the Alphabet Company in late 1917. Royle had been one of the three officers who threw the switches on the electric detonators to the Hill 60 and the Caterpillar mines, two of the 19 massive mines that heralded the start of the Battle of Messines on 7 June 1917.

Lieutenant John Campbell Close was an electrical engineer by profession. He held a Master's Degree in Engineering from Cornell University and had worked with General Electric in the United States for nine years. When he enlisted in 1915 he was commissioned into the 7th Field Company of Engineers. On 6 August 1916 he was wounded in his left leg by a shell fragment at Pozières and given a 'blighty' — wound convalescence in England. He rejoined his company in November 1916 and was transferred to the Alphabet Company in March 1918.

Plates 17. Lieutenant John MacDiarmid Royle, formerly of the 1st Australian Tunnelling Company, who was attached to the Alphabet Company from late 1917 (AMW P02333.001.

The Alphabet Company had several vehicles at its disposal, including the Studebaker motor car shipped from Australia, one box car, four lorries and three motorbikes, and all of which were worked hard. The motor vehicles were the beating heart of the company, making endless return trips from headquarters to the front lines. Unit war diary reports show that, in the three months from January to March 1918, the company's motor vehicles travelled a total of 25,600 kilometres. This figure is all the more impressive given that the distance from Hazebrouck to Ypres in the north is only around 40 kilometres and from Hazebrouck to Arras in the south, approximately 60 kilometres. Each journey would have been frustratingly laboured as the roads and byways in rearward zones were always congested with the relentless passage of the massed, slow-moving human and mechanical traffic of war.

The Effect of 1916 on Victor Morse

Victor Morse paid a heavy emotional and physical price for his commitment to his work. This was particularly the case over the period between May and October 1916 when his small band of men was spread thinly over the front and he had no officer support to share his workload or responsibility. During that time, the little unit established a dozen or so engine rooms at some of the most dreadful sectors of the front — the dreadful conditions precisely the reason they were so urgently required. The front extended from the Yser Canal just north of Ypres to Vimy Ridge in the south. Victor Morse was, in effect, the sole technical officer responsible for establishing the sites, sourcing the manpower and equipment and maintaining these, as well as responding to requests for additional services.

Initially, the frenetic pace of establishing the unit and immediately responding to tasks from senior officers proved a significant challenge. In late July Morse wrote:

> The sets we brought with us are just what the doctor ordered and now I'm hopelessly pushed for staff electric mechanics, which includes a ton of business which is very satisfying. Last week with all gangs out I was up against it when a new job urgently came on, promptly set out to break another record and did so. I like being up against it, am in my very element then.

Morse initially travelled between his jobs on one of the unit's motorbikes, but the state of the roads was such that, where cobblestone pavement existed, each journey became a bone and machine-rattling experience. When the roads were wet or icy, the cobblestones were extremely slippery, adding another element of danger. Acting on authority from his Controller of Mines, he began to use the unit's Studebaker car, which had arrived in France with the Mining Corps. However its life proved brief and, by the middle of September 1916, it was reduced to a state beyond repair. Morse moved to his second vehicle, a Daimler.

Other than the Studebaker, none of the cars used by the unit during the war was new and, inevitably, all were driven into the ground. Most also bore scars from multiple near misses from projectiles and other vehicles. The day Victor Morse took charge of the Daimler he collided with a motorbike fitted with a sidecar, damaging the Daimler. Both drivers were at fault, with Morse admitting that he was 'in a bit of a hurry and in a lights-out area.' However, in October 1916 he managed to secure the services of a driver who relieved him of the exhausting and time-consuming necessity to drive himself.

the motorists dream of the French cobble roads

Plate 18. 'The motorists dream of the French cobble roads', a cartoon by Hugh Thurlow illustrating the reality for those forced to venture out on the paved roads in motorised vehicles (AWM 3DRL/4059).

Following the establishment of his new company and the drafting of a work program for his men, Morse settled on his own daily routine:

> I rise about 7 AM, breakfast 8 to 8:30, then to shop [workshop] for as long as is necessary, often only a few minutes then away in the car to the trenches at one place or another on a pretty wide front, lunch often

obtained in dugouts very much in the bowels of the earth, some of Fritz's [shells] go very deep so we burrow well. When finished, perhaps 2 or 3 different places, I return, sometimes driving myself, more often as not, walking 10 to 20 miles on duck-boards hoping to prolong the day and the long travelling, often 100 miles a day, is quite satisfying enough even for the biggest glutton – well then back, if before 7 PM (seldom), mess, if not, 'tis generally bed right after morrow's necessary paper is fixed up.[14]

His suggestion that he returned in time for mess at 7.00 pm after a 12-hour day was an ambitiously optimistic assessment, and what may have commenced as 12-hour days soon became 16-hour days, worked continuously for long periods. With each passing week, as the list of jobs increased, the pace of his life and the strain of his mounting responsibility but diminishing time-frame in which to have his tasks completed, became more telling:

7 August 1916: We've been keeping very busy with our lot and what we've got his,[15] but oh the same old story, always the same, short-handed, hopelessly so.

By October 1916, when he finally managed to secure more officers to share the burden of his responsibilities, his workload as the lone field officer for five months had already affected him physically. His love and pride for what he and his small band of men were doing was the only force that sustained him emotionally — but only just. On 6 October he wrote to his wife using words that conveyed the cracks that had begun to appear in his emotional veneer:

… I'm getting to the 'played out' stage … you know just absolutely tired out, fed up and full. As soon as things become settled I'll try to get to Blighty for my leave.[16]

Two weeks later, in another letter, at a time he should have been celebrating his new command, he wrote:

It has been hard work and the last few weeks very bad luck, it dogged my footsteps for 3 weeks, some of my best went out to it, and some plants tried to give trouble. I saw very little of bed during that time and I was supposed to be down with the Flu … I'm not just in a state to appreciate it all as I should. I had to hopelessly overstep it in the latter part and consequently am stale, fed up, etc, etc.[17]

Even with the new influx of officers, the demands on the unit and its consequent heavy workload continued to increase, with no relief from the pressure. Morse managed to push himself on as winter set in and conditions across the front deteriorated to the point at which mere survival became a terrible struggle, let alone fighting a war. In early January 1917 he wrote:

Our officers & non-comms are at it more or less day and night, our Hdq 8 AM to 10 PM working Sundays included and by the phone all night ... The other day I was about 16 hours riding in the car through sleet, snow, rain and the last 4 hours 10 PM to 2 AM was driving in the dark myself to ease my man who was about done.[18]

The winter of 1916–1917 into which Morse plunged himself on a daily basis, was notoriously cold, particularly January 1917:

The whole country is frozen hard and white and we've had days of 10° F [-16°C]. 'Tis now 22°F [-5.5°C] and we are preparing for a thaw. I hope it warms up a bit soon, 'tis a couple of hours ride in the car, the clothes just cake with ice around you … ice, in some places 18 inches thick, yet water is fearfully scarce due to the ice. Radiator of the car freezes up, lamps freeze up. We've lost a couple of engines through their bursting owing to ice.

Plate 19. Lieutenant George Norfolk, MC (standing left), and Major Victor Morse, DSO (right), at the Maroeuil workshops in late 1918, standing next to one of the five motor cars the officers managed to wear out during daily trips to the front. The driver is not identified, but it is possibly No. 2346 Sapper Robert 'Cobby' Cobcroft (Victor Morse collection).

Added to the workload and the conditions in which he and his men had to work, was pressure from the largely unseen enemy whose primary objective was to kill or maim. This was perhaps the most insidious and pervasive element of stress which compounded the pressure on Morse and his men. Near-death experiences were commonplace, each sending its own shockwave through the men's psyche, denting and weakening it. Bravado and 'stiff upper lip' was the name of the game, coolness in the face of danger and the ability to react nonchalantly to horrific experiences were crucial despite the reality that these scarred the men's consciousness and cumulatively eroded their ability to cope with each new event. As Morse wrote:

Had a bit of luck a few days ago, was underground when the Hun blew a mine on us, bit nervy and unsavory as the whole ground rocked, and timbering commenced breaking, wondering if you're caught like a rat in a trap. Yesterday I was sliding down the iced up duckboards looking down when I got a rotten bash,[19] the steel helmet saved me other than the usual spot on my nose being skinned, but it knocked me almost silly for a bit and I had a lovely old clean out vomit all night for which I feel much better today.[20]

Five days after writing these words, Morse's fragile health collapsed. On 9 February he was admitted to a casualty clearing station and diagnosed with bronchitis and exhaustion. He was immediately despatched to the south of France to recover, well away from any evidence of the war.

Morse spent a month at the Michelham Home for convalescent British officers located in the Hotel Cap Martin at Menton, on the French Riviera. In an environment that both stimulated and invigorated the senses, Morse had time to repair himself physically and emotionally. It was during this time of emotional relaxation that he finally paused to reflect on how close he had come to being driven to a state of utter exhaustion:

I've been taking plenty of exercise more or less with the purpose of cleaning my system right out, at first it took some forcing myself, but I can notice some effect already as I can take fatigue much better now. Up north, 'tis mud, mud and filth all the time and I think once you are down, it's almost impossible to pick up decently, and I think I got to the stage where I'd take anything when they nabbed me for that pneumonia stunt.[21]

It was only once he returned to Hazebrouck in late March 1917 that his subordinate officers admitted their suspicion that he had been a spent force even prior to the arrival of winter. But there had been little any of them could do to persuade him to rest or to ease his situation, and they were forced to watch helplessly as he drove himself to illness. On his return to his unit he was far more conscious of his limits and the need to avoid over-committing himself. His experience also made him personally aware of the effects of overwork, the way it could affect his men and their emotional and physical wellbeing. Every day at the front was sufficiently dangerous without the added stress of unrealistic and excessively long periods of work. It was a lesson that Morse needed to learn as he would be required to call on all his reserves of inner strength time and again before the war ended.

Close Shaves

Every officer in the company — and Victor Morse in particular — endured an enormous and relentless workload. The officers made constant, almost daily tours of their assigned sectors seeking ways to reduce the pressure on their front-line squads and minimise the dangers inherent in their environment. While the men worked in cramped and noisy holes in the ground or cellars below precariously balanced landfills of masonry rubble, the officers travelled by car or motorbike over muddy, crowded, cobbled roads which were frequently shell damaged. As they approached the front, they were forced to leave their transport at the head of a communication trench to walk for several tortuous kilometres along the web of snaking trenches to the front lines, their return journey usually made in the dark, with shellfire and sniping intensifying the closer they moved to the front.

However German artillery fire was not solely the preserve of the front lines. In fact, while short-range trench mortar fire was exchanged between front-line positions, long-range artillery fire was generally not concentrated on the front lines, but was directed at the support and reserve lines behind the fronts where the bulk of forces waited in reserve. Both sides selected artillery targets that extended for many kilometres behind their enemy lines, targeting roads and buildings, as this was where men were likely to congregate, particularly at night. Artillery batteries were usually scattered throughout the countryside, their gun crews also constantly focused on the destruction of opposing batteries. Shellfire was thus a constant, lurking danger for everyone passing through or inhabiting the rear areas within four or five kilometres of the front lines. The very large calibre, rail-mounted naval guns would also pound towns many tens of kilometres behind the lines, their effect, like the slow drip of a tap, gradually reducing buildings to stumps of broken walls and dusty mounds of masonry.

A condition that tortured the minds of those who spent time within machine-gun, or more pertinently, artillery range of the front lines, was the apprehension of sudden, violent and apparently random death or maiming. Some men were able to deal with this fear better than others, some surrendered their lives to fate and pushed it from their minds. However, it left its mark on all as the toll of casualties around them rose, victims of war's great lottery. Experience and advice from veterans taught them tricks and techniques to enhance their chances of survival, however fate ultimately held the upper hand.

In the course of visiting the various sectors along the broad front where his men were at work, Victor Morse met many of the COs of front-line units and also liaised closely with the COs of the various resident tunnelling and engineering companies. Invariably, he became acquainted with most and a friend to many and it was common for him to be invited to lunch or dinner in the dugout of a front-line battalion commander and his staff. At one point, Morse reminisced about such visits to the front line in a letter to his wife:

> … by heavens it is often 'hell' with an occasional touch of heaven, when whilst Fritz is shaking the whole ground with metal and you manage to reach an officer's dugout 20'0' [feet] underground or more in dim candle light, you enjoy a smoke and tucker midst the latest tunes on a gramophone. No mess is complete without its gramophone.[22]

In his letters to his wife, Morse downplayed the effects of living close to the front, describing with a casual air his or another man's close calls with shot and shell. However, in a frank missive to his father in late June 1917 when the Battle of Messines had just drawn to a close, he revealed his true thoughts on the ever-present threat to life and limb:

> … lately I've felt it pretty severely, have lost a couple of my best friends within a week both the same rank as self, the last one the usual tho' it ended right, he got a piece of an 8' shell in the back between the shoulders and the spine and was paralysed from there downwards, fortunately he went out of it in 3 days.[23]

Morse was referring to the wounding and subsequent death of his friend Major Alfred Wraith, CO of the British 254th Tunnelling Company. He described the circumstances in which Alfred Wraith was mortally wounded in a letter to his wife:

> … he was on one of the worst parts of the front for over 12 months, many a time we've crouched in a trench or dugout or cellar when caught in one

of the Hun's hymns of hate and each time have come out smiling. His coy were moving to another part, and going on his motor bike through a town which had long since ceased to be a town a long range shell chanced practically on him. He was a fine man.[24]

This scenario was by no means unusual. Later in the year Morse mentioned his former comrade and adjutant of the Australian Mining Corps, Major Norman Macrae, who went on to command the 4th Australian Pioneer Company and who was killed during the Third Battle of Ypres on 4 October 1917 when a shell hit the house in which he was billeted, well back from the front line. Morse reflected in a rare unguarded moment: ''tis just the luck of we front line men to come back and get knocked miles away.'[25]

Plate 20. Major Victor Morse, DSO (back row, centre), with a group of officer acquaintances from a variety of British regiments (Victor Morse collection).

Through the latter part of 1917 Morse suffered as friend after friend was killed. Leslie Coulter, CO of the 3rd Australian Tunnelling Company, was killed in action on 28 June, followed by Major Maurice Wilkinson of the Royal Engineers, killed in action on the opening day of the Third Battle of Ypres. By late 1918, other sinister forces were taking the lives of men, including Morse's friends, in the wake of the retreating German armies, who were using booby-traps as an insidious method to kill or maim their foe. It became the task of the various tunnelling companies to locate and defuse these devices. However, before the nature of booby-trapping tricks and techniques was fully understood, they took numerous lives, including those of officers intent on learning the art of defusing them. One victim was Morse's friend the long-time CO office of the British 170th Tunnelling Company, Major Robert Manning, DSO, MC, Legion of Honour, who had a leg almost taken off by a booby trap and died of his wound on 6 September 1918. It was yet another funeral for a friend that Victor Morse was compelled to attend. Like any soldier at the front, Morse and his men lived with the constant threat of death and numerous close shaves. Morse described a number of instances involving his car, which could only take him to within a mile or so of the front line before he had to walk the rest of the way through the sinuous network of communication trenches. The events he described occurred some distance behind the front:

> ... one day we got under shrapnel which only perforated the car in 30 places and it was no joke standing looking on at the driver[26] mend a couple of tyres which had been pierced (including our spare wheel) with it bursting all around ... the next day he [German artillery] got another 10 holes in the car and still did not put her out of action, but you should have seen the windscreen it was a picture, and the footboard alone had 7 clean through it ...

The unit's headquarters in Hazebrouck were also far from immune to the probing effects of long-range artillery. A new mess had just been completed in late June 1917 when, the evening before its first use, a German shell riddled it, providing, in Morse's words, 'better ventilation'. Other close shaves occurred while Morse was visiting front-line trenches, experiences that would have been commonplace to his men along the line:

> Thought my end had come last week. We were wandering along a very battered front line trench with one eye upwards for the great miniwerfer[27] that goes skywards, then straight down, when everything else goes skyward. We both saw it coming but the trench was too broken to get shelter. It landed about 10 yards away and — didn't go off — we resumed walking — a little faster. It's wonderful watching these sorts of things ours and theirs, great masses hurled wobbling hundreds of feet in the air, then steady & comes straight down, with the huge upheaval on landing.[28]

While it may have been extraordinary watching the flight of German shells in the distance, had that mortar detonated, it would have killed Morse and his companion, a common occurrence among those men whose task it was to man the front-line fire-steps and dugouts. Close calls with unseen, high velocity hardware inevitably prompted consideration of the odds of survival and the fatalistic belief that there was a shell or round which fate had assigned to every man. Many men referred to the shell or bullet with their 'name on it' which they were convinced must inevitably come their way. The awful truth was, however, that they never knew what form this might take and where it might reveal itself.

Men who believed that their time was up and that it was their turn to be killed or, in the parlance of the day, 'go west', became morose, distracted and inclined to hesitate to perform any action that would place them in harm's way. While in modern times this would be classed as a form of post-traumatic stress disorder, at that time, such men were referred to as being 'windy'. Men on the front line were careful to avoid being classed as 'windy' by their peers. Victor Morse, like most men, endured periods of doubt over his own mortality, although he did not admit this to his wife. On receipt of news of the deaths of his friends, he reflected:

> When this sort of thing happens too often, consecutive days, and the men 2' [feet] away from you get it and you miss it, you begin to think that your turn is just coming along.[29]

Many of his very close calls were simply that, but there were at least two occasions when Morse should have reported to a dressing station, both times for gas poisoning. The first was on the opening day of the Battle of Messines (7 June 1917) when his unit assisted in the mining sectors where the 19 massive Messines Ridge mines were detonated that morning. As was his way, he visited his men along the front where the battle raged and was caught in the German shelling that followed. Over the course of the day he inhaled the gas that permeated the battlefields. He admitted to his wife:

> Yesterday I had one of the toughest afternoons of my life, got caught properly in his [German] shelling, walked miles dodging them and got caught in his gas shells, it's made me anyhow [ill] and my eyes have been hell since, but I cannot afford to be sick again, not now.[30]

Despite suffering the effects of gas, Morse's characteristic commitment to his men at a crucial time drove him on. Soon after, when his unit was stretched to capacity in the Ypres salient, in the days leading to the opening of the Third Battle of Ypres on 31 July 1917, a massive artillery duel raged that also featured German gas shells. Once again Morse admitted that:

... we are all out just now more than ever before when I say that even my shop foreman and storeman is up the line, and the fates have been unkind lately with gas casualties[31] ... a couple of days of his gas and I guess I've felt pretty rotten, stayed in bed yesterday morning and again this afternoon so I should be right to see it through now ... [32]

But he was not 'right to see it through', and told his wife a week later that he had been so ill with a sore throat and chest and dysentery brought on by this latest gas poisoning that a doctor had confined him to bed for several days, suggesting also that he should admit himself to hospital. He dismissed both suggestions, opting for a day of rest. Both occasions should have seen him attend a dressing station and be registered as wounded. Indeed his decision at the time to avoid proper treatment due to his work commitments meant the impact of the war on his long-term health was not formally recognised nor taken into account after the war, and probably contributed to his early death in the decade following its close.

The Comforts Fund

As the Australian tunnellers waged the war underground in distant and foreign lands, their families and friends at home collected and sent comforts in the hope of alleviating the hardship of life in the trenches. Australians overwhelmingly displayed strong support for their fighting troops and the provision of comforts from home took many forms, ranging from the quaint and often home-made comfort parcels sent by families and concerned individuals, to the organised formation of specific comfort and patriotic funds. Money was raised for patriotic funds primarily through charitable donations made direct to the fund agency or through organised events. During the war, 156 funds were established across the six Australian states to raise money for the purchase of comforts to send to the front. These funds ranged from large, national agencies such as the Red Cross to numerous state-specific funding bodies, many of which were splendidly named, including the Sandbag League (Queensland) and the Plum Pudding Fund (Tasmania). Such funds raised a phenomenal £13,800,000 during the course of the war, the equivalent of some $1.3 billion in today's currency.[33] In addition to donations for the purchase of comforts, hundreds of thousands of items, such as hand-knitted socks, scarves and gloves, fashioned by countless hands in sitting rooms and parlours across Australia, also found their way to the men at the front.

The driving force behind many of these fund organisations comprised women whose husbands, fathers and sons were away, fighting in the war.

Foremost among the comfort organisations was the Australian Red Cross, whose aim was to provide humanitarian aid to soldiers and civilians in war zones. There were other patriotic funds, such as the Australian Air Squadrons' Fund, which raised money for the provision of military hardware — in this case aircraft — to bolster the military supplies and equipment of the fighting troops. For the most part, however, such organisations aimed to provide gift parcels of clothes, food and little day-to-day luxury items to the troops at the front. The numerous comfort funds that sprang up spontaneously in the early months of the war were eventually coordinated under a single distribution body, the Australian Comforts Fund, which was formed in 1915 and established its headquarters and main distribution centre in London.

Local comforts fund or patriotic league committees were organised with headquarters in state capital cities. One such local committee in Melbourne established a depot on the sixth floor of 317 Collins Street and placed a newspaper advertisement calling on the friends and relatives of tunnellers to help with comforts packaging three afternoons a week.

Plate 21. Victor Morse's wife Aileen (centre row, right) with fellow members of the 'Cheeros', a wartime performing whistling troupe that raised funds for the men at the front (Victor Morse collection).

On 3 October 1916, a fundraising concert was held at the Sydney Town Hall to raise money for the Australian Mining Corps Comforts Fund — although by this time the Australian Mining Corps had ceased to exist in its own right. The concert was patronised by no less than the Governor of NSW, Sir Gerald Strickland, and the Chancellor of the University of Sydney, Sir William Cullen. The musical program included a whistling solo by Mrs Aileen (Mina) Morse, performing the aria 'Casta Diva' from the opera *Norma* by Bellini.[34] Mina was the wife of Victor Morse who, at the time, had just been appointed to command the Alphabet Company in Hazebrouck. She was a member of a performing troupe, called the 'Cheeros' who gave public whistling performances to raise funds. Mina's rendition was undoubtedly well received, the reception all the more heartfelt given her husband's position at the front. The concert ended with a selection of tunes by the Engineers' Depot Band.[35]

The concert program for the evening was a printed leaflet, its cover illustrated with a photograph of the CO of the (by then disbanded) Australian Mining Corps, sitting confidently astride a horse, a photograph taken before the Mining Corps left Australia. However, in his time as CO of the Mining Corps, Colonel Fewtrell had attracted such ill-feeling from his men that Victor Morse wrote in a letter home:

> I was glad that the concert was a success and that your items were appreciated, the programme was nicely put up, thought the front page, unknowingly to you, insulted every miner, as one said, 'tis a fine horse.

However, the distribution of comforts, an issue over which he harboured strong opinions, was to plague Victor Morse, who was determined to make every effort to ensure that his men and those of the Australian tunnelling companies received regular comforts from home to boost morale. With the disbandment of the Mining Corps, any coordinated system for distributing comforts to the tunnelling companies seems to have disappeared. The failure to equitably distribute comforts to their intended recipients not only affected the fighting men, but also those dedicated souls, generally their wives, whose time, energy and emotion were channelled into the provision of comforts to their loved ones so far away.

Comforts were collected, packed into cases and despatched to London to be forwarded to the front under the control and coordination of the War Chest Commissioner, at the time, Mr Henry Budden. By October 1916 however, having served at the front for some six months, the men of the

Australian tunnelling companies had yet to receive any comforts. Central to the problem was which unit would receive the comforts and how they would be distributed equitably. A potential complication arose from the fact that each tunnelling company had drawn its quota of men disproportionately from one or two states, a result of the way the country had been divided into recruitment districts. The bulk of men in the 1st Tunnelling Company were from NSW and Queensland, the 2nd Company was dominated by Victorians and the 3rd Company overwhelmingly comprised men from Western Australian. The Alphabet Company had men from all states, with no state over-represented. The population profile of Australia in 1916 was similar to its current profile, albeit a quarter of the size. The largest populations were in NSW, Victoria and Queensland. In 1914, these three states contained 80% of the Australian population and contributed 75% of donations to the comfort funds. Western Australia contained a mere 7% of the population and therefore its comforts contributions were proportionately modest given its smaller population base.

Had comforts been sent directly to the tunnelling companies from their source states, those men from the larger capital cities (Melbourne and Sydney) would have received a larger number of packages than those from the less populous states. Victor Morse was keen to take control of all comforts and distribute them on an equitable, pro-rata basis among the three tunnelling companies and his own Alphabet Company men.

The Alphabet Company was best placed to perform the task of centralised comforts receipt and distribution since all the tunnelling companies interacted with this unit almost on a daily basis at the Bailleul mining lamp charging station, which the company manned and operated 24 hours a day, seven days a week. When a consignment of comforts arrived, Victor Morse would deliver comforts to his fellow tunnelling companies when mining lamps were exchanged at the charging station. It was a simple solution to what might otherwise have been a logistical nightmare.

One of Morse's first acts after settling in as the new CO of the Alphabet Company was to meet with the commanders of the three Australian tunnelling companies to discuss a solution to the distribution of comforts. With some reservations, all agreed that the Alphabet Company was best placed to coordinate comforts on behalf of all the men. Morse immediately wrote to Commissioner Budden in London to advise him of the new arrangements for receiving and distributing comforts for the tunnellers at the front. He also enquired into comforts previously sent to the tunnellers which, according to the pamphlet that accompanied the Australian Mining Corps Comforts Fund concert, had been 'gratefully acknowledged' by the tunnellers. Such grateful acknowledgment was a mystery, since no comforts had been received by any tunnelling company.

Commissioner Budden responded, stating that he was despatching 22 cases of comforts to Morse for distribution, in addition to the lots that had previously been sent. However these had not arrived and no-one seemed to know where they were. The first installment of comforts arrived in early November and consisted of 'mostly shirts, a box of balaclavas and I think a little fruit.'[36] Following a vigorous exchange of letters with Commissioner Budden, a consignment of 30 of the 'lost' boxes of comforts finally appeared in time for Christmas 1916.

However the distribution of comforts proved an ongoing sticking point for the Australian tunnelling companies throughout the war, with continuing perceptions by one company CO in particular that distributions were not equitable. As late as January 1918, Morse became aware of requests to Australia asking that comforts be sent directly to tunnelling companies. Major Alexander Sanderson, MC, DSO, CO of the 3rd Australian Tunnelling Company, the predominantly Western Australian unit, proved to be the culprit. Only a meeting of all the Australian tunnelling company COs settled disagreement over the process which, after all, had been agreed to by the majority, and was then continued, albeit under a cloud of suspicion from elements of the collective.

Life at Headquarters

The men whose work was based at the workshop and office at company headquarters established routines with their own ebb and flow, quite separate to those based at the front. The five workshops, stores area and office had their own staff who worked long hours during the day. However, unless there was an urgent job request, they were able to lead a rather less frenetic existence, with the threat of violent death from shot or shell a mere spectre compared to the front.

The men at Hazebrouck were billeted in three nearby farm buildings, while officers rented rooms at the house where the headquarters office was located. Like most military establishments of the day, the sergeants had their own mess, as did the officers. In addition, each officer had his own 'man' — his batman or personal assistant.

Administrative and clerical positions were held by men who were left over from the dissolution of the Mining Corps and whose professional training was not suited to the technical electrical or mechanical works. These included former members of the corps band as well as No. 5 Lance Sergeant Penleigh Boyd, the accomplished Australian landscape artist. Boyd had been the Mining Corps transport sergeant but, with break-up of the corps and the division of transport assets among the tunnelling companies, he was assigned the role of the unit's stores inventory manager.

In the early months of the unit, prior to its expansion or formal designation, he described his role in unflattering terms to his wife:

> My work now is absolutely unexciting and although I like it all right there's nothing interesting. I just wander round the workshop most of the time counting bits of machinery and things and entering them in books. The alternative job offered to me was Billet Sergeant. I would have hated that, as the work mostly consists of making yourself unpleasant to everybody. At present as regards promotion I am at a dead end.

> Now that I'm stuck here all the time scarcely anything happens and I never see anything worth relating. It's just like ordinary civilian life except that I've never kept books in my life & the other chaps from the blacksmith's striker who is a Sydney orchestra player or something in civilian life to Torzillo[37] the guard and general fatigues hand, lately earning about £40 a week as a harpist, are almost all doing jobs they've never done before.[38]

Plate 22. Self-portrait sketch by artist Penleigh Boyd reflecting his despondency over his role in the Alphabet Company (AWM PR84/272).

But with the arrival of more men and the expansion of the unit's workload across the front, there was a huge surge in demand for stores and a constant influx of equipment, both new and old, passing though the storeroom. As Boyd described it:

> My job is sort of Q.M.S. machinery.[39] It's very interesting. I've got to keep all the books about the machinery and keep ordering stock for the store whenever I think anything would be needed. There is a tremendous lot of stuff always coming in and going out … its rather fun ordering electric lamps by the thousand and electric cable by the mile when you don't have to pay for it.[40]

However, men permanently stationed at the headquarters soon discovered that their presence there could be a double-edged sword. On the one hand it was comparatively safe, they could enjoy regular meals and, when time permitted, access to the delights of the local surroundings. On the other hand, there was limited opportunity to relieve the monotony of work, seek promotion and, more importantly, attract honours and awards. In July 1917, in one of his letters, Morse proudly includes a running tally of the awards the company was gradually amassing:

> I've got 3 more medals in the coy for the Wytschaete & Messines stunt, Denton, the DCM and Grieve and March[41] the Military Medal … it at any rate shows that we don't shirk front line work and I guess we won't whilst I'm alive … one lad after being in the line for 9 months, was brought in to the shop for a rest, the 2nd day he wanted to know when he was going out again, as there were no medals to be got in the shop.[42]

Unfortunately, there was a hierarchy, not only in terms of rank but also in the relative worth of skills brought to the unit from civilian life, which capped promotion for those at headquarters who did not possess key skills. The only way to circumvent this obstacle was through outstanding conduct in the field. Consequently, those stationed at the headquarters also harboured a certain degree of envy towards those employed at the front. As Penleigh Boyd lamented: 'The cocks of the walk are the real blacksmiths and carpenters. They are the tradesmen and the others are their labourers.'[43] In an effort to secure promotion and the opportunity for more exciting work, Boyd sought a transfer:

> I sent in an application a week or two ago for transfer to an officers school in England. They do transfers 12 out of every division once a month now

but as there are 20,000 or so in each division & one is sent out of each 1,000 of which 12 are finally selected, I did not think there was much hope … I couldn't even be made a full Sergeant in the Mining Corps because there was a regulation that all Mining Corps Sergeants must be shift bosses in civil life or works foremen or something. As I don't think I've ever heard of either occupation before I couldn't claim to be either. This came in I believe after I had enlisted. Now it's the same in this new company. All Staff Sergeants or higher ranks have to be electricians or certified artisans.[44]

While Penleigh Boyd was not selected for officer training, he eventually succeeded in breaking free from the bonds of headquarters and seeing action at the front. Ironically, this longed-for action saw him gassed during the Third Battle of Ypres in September 1917, repatriated to Australia and discharged from the forces.

The company officers, who made the daily trips to and from the front, lived a double existence that alternated between relative safety and extreme danger. On the one hand they slept in beds fitted with sheets, had a solid roof over their heads and windows fitted with glass, and generally ate at a table in a mess. On the other hand, each journey to the front was a gamble with death. They began to accumulate so many near-death experiences that each new incident became just another talking point at the end of the day.

However life in the billets and workshop was not without its own dangers. Hazebrouck was well within range of large-calibre German artillery, and the town was routinely shelled throughout the war. Victor Morse describes a typical scene during shelling at a dwelling where officers were routinely billeted:

When they commence raining down, there's a scatter in the house, and if there is no cellar, the old dame sits in one corner of the ground floor room, counts her beads and 'Hail Mary' all the time, the old chap sits in the other corner blaspheming at all eternity the hun, new oaths coming as each fresh window smashes in or the house next door disappears, only leaving the door handle, the batman stands in the doorway watching the fireworks, the officer, if he is B.E.F., most are, stays upstairs in bed. Trying to be brave as a morale boost for the others, and to kid the civilians there's nothing to be frightened about.

We've just built a new mess and the night before we went into it the bosche simply riddled it through and through, it's given us better ventilation.[45]

But death could strike the workshop in far more insidious ways and it was not immune from workplace accidents simply because of the war setting. On 10 May 1917, No. 2350 Sapper William Fisher, an electrician working in the workshop at Hazebrouck, was badly burned, possibly due to an electrical discharge. He was taken to the 13th Stationary Hospital at Boulogne.

As if to compound the tragedy, Fisher's sister Mary was working as a nurse at the 3rd Australian Auxiliary Hospital in nearby Wimereux. She visited her badly injured brother and, given her training, recognised the gravity of his plight. Victor Morse met her six weeks after the accident. She told him that, as soon as she had seen her brother, she knew he had little chance of surviving. Her prognosis proved correct and, on 18 May, he succumbed to his injuries.

Morse soon discovered that one of the few perks of being a CO was the ability to 'recruit' men from other units for the benefit of his company. He could also have men transferred for personal or family reasons. There were at least two occasions when Morse exercised this privilege, the first at the request of one of his older men. At the age of 44, No. 2844 William Northcote became the leading carpenter workshop foreman at Hazebrouck and was regarded as a father figure, always willing to help and offering kind and wise words to the younger men of the unit. He assumed the role of president of a self-improvement and social group at the headquarters and was likewise admired by his CO. Northcote's 19-year-old son, Thomas, arrived in France with the Australian 1st Pioneer Battalion in early 1916, and his father, fearful for his son's safety, asked Morse if Thomas could join him at Hazebrouck. Morse agreed, arranged the transfer and Thomas Northcote duly arrived in September 1916, the father and son partnership destined to survive the war.

Morse's assistance with the posting of family members did not stop with his men and later extended to his 25-year-old brother-in-law, Clive Neill, who had enlisted with the Australian artillery. In January 1917 Clive arrived in France as a gunner with the 3rd Division's 26th Battery, 7th Field Artillery Brigade. Victor located him soon after his arrival, and they discussed a transfer to the Alphabet Company. At the time, Neill decided to remain with the guns; by July, however, his attitude had changed and he agreed to join the Alphabet Company. A month later he had been transferred to Hazebrouck, just as his former artillery brigade was to see action in the Third Battle of Ypres during the Battle of Menin Road. Having secured his wife's brother a transfer from doing battle with military hardware to doing battle with military bureaucracy, Morse wrote reassuringly:

I hope 'tis for the best, I think it is, though as regards safety it may mean out of the frying pan into the fire. He had it close getting here, when I saw him he still had a lot of dirt to shake off, thanks to the efforts of a shell alongside him.

After initially being sent out into the Wings Way sector between Loos and Givenchy (Givenchy-les-la-Bassée, not to be confused with Givenchy-en-Gohelle) for a few months, Neill returned to the headquarters. There he assumed a role more suited to his civilian profession, becoming the company's orderly room sergeant, an important administrative role. He was among the last handful of the unit's men the leave France along with his brother-in-law the CO.

Troubles at Headquarters

Through the frantic days and months of 1917 and the succession of major British offensives — Arras, Messines and Third Ypres — the company quietly and consistently completed its assigned tasks and accumulated rewards for its efforts. Pride in the unit grew as the men cultivated their expertise in their particular battlefield craft. But, as the last of the great battles of 1917 was drawing to a close, an incident occurred that shook the unit's headquarters to its core and affected the morale of its officers, in particular, Major Victor Morse, for many months to come. The events of the evening of 27 November and the precursor to these only came to light at the General Court Martial of No. 1291 Company Sergeant Major William Curtis just two months later.

William Curtis had been with the Alphabet Company from its earliest days, having left Australia as the bandmaster of the Australian Mining Corps band. With the demise of the corps and, by association, the demise of the band, he and his fellow band members remained with the remnants of the corps headquarters to fill other roles, mostly in administrative positions. Prior to enlisting Curtis had served 15 years with the military, 12 as a regular soldier, a bandsman with the 1st Battalion, East Kent Regiment (The Buffs). He migrated to Australia in 1909, married and, by 1915, had three children.

Following the disbandment of the Australian Mining Corps, Curtis spent some three months working as the sergeant in charge of one of the water boring parties, returning to Hazebrouck when the unit officially became the Australian Electrical and Mechanical Mining and Boring Company. He was then appointed Company Sergeant Major. In November 1917 he was acting pay sergeant during the absence of No. 4033 Sergeant Thomas Dowling who was in England at the time, attending a pay sergeant's course. All monies held by the company for pay and the purchase of equipment along with any important maps and plans were kept under lock and key in the headquarters office, in what was known as the plan box, a wooden box that was kept under the desk in the office. There was only one key, at that time entrusted to the care of William Curtis.

On the night of 27 November the plan box contained 3160 francs — the company's imprest money, which covered payments for equipment and supplies as well as the men's pay. As it was public money, documented evidence of any expenditure was duly required so that expended funds could be replaced from the public purse through the War Office. The plan box also contained an envelope with another 284 francs in contributions from the men for canteen purchases. A third envelope contained 180 francs belonging to the absent Sergeant Dowling. In today's currency (2014) the total monies in the plan box amounted to almost AU$10,000. Of this AU$8,500 was public money for which ultimate responsibility lay with the unit's CO, Victor Morse.

On the evening of 27 November William Curtis paid leave money to the workshop foremen, Corporal Sinclair and Sergeant Hugh Thurlow, who were going on leave to Paris the next morning. Curtis then placed the plan box in its usual spot under the office table and the unit was closed for the night, its staff retiring to bed. Sapper Clive Neill, Victor Morse's brother-in-law and the orderly room clerk, slept in a room above the office. At 1.00 am, Mademoiselle Geus, the owner of the building, woke Neill in a state of high excitement and, rushing downstairs, they discovered the office full of smoke. The source of the fire was found to be on top of the wooden plan box and in the waste paper bin under the office table. The fire was extinguished and, although the top of the box was badly charred, the lock was intact and the lid remained secured. Victor Morse was summoned and, after surveying the superficial damage to the room, he checked the lock and then placed a seal over it. Morse wrote to his wife a few days later describing subsequent events:

> I've had the worst possible thing happen to me that could, I've had about £150 of the mess pay stolen and worst of all, the room strewed with petrol and set alight to cover the theft, and with the knowledge that it might mean certain death to some occupants sleeping above … and probably the whole terrace. I don't know a more dastardly act.

After breakfast on the morning after the fire, Morse summoned William Curtis and instructed him to open the box. The seal was removed and the box duly unlocked with the only key. All the money and envelopes were missing.

Victor Morse immediately ordered a Court of Enquiry overseen by Captain Stanley Hunter and Lieutenant George Norfolk.

Over the course of the next few days, two officers, nine other ranks and three French women, including the building's owner, were interviewed as witnesses and all the details recorded. After the enquiry, William Curtis was left in no doubt that he was the prime suspect as all the evidence pointed to him. The fire had occurred on Wednesday and in the early hours of the following Sunday, William Curtis quietly made his way to where he had buried the money outside the office, dug it up and absconded.

Curtis was later apprehended and, at Poperinghe on the morning of 29 December and in the presence of Assistant Provost Marshal Captain Strachen, he stated that he had recovered the cash from the imprest box and bolted. He had just 935 francs on him when he was arrested. His reasons formed part of his defence at his court martial a month later. Foremost were his feelings of dissatisfaction at his treatment by his CO. He told the court that his daughter had died in Australia in late 1917 and he had been refused permission to return home. He had also formed the impression that, during his time as company sergeant major, he had been overlooked for leave and pay privileges afforded to others in the unit. His history of good conduct for prior military service was taken into account, but he pleaded guilty to receiving stolen money and being absent without leave. He was sentenced to reduction to the ranks and two years' imprisonment with hard labour at No. 10 Military Prison, Dunkirk.[46]

While this incident illustrates that grievance and temptation were just as prevalent in the military as in civilian life, at a personal level, the consequences of the theft were deeply felt. The loss of the unit's money weighed on Victor Morse, who accepted full liability, and the pall of depression caused by the theft lingered for many months. He knew what the theft meant to the men, as did his fellow officers. He later wrote,

> ... saw Major David a day or so after and he told me that he would consider it a very unfriendly act on my part if I did not allow him to share my loss ... but I definitely refused his offer. Hunter and my own officers have offered to do the same, and their offers have likewise been turned down. I guess it's a poor spirit that can't stand by his own responsibilities ... but isn't it grand to get these offers, and from dear old Major too, who though so close to our hearts, has nothing to do with us. Well it's no use moping over it, but I would like to handle the culprit.[47]

A Court of Enquiry was subsequently convened on 1 March 1918 to consider whether there had been a breach of the King's Regulation 112 in relation to the considerable responsibilities of a CO. The court found:

> Every company, etc., commander, even if the appointment is held only temporarily, is charged with the equipment, ammunition, clothing, and public stores appertaining thereto, and is accountable for them to his C.O. He is responsible for his men's messes and necessaries being properly provided. He will pay attention to the cleanliness of the men and to that of their clothing, arms, accoutrements, and barracks or quarters. He is bound to take charge of all money received on account of his company, etc., and is responsible for the safe custody of such money, and for its being expended in conformity with regulations and with due regard to the interests of his men. A N.C.O. is not to be subjected to the risk of loss by having public money placed in his hands.

At face value, placing public and private money in the hands of an NCO is exactly what Victor Morse had done. However, in his defence, it was explained to the members of the board that the special needs of the Alphabet Company required all its officers to be away from the headquarters for extended periods of time to attend to matters of a highly technical nature over a large section of the British front line. The CO had little choice but to delegate responsibility for the company's funds to an NCO — in this case a sergeant. The court considered the appeal with some sympathy. The verdict, which took two months to filter though to Morse, was that the stolen money would be reimbursed by the government and he was not liable for its repayment. This must have been an enormous relief after many months of anxiety.

As history would have it, and by Victor Morse's own admission, the pay sergeant, Thomas Dowling, who was in England at the time of the theft, was also one of a small handful of his charges who had caused the CO much grief since the early days of the unit. While on the pay sergeant's course, Dowling was charged twice for absence without leave and, following his return, was involved in a fight. That was the last straw and, in April 1918, he was court-martialled, reduced to the ranks and sentenced to six months' hard labour. Another bad apple had been removed from Morse's care.

Unfortunately for Morse, the theft of the company's imprest money in November 1917 was just the first of two monumental events involving the loss of important documents at company headquarters as the consequence of an individual's poor judgement.

By April 1919, the war was over and the company's headquarters and workshops had been established at Maroeuil outside Arras since the previous November. The process of demobilisation had been under way for over a month and men were gradually leaving for Australia via England in batches. The process was two-thirds complete and, among the last hundred men awaiting their turn, some were beginning to become restless. At the time, Victor Morse was in the throes of finalising the unit history in preparation for handing the completed set of documents to the War Office once he finally left France. He had accumulated a huge collection of relevant documentation, daily diary entries complied for each month along with their appendices of orders, administration records, maps, plans and photographs. He had been completing the diary entries, a job he had delayed for many months until the time deadline had forced his hand.

In the early hours of 6 April, three men from the unit, drunk and looking for mischief, broke into the mess, doused it with petrol and set it alight. Because of the space it afforded, Morse had been using the mess as a workplace to lay out all the accumulated paperwork of unit history records. Soon, the building and its contents were ablaze. The company's cook was sufficiently level-headed to grab whatever he could before being forced out by the heat and managed to save a clutch of the company's letters. Some of Morse's handwritten diary notes and, importantly, a number of marked maps, now in the possession of the Australian Archives and War Memorial collections, were not in the mess at the time. However everything else, including personal items belonging to Morse and George Norfolk, along with £170 in cash, was reduced to little more than a cloud of sparks and ash rising into the cold night sky. The three instigators of the fire were arrested, but this was little consolation to Victor Morse, as the responsibility for furnishing a unit history to the War Office remained and he could not return to Australia until this task had been completed. The mission now weighed like a granite yoke around his neck and, in the days that followed, the prospect of returning home must have seemed almost beyond reach. But, like all the challenges the war threw at him, following the initial shudder of shock, Morse drew on an inner strength and simply started again. However, the historical consequences of what was the senseless act of three now nameless men have continued to reverberate. So much of the intimate detail of the workings and operations of the company were lost, detail that Morse on his own could not be expected to resurrect and did not. That intimate knowledge was also lost to later generations.

Fraternisation

For men stationed for extended periods at headquarters, particularly in places such as Hazebrouck where a large portion of the local population remained during the war in spite of the shelling, those towns and their inhabitants offered an inviting source of distraction. This was one of the few perks of being headquarters-bound. The soldiers were a long way from home and from their spouses, sweethearts or friends and the comforts they offered. The men also had ready access to cafes and estaminets where cheap wine could be purchased with food, usually at inflated prices for the cashed-up soldiers who grumbled but tolerated their exploitation by enterprising shopkeepers seeking to earn a little extra money while their establishments still boasted a roof and four walls.

The towns in which the men were billeted and with whose inhabitants they interacted on a daily basis also boasted numerous diversions that could be readily accessed when free time permitted. These attracted many soldiers, among them the sappers of the Alphabet Company. On occasion, the officers of the unit were compelled to employ delicate negotiation to resolve problems that arose in their dealings with the civilian population. Women were usually at the heart of the matter and indeed, for those inclined, women were never far from their thoughts — that is, when not focused on other important issues such as the prospect of imminent death.

Plate 23. 'Now, do the French and Australians really fraternise?' A sketch by Sergeant Hugh Thurlow illustrating the comforts of the local female population and the passions they aroused. This presented a constant headache for any CO (AWM 3DRL/4059).

Local women who found themselves in an altercation were often either the innocent victim of a sapper's affection or the instigator of demands arising from amorous liaisons where expectations on the part of a flower of France were mismatched with those of a lion of Australia. Either way, problems resulting from fraternisation proved distracting for the company's officers who were generally more preoccupied with other more pressing issues, such as winning a war. At times the men sought their officers' assistance with problematic indiscretions while, at other times, it was the aggrieved belle who sought intervention to resolve an impasse.

On one occasion, Victor Morse noticed that his batman appeared dejected, and the cause soon became apparent. The man had become romantically entangled and, during the course of the relationship, had been borrowing money from the object of his desire. The sum was of sufficient magnitude that its repayment was subject to a condition: her agreeing to engagement — hardly an endearing strategy for winning the heart of a loved one. The young lady was caught in a difficult position. She could not admit the situation to her mother for fear of a severe reprimand for her foolhardiness. However she may have been reluctant to marry a man who would resort to such a ruse to win her hand. This tactic had been deftly employed by the desperate Australian, the terms of marriage and repayment used almost to blackmail her into deciding in his favour. Ultimately his gamble backfired, succeeding only in backing the blackmailed party into a corner and raising her ire. She sought out the man's CO, before whom the whole sorry story was recounted in dramatic fashion, resulting in the abashed blackmailer losing in one blow the money borrowed and, more devastatingly, his intended bride. The dejected lover later embarked on 14 days' leave in England and returned a married man, the news of which prompted his puzzled CO to muse, 'lord knows what he picked up in London.'

On another occasion, one of his 'shop birds', as Victor Morse referred to his headquarters-bound men, developed a misjudged attachment to one of the women of the town notorious for sharing comfort and pleasure with any man willing to pay. The naïve soul revealed his intention to marry the lady in question, a fact brought to an officer's attention by a concerned mate. The soldier in question was promptly reassigned to a front-line position well away from trouble and from certain heartbreak. Conversely, there was an at least one occasion when Victor Morse was asked by one of his men for reassignment to a distant sector. The self-imposed banishment from mates and the comforts of well-established billets was the price this sapper was prepared to pay to avoid the problems he envisaged if he should remain exposed to temptation. Another of the company's batmen was responsible for a local girl finding herself 'in trouble' after the company had moved from Hazebrouck to the countryside at Assinghem. Victor Morse only discovered this once the company had again moved on, although at least the man had the decency to seek permission to marry the unfortunate girl. When Morse travelled back to investigate, he discovered other ladies similarly afflicted and was surprised to receive a cold reception. He later found out that his men had been claiming that their CO would not permit them to marry, using this as an excuse for not fulfilling their moral obligation to these women.

Officers generally had less opportunity to develop relationships than their men due to the frenetic pace of their workloads and the fact that they were almost constantly on the move. This is not to suggest that officers did not fraternise, nor that successful relationships did not occur between the men and local women. There are many stories of men returning from the war with European brides. Captain Garnet Adcock, adjutant of the 2nd Australian Tunnelling Company, returned to Australia with a Belgian wife, while Major Alexander Sanderson, CO of the 3rd Australian Tunnelling Company, returned to Australia with an English wife. For most men however, the consequences were less rosy and indeed many a service record bears the conspicuous letters 'V.D.' (venereal disease) as a line entry beside dates and the name of the hospital where this insidious consequence of intimate moments was treated. However, it is also clear that the consequences of fraternisation took many forms and left many a man unscathed. Those of the Alphabet Company were no exception.

Socialising

Plates 24–26. Three depictions of Christmas 1917 by Hugh Thurlow: 'Xmas Eve', depicting Christmas at Alphabet Company Headquarters; 'Xmas 1917'; and 'Since Xmas our MO has been working day and night' (AWM 3DRL/4059).

Life at headquarters, while busy for everyone stationed there, was still a refuge from the horrors of the front and, when the opportunity arose, the front-line long-termers were rotated through for some rest away from being constantly on call and in the thick of the action. The men stationed at the front developed close working and social relationships with unit colleagues in their sector and men from the resident tunnelling company responsible for that sector where the Alphabet Company was embedded. The men were routinely billeted with and messed with men from the tunnelling companies, usually British or Canadian, for months or even years on end and only reconnected with the men from their own unit during the occasional return to headquarters for a rest.

Those permanently stationed at headquarters endeavoured to make their lives as comfortable as possible under the circumstances. Like most military establishments, the lower ranks, sergeants and officers each had their own billets and mess. The officers in particular made the most of the opportunity to live life to the full while they could and delighted in the company of their fellows when fortuitously assembled in the same place. Festive seasons in particular were celebrated in style and none more so than Christmas, when they sought some form of compensation for the fact that they could not be at home with their families. This compensation took the form of a bounty of food and drink of surprising sumptuousness given the war-induced austerity of the surroundings in which they found themselves. Much of the food was provided in parcels from home, pooled and shared among the members of the mess. This was augmented with foodstuffs and other luxuries that arrived via the Comforts Funds.

It was not unusual for each unit to produce its own Christmas cards and the Alphabet Company was no exception. The unit also had at its disposal a world-class professional artist, and Penleigh Boyd produced a set of lightning sketches, caricatures of the officers, which were then auctioned at the unit's Christmas Day concert in 1916 with all proceeds donated to the mess. The auction was held after Christmas dinners with menus that boasted such delicacies as suckling pig, duckling, goose, pies, nuts, puddings, cakes and chocolates. Victor Morse and Stanley Hunter bought their own caricatures for a total sum of 36 francs. Such was the high esteem in which Morse was held by his men that he was treated to a round of three cheers and a rendition of 'for he's a jolly good fellow' which, by his own admission, brought a lump to his throat.

The following Christmas, Major Edgeworth David accepted an invitation to brave blizzard conditions and travelled the 130 kilometres from GHQ to spend Christmas dinner with some of his old officer friends from the Mining Corps days. Dinner was the culinary creation of Officers' Mess cook No. 1477 2nd

Corporal Joseph Lord. Before settling down to enjoy a spread of soup, chicken with vegetables, roast beef, sweets, stewed fruit, lollies and coffee, Edgeworth David made a speech to members of the unit who had assembled for their dinner in a large church tent. Officer friends from other units dropped by to join the festivities, including Major (later Lieutenant Colonel) Thomas Lowry, DSO, MC, CO of the British 173rd and 174th tunnelling companies.

Plate 27. Alphabet Company Officers' Mess, Hazebrouck, Christmas dinner 1917 (AWM H12765).

Other ways in which the men strengthened social bonds included through sport and news. Inspired by the success of the wartime satirical newspaper, the *Wipers Times*, and the humorous distraction it afforded men in the most dreadful of circumstances, the Alphabet Company turned its hand to producing a newsletter for its members, with articles invited from both the unit's aspiring writers and its collection of wits and wags. References to humorous incidents and the peculiarities of well-known members of the unit were encouraged, although advice or commentary on more serious issues was also welcomed. The monthly journal was called *The Vivid Flash* and the first edition was printed in October 1917 during the height of the Third Battle of Ypres (Passchendaele), at a time when parties of men from the unit in the Ypres salient would have been worked to the bone. The introductory note to the first edition explained the purpose of the publication:

Some of us have the luck to be able to indulge in 'Spare time', whilst others less fortunate will, on the advent of this Journal, probably gain a few moments pleasure from the results of our aforesaid 'Spare time'.

The journal contained smatterings of poetry, unit news, the current list of unit honours, advice into matters of importance such as hygiene and sanitation, and frivolity of all kinds ranging from the parodying of various NCOs to nonsensical classified advertisements, many invoking reference to the opposite sex, such as:

For Sale: A shop-soiled baritone voice. Owner giving up business.

Apply. L/Cpl. Workshops

Wanted: At once. Assistant for night work. Female preferred.

Apply Bob Lee[48] Workshops

Wanted: Electrician. One used to maintaining steady supply in Residential Flats. Permanency to suitable man.

Call or Write. Billet.

For Sale: For immediate disposal. Fully stocked Poultry Farm. Splendid egg trade.

Apply. Joe Lord. Officers' Mess.

Typewriting: Young ladies urgently wanted to learn typewriting. No fees. Avoid so-called colleges. Instruction & success guaranteed. Ladies taught at home or in private apartments if desired.

Apply Sergt. Major Hd. Qrs.

Wanted: Young lady for post office work. Free tuition

Apply. Company Postman Hd. Qrs.

Wanted: Young lady with experience in men's trousers.

Apply: Q.M. Stores

Sport, particularly soccer, rugby (union) and cricket, depending on the season and weather, was another form of socialising and further strengthened the bonds between the men. Sports of every variety were played by soldiers of all ranks across the entire front. There were competitions both within units and between local units with unit pride fiercely contested and defended. There were also regular competitions in other sports such as boxing, musketry and tug-of-war in which, once again, the pride of the unit was the usual prize. One unusual sport in which the Alphabet Company indulged was water polo. When

Hazebrouck was under threat of being overrun during the German spring offensive in April 1918, and the company workshops and headquarters were evacuated to the tiny village of Assinghem, the new base was situated on the banks of the River Aa. The proximity of water and the onset of warm spring weather combined to encourage all sorts of water-based activities, including competitive water polo. Matches were played against staff from nearby casualty clearing stations, including No. 2 Casualty Clearing Station and, on at least one occasion, a French team was challenged and defeated before the match was abandoned due to a cold snap.

By 1918 the company had also arranged the use a military rest camp on the French coast for groups of officers and men on leave as an alternative location to England or that other favourite leave destination, Paris. The rest camp was invariably far cheaper than the big cities and the men could also spend their free time with larger groups of friends.

Given the dispersed nature of the unit's work, the company never assembled at full strength at its headquarters, or anywhere else for that matter. One rare occasion when a respectable proportion of the company was assembled at headquarters occurred during the period when it was based in Assinghem, and a large number of men gathered for a medal presentation on 29 August 1918. On that occasion over 100 men — around 40% of the company's strength — were assembled and, the morning before the presentation, put through a rapid rehearsal drill. A number of men were brought in from distant jobs to witness the presentation of medals to 13 members of the unit. The presenting officer was none other than General Sir William Birdwood, then General Officer Commanding (GOC) the British Fifth Army, and another friend of Victor Morse. The next time any significant number of men gathered at headquarters was in the early months of 1919, with the war over and the company already commencing its slide into history.

CHAPTER 4

MESSINES RIDGE

The mainstay of the Alphabet Company's front-line work was its 'engine rooms'. These were dugouts, usually located underground, that housed the petrol-driven engines and generators that were connected in turn to the local mining and dugout systems via electrical cabling and controlled by a wall-mounted switchboard. To reduce the cabling's vulnerability to damage by shellfire and random bullets, engine rooms were constructed in whatever converted cellar or hole in the ground was available, as close to the front line as possible. They were, for the most part, hot, oily, noisy, smelly and cramped little places from which tangles of electrical wiring would sprout and head off in all directions. Many of the larger dugout systems that eventually populated the ground below the fields and hills of France and Flanders had engine rooms custom-built at the time of their construction which made life easier for the Alphabet Company crews tasked with manning them. Many others, however, were constructed from makeshift materials in hasty excavations in sometimes less than salubrious locations.

A week after installing its first permanent power supply at the Second Army Mine School on 20 May 1916, the Alphabet Company began its long association with underground workings. Its first tasks concerned the mining systems that had been established along the British front below the Messines Ridge.

The concept of the Messines mines evolved following the Second Battle of Ypres in April 1916 which involved the failed attempt to capture and retain one of the most contested sites of the war — Hill 60 on the northern edge of the Messines Ridge. Hill 60 was one of several select locations on the Western Front that claimed legendary status in the annals of the First World War. Situated atop the Messines Ridge — or, as it is more accurately known at that location, the Zandvoorde Ridge — on the southern edge of the Ypres salient, it was a vital German observation post into the southern part of the salient.

While the ridge remained in German hands, any British plans for a large-scale frontal assault were immediately stymied by German observation of British troop movements and the consequent threat of a crippling artillery barrage. Artillery and observation were the keys to winning the war. The ridge, and strategic positions along it such as Hill 60, quite simply *had* to be taken from the Germans. The battles that raged at Hill 60 between 1914 and 1917 saw many thousands of lives lost in attempts to capture and defend it.

The 'hill' was, in fact, one of three soil dumps — spoil from excavation of the Ypres–Comines railway embankment where the railway cuts through the ridgeline. The excavated soil was disposed of simply by dumping it on either side of the cutting. Hill 60 was the northernmost of the three dumps. It rose to a height of around four to five metres above the natural ground level and sloped slightly downwards from its northern to southern side. It was shaped like a badly formed rectangle, elongated along its west-east axis with its rounded, western end facing the British front line. The long axis of the hill, which ran away from the British front line, was around 160 metres in length and 100 metres wide.

A second large dump known as 'the Caterpillar' lay on the southern side of the railway cutting but offset to the south-east of Hill 60 by around 100 metres. Shaped like a long, thin sausage, it lay parallel to the railway embankment, extending away from Hill 60. A kink in the middle of the dump gave it the appearance of a caterpillar, hence its name. The western end of the Caterpillar, which the Germans called Hill 59, also formed part of the German front line and, together with Hill 60, these comprised a highly valuable strategic position. The third and smallest soil dump, unimaginatively called 'the Dump', lay inside the British lines around 450 metres north of the Caterpillar. Looking from the British lines, Hill 60 and the Caterpillar together formed a curious if not unique position on the Western Front: two flat-topped mounds rising abruptly from the sides of a deep railway embankment and all situated atop a gently rising, almost undiscernible ridge.

The small village of Zwarteleen lay to the immediate north-east of Hill 60 and the equally small village of Verbrandenmolen lay half a kilometre north-west of Hill 60. The two villages were connected by a road which swung around the western side of the hill and crossed the railway embankment by a small bridge adjacent to the south-western toe of the hill. The deep railway cutting forced a break in the front lines. By the time the Australian tunnellers arrived, both villages had been pulverised.

Given its strategic importance in affording a view of the entire Ypres salient, it is not surprising that Hill 60 was the scene of fierce fighting, particularly during the first year of the war. The French had originally fought in the area in December 1914. When the British relieved the French in February 1915, the Allied front line ran from the north-west through the southern side of Zwarteleen, around the western toe of Hill 60 and across the small bridge over the railway cutting. From there the front line continued its meandering course to the south-west.

Alexander Barrie describes Hill 60 as it appeared in February 1915:

> ... a mean misshapen triple hummock that was on its way to immortality for the multitude of young men who were to die there. Already it was thinly littered with decomposing foul-smelling British, French and German bodies.[1]

On 5 May 1915 the first gas attack of the war was launched by the Germans with devastating effect. The precarious gains made by the British and the sacrifices made at the hill over the preceding two and a half weeks were lost. The Germans won back the hill and consolidated their position. From that time until June 1917, the hill remained in German possession. Its loss was a heavy blow to the British. They understood that failure to control it and the rest of Messines Ridge would exact a high price.

Despite their appalling losses, the British retained their conviction that the ridge had to be taken — the question was simply how.[2] A British engineering contractor and the founding force behind the British tunnelling companies, John Norton-Griffiths, delivered the answer. Norton-Griffiths was an unconventional man and, true to character, strove to achieve his goals beyond the scale most men would seriously consider. He devised a plan — the 'Messines Plan' — an idea which came to him one rainy day in May 1915 during an inspection of the British line. He looked up towards the ridge and pondered the outcome of an attack on Hill 60 a month earlier during the Second Battle of Ypres. In his mind's eye he pictured the ridge as it was, an arc bulging into the British lines extending from Hill 60 to just south-west of the town of Messines. In the centre of the arc and sitting atop the ridge, was the town of Wytschaete. The Germans looked down over the British from the western rim of the ridge. Dislodging the enemy from such a position of ascendancy using a conventional frontal attack had already proven almost impossible without massive loss of life. To Norton-Griffiths the answer was obvious. The lamentable attacking position of the British infantry was, in fact, a gift to the British tunnellers. He pictured the British tunnelling directly into the ridge under the German positions, not at one point, but a multitude of points and, when the time was right, literally blowing the Germans off the ridge. Given sufficient resources to undertake such a massive and daring operation, he was convinced that his scheme would succeed.

Norton-Griffiths presented his idea to Robert Harvey who, at the time, was still the assistant to the Engineer-in-Chief, Brigadier General George Fowke. He sought Harvey's assistance to persuade General Fowke to support his plan. Despite Harvey's best efforts, Fowke dismissed the plan outright as utterly fanciful. But Norton-Griffiths was not to be deterred. He was so certain of the plan's merit that he kept its genesis alive through ongoing discussions with Harvey, who slowly began to appreciate the plan's potential. Gradually, he began to recognise that, in concert with a general infantry assault on the ridge, such a scheme might just work.

The breakthrough came in January 1916 when General Fowke handed operational matters for the tunnelling companies to the newly created Inspector of Mines. Robert Harvey was appointed to the position and promoted brigadier general. Harvey now controlled all British mining activity across the British sector of the Western Front. His appointment equipped him with the position and authority to see the plan he now championed presented to the British High Command. In a meeting of army commanders on 6 January 1916, the engineers unveiled their scheme. Over the eight months since its inception, Norton-Griffiths and Harvey had carefully defined and refined the plan. Norton-Griffiths argued convincingly that the ridge was, in technical terms, essentially a hill of soft, partially wet sand lying on a solid bed of the blue clay that was ideal for tunnelling. He believed that the shock waves caused by a succession of massive mines along the ridge would have the same effect as an earthquake. The objective now was not to *blow* the Germans off the ridge but to *shake* them off by causing a man-made earthquake. He argued that a frontal attack of infantry that followed on the heels of such an explosion would succeed because of the damaging and demoralising effect of the mines all along the ridge.

The generals at GHQ listened patiently to Norton-Griffiths' extraordinary proposal and, to his immense relief, approved it. The Messines Plan became a reality and marked the start of one of the most visionary and audacious operations ever adopted in the First World War.

Work soon commenced to place a series of massive mines in the arc below the German front line extending from Hill 60 to Trench 121 adjacent to the southern corner of Ploegsteert Wood, a distance of around 12 kilometres. At existing mining hotspots on the ridge such as Hill 60 and St Eloi, the relatively

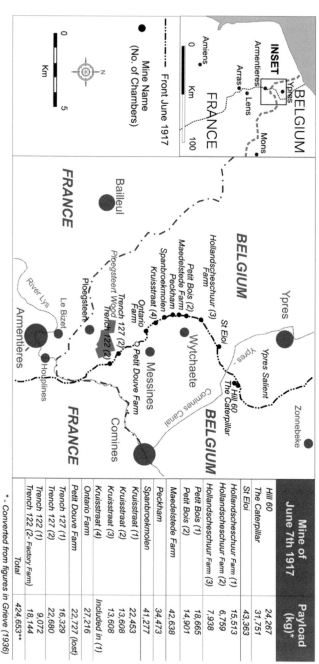

Mine of June 7th 1917	Payload (kg)*
Hill 60	24,267
The Caterpillar	31,751
St Eloi	43,363
Hollandscheschuur Farm (1)	15,513
Hollandscheschuur Farm (2)	6,759
Hollandscheschuur Farm (3)	7,938
Petit Bois (1)	18,665
Petit Bois (2)	14,901
Maedelstede Farm	42,638
Peckham	34,473
Spanbroekmolen	41,277
Kruisstraat (1)	22,453
Kruisstraat (2)	13,608
Kruisstraat (3)	13,608
Kruisstraat (4)	Included in (1)
Ontario Farm	27,216
Petit Douve Farm	22,727 (lost)
Trench 127 (1)	16,329
Trench 127 (2)	22,680
Trench 122 (1)	9,072
Trench 122 (2 - Factory Farm)	18,144
Total	424,653**

* - Converted from figures in Grieve (1936)
** - Excludes the Petit Douve Farm Mine

Map 5. The Messines Ridge mines.

uncoordinated mining work took on a fresh impetus and new shafts commenced around the arc of the ridge into late 1915 and early 1916 as more and more tunnelling companies came into existence.

In total, 26 mine chambers at 13 locations extending from Hill 60 to Ploegsteert Wood were dug, charged and tamped in readiness for firing in early June 1917. The payload from these mines totalled a staggering 507,200 kilograms, with individual mines ranging in size from a meagre 6759 kilograms in the Hollandscheschuur (No. 2) chamber to a massive 43,363 kilograms in the St Eloi chamber — the biggest mine laid in military mining history. Each of the great mines carries its own tales of the dramatic scenes that marked its installation and protection.

By the eve of their detonation, only 19 of the great mines, with a combined payload of just over 424,500 kilograms (424.5 tonnes) had been earmarked for detonation. A second mine chamber at Peckham had been charged with just over 9 tonnes of explosives when wet ground conditions caused the gallery leading to the chamber to collapse. The mine was lost and attempts to recover it proved futile. To this day, the mine remains like a sleeping giant, lying below the ground next to the water-filled crater of its long-exploded partner. At a German strongpoint at La Petite Douve Farm, just south of Messines, a mine chamber containing just over 22.7 tonnes of explosives was also lost when the mine chamber was irreparably damaged by German counter-mining. This mine also lies dormant under Belgian soil.

As early as June 1916, four mines with charges totalling 50.8 tonnes had been placed under another German strongpoint known as 'the Birdcage' at Le Pelerin, opposite Trench 121. The mines lay in the sector taken over by the 1st Australian Tunnelling Company soon after it began operations in France. These mines were later considered too far south to be of any material use in the Battle of Messines and were kept in reserve for another opportunity. That opportunity never arose and, before the mines could be recovered and rendered harmless prior to the German offensive in the spring of 1918, they were also lost. In July 1955, one of the mines blew when lightning struck a power pole unwittingly placed directly above the 40-year-old mine chamber. The electric charge that surged through the ground was sufficient to activate the still-live detonator at the centre of the 11.8-tonne mine below the pole. The result was an immense explosion that blew a hole in the centre of a field. The remaining 39 tonnes of high explosives in the other three mine chambers remain, lurking somewhere below the fields.

Peckham Farm
Company Tour of Duty: Peckham Mining System

The first front-line mine sector in which the precursor unit to the Alphabet Company established itself was the Peckham Farm (Peckham) mining system in the centre of the arc of Messines mines. The British 250th Tunnelling Company began work on the mine system in December 1915 in an attempt to target a German strongpoint established in ruined buildings on the German front line known by the British as Peckham Farm. A shaft 21 metres deep was sunk, followed by a second shaft, both of which were connected to the main drive which was angled towards the farm, south-east of the shafts.

The mining conditions at this location were difficult from the outset. The blue clay — the sought-after compact and relatively water free clay layer below the ridge — was soon found to swell more extensively than at other mine systems. Once exposed to air, the clay swelled so much that it crushed timber supports and strained cables and leads. The Peckham mine system was also notoriously susceptible to flooding.

The mine shaft descended 20 metres into the side of the ridge before the mine galleries extended out below the German lines for distances of between 350 and 400 metres. Below no man's land, the main mine drive branched. 'A' branch continued towards Peckham Farm, while 'B' branch headed north-east to target a small German salient which thrust into no man's land just north of the farm. The mine gallery at the end of 'A' branch was successfully completed below the farm and packed with a staggering 34.5 tonnes of explosives. The wiring for the mine detonators was completed by the Alphabet Company.[3]

The 'B' branch drive, however, had advanced just 120 metres when it unexpectedly intersected 'bad' ground — a small geological fault. The resulting offset in the sediments caused by the fault meant that waterlogged sand occurred deeper than expected and water poured into the drive from the saturated sand at the face. The gallery was unrecoverable and a dam was constructed back from the face in an attempt to hold back the water. It was only partially successful. After several attempts, a second mine gallery was finally completed in September 1916 at the end of 'C' drive, which ended just north of the Peckham Farm buildings and was packed with 9 tonnes of explosives. Water inflows and unstable ground were a constant problem at Peckham, so much so that on 23 October 1916 the main 'A' drive collapsed, cutting the leads to both mines, and water inflows flooded the drive. The drive had to be 'dewatered' (drained) and a second drive dug from behind the collapsed section to bypass the lost drive. Fortunately the leads to the main 'A' mine chamber were relocated and electrical contact re-established. More collapses had further isolated the smaller 'C' mine chamber and there was no attempt to reconnect it. That mine still remains below the soil in Belgium.

The Peckham mine system was the first front-line sector in which the Alphabet Company was tasked to provide power for lighting and, more importantly, mine dewatering. The company established the first of its front-line workings at Peckham on 29 May 1916, barely three weeks after arriving in France. A makeshift engine room, with sandbag walls and corrugated iron roof — poor protection against a high-calibre shell — was established off a main communication trench 600 metres from the front line. A second engine room was later established closer to the front, but was quickly deemed too exposed to enemy fire and that site was abandoned and the first engine room re-established. To avoid interference from troop movement and shells, electrical cables were run on poles along the sides of the trenches and two to three metres above the top of the parapet. In this way, 2700 metres of electrical cabling were eventually laid and maintained by the company within 550 metres of the front line.

The first of the mine dewatering pumps was a salvaged pump which had to be located in the cramped space at the bottom of the shaft on the main mine drive. The conditions were dreadful. The pump was constantly choked with fibres from sandbags and other detritus that washed into the various mine galleries and had to be cleared every few hours in the wet, cramped and muddy shaft with working tunnellers trying to move around and over the unfortunate individual whose task it was to clean and restart the pump. Eventually, and after numerous experiments, a charcoal-filled filter box was installed at the pump, reducing the need for clearing from every few hours to every few days.

By October 1916, No. 382 2nd Corporal Richard Grieve, No. 375 Sapper William Cairns and seven other ranks from the Alphabet Company were busy maintaining lighting and water pumping at the Peckham system. The two men were electricians by profession and, by virtue of their skills, had been transferred to the Alphabet Company from the 1st Australian Tunnelling Company.

The Peckham mine system eventually used seven electric pumps to control water inflows, the largest number installed in a single mining system by the Alphabet Company. Power was also used to provide lighting via 90 lighting points. A maximum power supply of 13 kilowatts was achieved by October 1916.

By the time of the Battle of Messines in June 1917, the unit had expanded its connection with the Messines mines, with Grieve and Cairns maintaining four electric power plants in the vicinity of the Peckham mines below the Messines Ridge. For their work at the Peckham mine system, particularly their timely action in the aftermath of the sudden collapse and flooding of the mine galleries in late October 1916 when Grieve worked furiously to pump them clear, he was awarded the Military Medal (MM) and William Cairns the MSM.

Hill 60
Company Tour of Duty: Hill 60

Hill 60, the northernmost of the Messines mines, was one of the first locations in which British tunnelling companies began mining operations in any organised fashion. In February 1915, the first contingent of men from the infant 171st Tunnelling Company arrived at the hill. In July 1915, they were relieved by the 175th which was relieved in turn in April 1916 by the 3rd Canadian Tunnelling Company. By that time the Messines Plan had been approved and, during the summer of 1916, the Canadian tunnellers had placed and tamped the 56 tonnes of explosives in the two mine chambers below Hill 60 and the adjacent Caterpillar.

The Alphabet Company was called on to assist the 3rd Canadian Tunnelling Company at the Hill 60 mining system and arrived on 22 September 1916. By this time the shattered hulk of the hill itself had been in German hands for 17 months. The 6-kilowatt Gardiner generator was housed in a 2 metre x 4 metre engine-room dugout six metres below ground level, in a mine shaft situated just 100 metres behind the front line.

For several months the men maintaining the generator and ancillary equipment were forced to use the engine room as their sleeping quarters because the tunnellers were so involved in 'hard underground fighting' that they could not be spared to build another dugout. A significant problem associated with having the engine room located so close to the front was the need to conceal the generator's motor exhaust so that the location of the important mine shaft and nearby dugouts would not be betrayed by either noise or fumes from the motor and draw the attention of the much-feared German trench mortars (*minenwerfers*, known as 'minnies'). The solution was to place two silencers in the exhaust pipe to muffle the noise and extend the end of the pipe above the ground, running it horizontally away from where it emerged from the engine room to a sunken earthen chamber where the exhaust could disperse into the atmosphere. However the exposed pipe was constantly cut by shellfire and repairs had to be effected as quickly as possible. These were generally completed under cover of darkness if the breakage was far enough from the engine room. Those breakages that occurred close to the room were repaired during the day, the men using shell holes as cover. Either way, the prospect of having to leave the trenches and work above ground anywhere within 500 metres of Hill 60, with German eyes peering over the parapet, would have been disturbing for any man.

In early November 1916 the 1st Australian Tunnelling Company replaced the Canadian tunnellers, their task to extend the three levels of mine galleries at Hill 60 and guard the two great mine chambers the Canadians had so skillfully placed. The hill was still heavily contested, a formidable and deadly location, pockmarked with the scars of innumerable artillery shells and punctuated with the remains of larger craters from almost two years of mining and counter-mining activity.

Like many of the Messines mine sites, the geology of the place significantly influenced the progress of mining efforts and the problems encountered. The ground facing the toe of Hill 60 was found to consist of an uppermost layer of a wet, clayey sand, one and a half metres thick. Below this upper layer is around nine metres of a drier clayey sand which in turn is underlain by around five and a half metres of saturated sand, known as the Kemmel sands. The Kemmel sands posed a persistent problem to both the British and German miners. Considerable time and effort were spent overcoming problems with digging through and trying to control groundwater inflows into the workings. At the time the 1st Australian Tunnelling Company arrived at the hill, hand-pumping to control the inflow of water into the workings from the sand occupied 60 men.[4]

Below the Kemmel sands are three and a half metres of a moist, clayey sand. Below this is dry clay, the clay that the tunnellers considered ideal for tunnelling and the clay that they sought when tunnelling in Flanders. Known technically as Ypresian clay, but to the miners as 'blue clay', it was ideal for the clay-kicking digging technique, its texture firm and moist like plasticine. At Hill 60, the blue clay is around 26 metres below ground level.

The immediate support trench leading to Hill 60 was known as Bensham Road. The main audit or entrance to the deep mine system commenced in the Bensham Road trench, 15 metres from where the trench joined the Ypres–Comines railway cutting. The audit measured a mere 1.9 metres in height and was 1.1 metres wide.

From this entrance, a long tunnel, known as the 'Berlin sap', was driven horizontally and parallel to the railway cutting 158 metres directly into the shallow slope leading towards Hill 60. At its end, the sap had an overhead cover of six metres of earth. At this point the tunnel was dug on a downward incline for a distance of around 145 metres. The foot of the sap lay at a depth of just over 27 metres and directly under no man's land near the railway cutting. At that point it branched into the three deep mine galleries. The first of these led towards Hill 60 and was called 'A' gallery. The second, 'B' gallery, pointed towards the Caterpillar. Each gallery measured a claustrophobic 1.3 metres high by 0.7 metres wide. The third gallery, 'C' gallery, angled sharply to the right and accessed the shallow gallery system on the southern side of the railway cutting in front of 'I' shaft.

'A' gallery was then driven for a distance of 73 metres and, at its end, a 'chamber' comprising six smaller chambers was excavated. Three were dug off one side and two off the other side and at right angles to the gallery, each extending a distance of around six metres. The last chamber was the end of the gallery itself. The chambers were dug parallel to one another and separated by walls of earth two metres thick. They were then packed with tins of explosives totalling 3.3 tonnes of guncotton and 20.7 tonnes of ammonal. Once the charge had been laid and wired, the gallery was tamped with sandbags its entire length back to the foot of the Berlin sap.

From the bottom of the Berlin sap, 'B' gallery angled slightly to the right and extended a distance of 155 metres until it lay below the western end of the Caterpillar. During the tunnelling process, the Canadians had to overcome the problem posed by the wet and running sand — the Kemmel sands. To avoid digging along and through the wet sand bed, which would have been virtually impossible at that depth, they dug vertically through it, dropping the level of the mine gallery by three and a half metres. They then continued tunnelling underneath the sand layer, enabling them to reach their target and excavate the second mine chamber. However, the sand layer above the gallery continued to leak water into the tunnel workings. The Canadians had to continually pump water from the gallery to stop it flooding while they worked.

Eventually three mine chambers were excavated. Again, each chamber was dug at right angles to the main gallery. They were then packed with just under 32 tonnes of ammonal. The chambers lay deeper than the Hill 60 chambers, at 33 metres below ground level. The mine gallery behind the chambers was also tamped with sandbags and the gallery and mine chambers below the Kemmel sands were then allowed to flood. They remained flooded until the day the mine was detonated almost a year later. As 7 June 1917 was to show, the work of the Canadian tunnellers at Hill 60 was of the highest order.

Water from the Kemmel sands aquifer still posed a problem in other areas of the deep workings and the number of men required to man pumps to keep the mine system free of water represented a serious waste of resources. The Australians were determined to solve the problem. Where the Berlin sap incline commenced its long descent, they excavated a shaft chamber known as the 'Sydney' shaft. It was around this point that the engine room, then occupied by the Alphabet Company, had been constructed weeks earlier. A 15-metre deep, steel-lined vertical shaft 1.8 metres in diameter was then pushed through the floor of the chamber. The steel lining was designed to stop the inflow of water from the Kemmel sands. The shaft chamber housed four large hydraulic jacks, each of which could exert a downward force of five tons. The steel shaft itself was delivered as a series of sections each 60 centimetres high and each bolted to the one below. The steel shaft was gradually pushed down by the hydraulic jacks. The soil — mud would be a better description — within the steel shaft was then dug out by hand. When the steel shaft had passed through the wet sand and had been bedded in the 'dry' blue clay, the process was continued using traditional mining methods and completed to a bottom depth of 38 metres with timber walls.

A two-metre-deep sump was constructed at the bottom of the shaft where mine water drainage was collected and pumped to the surface. Above the sump, pump and plant chambers were built to house the water pumps and ventilation equipment supplied and operated by the Alphabet Company. From these a long, narrow gallery, the 'Sydney' gallery, was driven to a point just below the bottom of the Berlin sap incline.[5] A hole was then bored upwards to connect the Berlin sap with the Sydney gallery. This breakthrough finally occurred in March 1917. From that time, water from the bottom of the Berlin sap flowed to the sump in the Sydney shaft where it could then be pumped from the workings. This system effectively freed the 60 men who would otherwise have been required to hand-pump the water from the bottom of the Berlin sap and it also vastly improved the usually appalling ventilation situation in the deep mining system.

The Sydney gallery was also used as the starting gallery for several new deep galleries dug by the Australians. It was in digging these deep galleries that the 1st Australian Tunnelling Company first used the famous 'clay-kicking' technique. At around 230 metres, the longest of the new galleries was the 'Brisbane' gallery. Its intended target was a nearby sharp prominence in the German front line known to the British as 'the Snout' just to the north of 'Knoll Road' and 430 metres to the north-east of the Sydney gallery.

A second gallery, which later branched off Brisbane, halfway along its length at a right angle, was the 'Perth' gallery which further branched into the 'Newcastle' and 'Hobart' galleries, intended as defensive galleries for the Berlin sap. Another gallery, 'Ipswich', was dug to connect the intermediate and deep gallery system near the junction of the A and B galleries.

Extending a distance of some 70 metres to the right wall off the Sydney gallery but further down from Brisbane, was the 'Adelaide' gallery. This gallery was intended for another German strongpoint to the right of the Caterpillar. Much to the disappointment of the Australian tunnellers, these deep offensive galleries were not completed in time for the Battle of Messines and the hard work that went into their creation remained unrewarded, despite the fact that they were a mere matter of weeks from completion.

Three hundred metres to the rear of Hill 60 was the shattered remains of a small wood known as Larch Wood. Larch Wood was a sinister and thoroughly unpleasant place. One of the British trenches leading up to the hill from the southern side of the railway cutting was called '4711 trench', a perverse reference, not to the sweet smell of the perfume that bears that name, but the lingering stench of rotting corpses. So great was the danger of being killed in the open that the approaches to the hill were mostly underground. A series of dugouts, including a battalion headquarters and an advanced dressing station, were constructed below the remains of the wood. A complex series of interconnected subways and dugouts was also constructed, extending from Larch Wood to the front line.

Private E.N. Gladden of the 11th Northumberland Fusiliers described underground access and accommodation at Hill 60 during the build-up to the Battle of Messines in 1917:

> The trenches on Hill 60 were not many yards apart, but conditions were so hellish that both sides had reduced their garrisons to a string of strong posts and held only the support lines in force.

> There was, under the hill on the British side, a wonderful system of saps and dug-outs, a veritable underground settlement. The concreted and

sand-bagged posts above were joined by wooden stairways to the narrow bunk-lined sleeping quarters of the forward troops. Further down, passages lined with wooden planks led to larger barracks, and here were the headquarters offices and dressing station, so far below the level of the ground that the heaviest shell bursting above caused but a distant tremor through the galleries. The whole place was illuminated by electric light and the chug-chug of the pumps keeping the water out of the galleries continued day and night.

The company had come down from the front line into deep support as it was called. We occupied one of these billets, a cavern divided into two stories by a wooden shelf some four feet from the ground and large enough to house a whole platoon. We slept, when we had the chance, in two layers, and there was a passage leading along one side right through the chamber.[6]

In April 1917, a second engine room was finally constructed by the 1st Australian Tunnelling Company to replace the original close to Sydney shaft near Larch Wood, 200 metres to the rear of the original site. It was better ventilated and bigger, as a second 16-kilowatt generator was added, raising the power output of the plant to 22 kilowatts. Separate sleeping quarters were constructed for the Alphabet Company's maintenance crew.

On the morning of 7 June 1917 the two massive mines below Hill 60 and the Caterpillar remained undiscovered despite the frantic efforts of the Germans to locate the deep mines they feared lay below the hill. The two mines lay in wait, along with 17 other massive mines that dotted a 15-kilometre front. Nine divisions of infantry — some 100 infantry battalions or around 80,000 men — also lay waiting for the signal to jump off and attack the Messines Ridge.

At 3.09 am, as the first faint glow of dawn began to light the eastern sky, Captain Oliver Woodward of the 1st Australian Tunnelling Company was gripped by nervous tension, hunched over an electric detonator switch, his eyes fixed on his synchronised watch. He was in a dugout 400 metres to the rear of the Hill 60 mine chamber. Lieutenant John Royle, a later addition to the team of officers of the Alphabet Company, and Lieutenant James Bowry each hovered over an older, back-up plunger detonator in case the main detonator failed. Brigadier General Thomas Lambert was present to oversee the firing and provided the countdown.[7] His brigade, the 69th (23rd Division), was to go over the top at Hill 60 at zero hour.

Nineteen of the 21 massive mines that had been secreted below the western slope of the Messines Ridge exploded over a 19-second period and 425 tonnes of high explosive evaporated in a maelstrom of heat, light, gas, noise and unprecedented destruction.

Today, the ground above Hill 60, the Caterpillar and many of the other 19 former Messines mines bears the scars of those explosions. A semi-circle of depressions, most filled with water, lie like pearls in a necklace around the western slope of the ridge. Those at Hill 60 are surrounded with lush copses of woodland and green grass, while trees now obscure the view to Ieper (Ypres) that once proved so deadly to many who were sent to the salient. Without the knowledge of the terrible history of those places, it is easy to regard them merely as tranquil and beautiful resting places.

By 9.00 am on 7 June, the Messines Ridge had been captured along its entire front, from St Yves in the south to Mont Sorrel in the north. Prior to the battle, the British High Command had estimated casualties among the troops engaged to take the ridge at between 50% and 60%.[8] The impact of the mines was so decisive that actual casualties were just a fraction of this estimate. It was only after the ridge had been taken that casualties began to mount, primarily due to the unforeseen congestion of British troops along the ridgeline.

The Alphabet Company played an integral role in the Second Army's preparations for the Battle of Messines. From the time it established its

Plate 28a. Panoramic view towards Hill 60 (left) and the Caterpillar (right) taken in April 1915 from just behind the British front lines (IWM Q44172).

headquarters in Hazebrouck, the company supplied and maintained machines and equipment for lighting, the pumping of water and for ventilating most of the great mine systems fringing the Messines Ridge. It also wired the detonators for the Peckham mine and the electrical firing mechanism for the Hill 60 mine. The Alphabet Company was subsequently honoured with a number of awards for devotion to duty leading up to and during the battle.

Outside and to the south of Ypres, the company's No. 831 Staff Sergeant Fred Whitwell and No. 370 Sergeant William Millar were responsible for providing power to the Railway dugouts and the Hill 60 tunnels from as early as September 1916 to the blowing of the mines at Hill 60.[9] During a German raid on 9 April, an extensive network of wiring and some 50 lights in the shallow galleries were damaged. The lights were quickly restored and rescue efforts in the affected galleries proceeded almost without interruption. Both Fred Whitwell and William Millar were later awarded the MSM for their prompt action. Another sergeant from the Alphabet Company, No. 386 Sergeant Arnott Moody, was also awarded the DCM for overseeing and inspecting lighting and power plants during the monumental attacks that took place at Hill 60 on 9 April and 7 June 1917. The recommendation for his award was made personally by the Inspector of Mines, Brigadier General Harvey.

In the southern sector of the Second Army, the Alphabet Company also installed a number of power plants for lighting headquarters dugouts around Midland Farm outside the village of Wulverghem.

Plate 28b. Panoramic view towards Hill 60 (right) taken in April 1915 from just behind the British front lines (IWM Q44172).

The Battle of Messines lasted seven days and, by 14 June, the British objectives had been secured. The removal of the Germans and their artillery from the Messines Ridge saw an end to the immediate danger of direct artillery observation in the south-western quarter of the Ypres salient and, for the time being, the threat of being hit by a shell while pursuing the routine business of soldiering. At Hill 60, while life continued in the maze of trenches and dugouts, the location was no longer in the front line and its use turned from defence to support, its many dugouts occupied as sleeping quarters, mess rooms, company offices and dressing stations.

The letters written by Alphabet Company CO Victor Morse to his wife resonate with frustration at misinformation or misreporting of war facts in Australian newspapers which were mailed to many men by their loved ones. He was especially interested in reports of battles in which his unit had participated. Reports describing the Battle of Messines in particular attracted his criticism:

> I read a piece re[garding] the laying of the Hill 60 mines and how long the Australians were there, 'twas absolutely a patch of lies, the account of the Messines stunt, one would think we ran the show, some day ... the actual percentage of our troops will be given and I assure you that the smallness of it after what you read will surprise you.[10]

Morse's insistence on historical accuracy extended into his civilian life after the war. On one occasion he took particular umbrage over the commercial liberty taken by one Australian distributor of the Lister company's portable combustion engines, a number of which were used by the Alphabet Company to power generators at the front, including at Hill 60. When the company used this connection with the war effort to advertise its product in a respected Australian magazine, Morse was appalled.

In a letter to the distributor, Morse delivered a double-edged rebuke, making it quite clear that the facts as stated in the advertisement were incorrect:

> I was in charge of this work and wish to point out to you that no Lister Engine was used in that sector and that the statements in your advertisement are absolutely incorrect. This engine was used extensively in connection with our forward line work and proved one of the best, and I think that the qualifications of the sets are of such high quality that it is quite unnecessary to publish such incorrect statements. Many engineers in Australia and England have full knowledge of the plants mentioned,

and in their case this advertisement could only do more harm than good for English manufactured material which it is our desire to push ahead as much as possible.

This letter must not in any way be used as an advertisement.[11]

You get Reliability
because--
The Lister Engine is built to a high standard, and nothing is sacrificed to quantity production. Iron is not used where steel would give better service. Nothing is hurried in order to turn out a cheap job.

You get Service
because—
The Lister Equipment reaches the high-water mark of engineering. It has about 20 less working parts than other farm engines. It is equipped with High-tension Magneto, Throttling Governor, "Once a month" Oiling System, and Dust-proof Gears.

34 days & nights non-stop run!

How LISTER ALL-BRITISH ENGINES helped the Tunnellers at Hill 60 and refused to be shell-shocked.

IT takes a lot to make a Britisher blow his own trumpet. Here's a wonderful war story that has only just come to hand. Everyone who followed events in Flanders during the war will remember the gigantic efforts put forward in reducing the position known as Hill "60."

For 34 days and nights the Tunnellers worked at top speed in undermining the position. Every delay was fatal. But because Lister All-British Engines were used for driving the lighting and pneumatic equipment there was not a stop during the whole of the 816 hours' work.

At one time a shell demolished one of the engine huts, but the Lister Engine kept on running sweetly, and refused to be shell-shocked.

This wonderful Lister Record demonstrates the value of All-British workmanship. The Light Horse in Palestine proved this, too. Lister Engines were responsible for regular water supply for troops and horses from the Suez Canal to Jerusalem.

The Lister Engine is the safest investment for country work. It is wonderfully equipped in every way, and the dust-proof gears give you complete protection against trouble, no matter where it is used.

Send for Prices and all Particulars to nearest of the following:

Dangar, Gedye & Co., Ltd., 9-13 Young Street, Sydney.
Winchcombe, Carson, Ltd., Brisbane.

Malloch Bros., Perth.
A. W. Sandford & Co., Ltd., Adelaide.

Plate 29. The advertisement placed by the Lister company in *The Bulletin* in 1920, promoting its engines and referring to Hill 60 as evidence of their reliability under the most adverse conditions (Victor Morse collection).

Following the Battle of Messines, with the front lines pushed further east from Hill 60, the Alphabet Company remained in position to maintain power supply to the lighting, water-pumping and ventilation systems which were still needed in the largely underground structures. Later, in September 1917, when the area was being used extensively for support and reserve dugouts, the original, smaller generator was replaced with a larger 16-kilowatt generator, raising the engine room's power output to 32 kilowatts.

During its tour of duty at Hill 60, from September 1916 until its departure in April 1918, the company installed, maintained and provided power to a total of six water-pumping sets and seven mine-ventilation sets. Some 335 lights were fitted in the mine galleries and dugout systems and approximately 3400 metres of heavy and light electrical cables were laid and maintained until at least June 1917 in what had been one of the most heavily contested positions in the British sector of the Western Front.

The Bluff and Spoilbank
Company Tour of Duty: The Bluff and Spoilbank

The Bluff, a mere 1500 metres south-west of Hill 60, was another infamous location on the Western Front and was referred to by the Germans as *Die Grosse Bastion*. Like Hill 60, the Bluff was the product of soil dumped during the excavation and construction of a feature that crossed the Messines Ridge, in this case, the Comines–Ypres Canal. Soil was dumped along both banks of the canal, but on its northern bank, where the dump draped across the top and down the western side of the ridge, it formed an embankment platform that jutted to a height of around 10 metres above the surrounding landscape. It was one of the very few places where the British could overlook the German lines from their elevated front line — albeit at great risk.

The British 171st Tunnelling Company commenced mining operations at the Bluff in March 1915. A month later, the company was replaced by its sister company, the 172nd Tunnelling Company. The Germans began an aggressive offensive mining program against the position and, over the course of the next 18 months, an underground battle raged in which the German miners gained the ascendency on several occasions. Many of the early gallery systems were shallow, a mere five metres below ground. The reworked soil through which the tunnellers burrowed was soft and, when wet, quickly turned to a slimy mud.

As more mines were blown and more craters dotted the ground between the British and German lines, both sides dug shallow galleries that intersected the sides of the craters, allowing them to be used as observation posts — albeit very dangerous and exposed positions. The craters tended to pool water, resulting in seepage through to the underlying workings. Such was the magnitude of this problem that time and manpower had to be diverted to tunnelling through the crater walls into the adjacent canal in an attempt to drain the accumulated water.

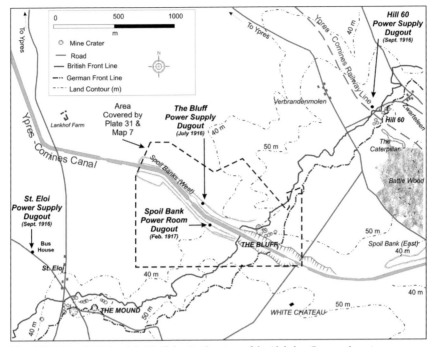

Map 6. Hill 60 to St Eloi and the Bluff showing locations of the Alphabet Company's engine rooms.

A permanent lake lay in what was known as 'B' crater, a scar on the face of the Bluff, the result of a series of German mines blown between October 1915 and February 1916. These mines had claimed the lives of a number of British soldiers, many buried alive.[12] The carnage of the mines constituted a deadly addition to the usual trench and artillery warfare waged along the front, particularly in the Ypres salient where conditions were hellish as a matter of course.

On 14 February 1916, the Germans blew three mines, further enlarging 'B' crater. The German *124th Regiment* then attacked and captured the Bluff along with all the British tunnel systems, an attack that inflicted almost 1300 British casualties.[13] The British 76th Brigade finally drove the Germans back on 2 March 1916. A month later, the 2nd Canadian Tunnelling Company relieved the 172nd Tunnelling Company and was then relieved itself soon after by the 1st Canadian Tunnelling Company.

This was the situation in July 1916 when the first Australians arrived at the Bluff. The men belonged to a small group of sappers from the Alphabet Company under No. 1431 Sergeant Hugh Thurlow, MSM,[14] whose task it was to install lighting, ventilation equipment and pumps in the gallery systems.[15] This was no easy feat and the experience of Thurlow and his men typified the problems associated with moving power plants to forward locations, often into conditions just as horrendous as the Bluff.

Plate 30. A sketch by Hugh Thurlow entitled 'The EMM&B Coy A.I.F. installing a power plant'. The sketch depicts the engine and electrical generator set being manhandled into a front-line dugout under cover of darkness. This was a familiar task for the men of the Alphabet Company (extract from AWM 3DRL_4059).

The power generating equipment, a 12-kilowatt Frisco Standard engine with its electricity generator, weighed around 1.3 tonnes and had to be moved into a dedicated engine room dugout located back along the soil bank on the northern side of the Ypres–Comines Canal and just 350 metres shy of the front line. On the night of 17 July the set was delivered under cover of darkness by lorry from Hazebrouck and unloaded at Lankhof Farm, some 2000 metres to the west of the Bluff. The routine shelling in that part of the line scored a lucky hit that night and the lorry was damaged, although the men escaped unscathed. The generator set was transferred to a narrow-gauge railway (trench railway), used to supply the Bluff and running parallel to the Ypres–Comines Canal, passing the ruins of Lankhof Farm. The small rail truck on which the equipment was loaded was pushed manually along the track in the final approach to the front. Shellfire had cut the tracks in several places and running repairs were completed using timber for the rails.

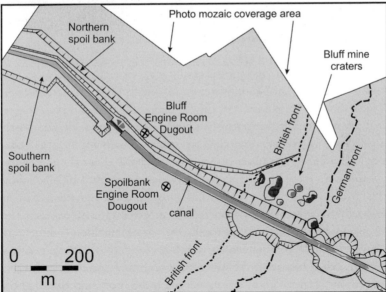

Top: Plate 31. Aerial photo mosaic of the Bluff taken in April 1917 showing the heavily shell cratered landscape, the result of intense artillery shellfire and larger craters from mine explosions in no man's land at the Bluff (part of photo mosaic IWM P005333).

Bottom: Map 7. Map of the photo mosaic area highlighting points of interest.

By dawn, the men and their precious equipment had covered just half the distance and, as any movement in the open in daylight was deemed suicidal, the generator set was camouflaged with tree branches and abandoned for the day. At dusk the men returned and that night managed to move the generator to within 200 metres of the engine room using the rail system. The set was then transferred to a pair of wooden skids. With the addition of rollers and much puffing and cursing, the heavily laden skids were manoeuvred across shell holes, tangled wire and even a small stream of muddy water, to the generator's final destination.

The engine room and adjoining sleeping quarters were far from luxurious and offered little protection from the effects of a well-placed shell. The soil cover over the roof above the engine room ranged from a meagre one metre to three metres, offering protection against only the smallest projectiles, bullets and shrapnel. In the 12 months the engine room was operational, it was partially destroyed twice by shellfire and finally completely destroyed on 27 July 1917. Fortunately, on all three occasions, no-one was in the room when it was hit. Adding to the general discomfort of the site, the level of ventilation in the dugout was found to be less than ideal and, soon after it commenced operation, the engine room staff were gassed by engine exhaust fumes. Unlike the deadly gases delivered by artillery, the exhaust fumes proved only temporarily debilitating and the men recovered quickly.

Some 400 lighting points were eventually installed in the tunnel galleries and dugouts at the Bluff. The lighting points were fitted with what was the standard 15 candlepower (approximately 13 watts) metal filament lamps. These were initially fixed to timber beams that lined the tunnel gallery walls but, given the concussions of the high explosive shells, the lamps had a short life due to filament breakage from the vibrations of the concussions. However hanging the lamps by their leads away from the timber extended their life and eventually around a month of continuous use was possible before replacement was required. By April 1917, when the embankment engine room was destroyed, a larger power supply had been installed on the opposite (southern) side of the Ypres–Comines Canal and this replaced the old Bluff engine room.

But in July 1916, with the assistance of the lighting, ventilation and a dewatering pump installed by the Alphabet Company, the underground battle at the Bluff continued unabated. The Canadians had succeeded in digging down to the Ypresian clay, some 30 metres below the surface, where the clay-kicking digging method could be used effectively. They then extended a deep gallery, the Bluff gallery, out underneath no man's land.

The German miners had also been busy. Undetected and with great daring, they had laid a massive 15,200-kilogram mine under the forward toe of the Bluff embankment, detonating the mine on 25 July 1916, six days after the Alphabet Company arrived at the Bluff. The explosion formed a distinctive bean-shaped crater which was subsequently known as 'A' crater. With the noticeable decline in German mining activity leading up to the detonation, the officer commanding the Canadian tunnellers had sensed that a 'blow' was imminent and kept the forward areas lightly manned. His caution was rewarded with few fatalities. Inexplicably, the blowing of the mine was not, on this occasion, followed by the usual infantry attack.

On 22 October 1916, the German miners blew another three large mines simultaneously, producing three craters which were nicknamed 'C', 'D' and 'E' craters. These mines represented the swansong of the tenacious German miners. The deep Bluff gallery continued to be extended out under no man's land to a point below 'E' crater where the gallery turned and headed in the direction of the canal for a distance of 100 metres. A mine chamber was placed every 25 metres along this lateral gallery. A total of 22,000 kilograms of high explosive was divided between the four chambers and, on 11 December 1916, the charges were fired. These camouflets formed an effective curtain of destruction, crushing the German tunnels above and separating them from the German tunnels behind the curtain. Over 200 metres of German galleries were captured in this way. This allowed the construction of an arc of listening posts in an intermediate-level gallery at a depth of around 10 metres. This gallery extended around the front of the old 'C', 'D' and 'E' craters. The deep system was also quickly recovered after the camouflets had been blown and the position was then converted to a series of deep listening posts. The two lines of listening posts and the capture of an important part of the shallow German gallery system all but secured the Bluff from further offensive German mining activity.

This was the situation when the tunnellers of the 2nd Australian Tunnelling Company relieved the Canadians on the northern side of the Ypres–Comines Canal in late January 1917. The Australians took over the role of guarding the Bluff, utilising and extending the defensive mining system painstakingly constructed by the Canadian tunnellers. The tunnellers worked carefully, fully cognisant of the fact that the ground through which they moved contained the remains of many men, both tunnellers and infantrymen, lost to the mining war. The great craters that deformed and dominated the landscape at the Bluff were perpetual and menacing reminders of this.

By early 1917 the 1st Canadian Tunnelling Company was in charge of underground activities on the southern side of the canal. The Canadians embarked on one highly unusual and supremely ambitious project which saw an Alphabet Company engine room constructed in the soil bank on the southern side of the canal.

By the outbreak of the war, mechanical tunnelling machines had been in existence in one form or another for decades and, in early 1916, the father of the British tunnelling companies, John Norton-Griffiths, initiated plans to trial some machines on the front, keen to free up tunnellers for other works. The softer clay and sandy soil conditions of Flanders were considered ideal for such a trial. The first machine was an air-powered Stanley Heading machine which was trialled by the British 250th Tunnelling Company in one of the Petit Bois mine shafts below the Messines Ridge. After several months struggling with the machine 36 metres below the ground, the tunnellers abandoned both it and the idea *in situ* after progressing less than 40 metres through the tight clay below the ridge.

A second machine, a Whitacre tunnel-boring machine, was also tried, this time by the Canadian tunnellers, to fill a gap that existed in the Messines Ridge suite of mines between Hill 60 and St Eloi. The objective was to drive a mine gallery from a shaft in the Lock Hospital located in the southern soil bank at Lock 6 behind a small cluster of farmhouses known as Norfolk Lodge.[16] The tunnelling machine was to dig the gallery 760 metres due south towards the German line in the direction of a farm known as Eikhof Farm which lay behind the German front line. Once close to the German front lines, the noisy machine was to be withdrawn and the gallery would be pushed another 500 metres further by the silent clay-kicking technique. Four mine chambers were planned, the most distant placed below a long, straight sunken road known as the Damm Strasse, which led to White Chateau. The Damm Strasse mine chamber would require an impressive 1470 metres of tunnelling.[17]

In March 1917, the Whitacre machine was transported to the Spoilbank, the soil pile in British territory on the southern side of the canal. Unlike the air-powered (pneumatic) Stanley Header machine, the motor that rotated its 5 foot (1.5 metre)-diameter cutting head, the spoil conveyor motor behind the cutting head, a bucket conveyor and two elevators (with 42.6 metres of travel, for the technically minded) were all electrically powered.

The Spoilbank engine room was constructed to house the power supply for the electrical generators to power the machine and its accoutrements. The Alphabet Company began progressively installing three 440-volt, 22.3-kilowatt generators which were fully operational by 16 March. However the power supply from the three generators responded badly to the sudden changes in power that resulted from the cutting head of the machine gripping and breaking through the clayey soil. After a week of work, only six metres of tunnel had been cut and timbered. A fourth engine and generator, a 500-volt, 30-kilowatt machine, was added at the end of March. Three electrically driven soil haulage units and two air ventilation sets were also eventually brought up to assist.

Aside from the power supply issues, the Whitacre machine, like the Stanley machine a year earlier, struggled with the conditions and constantly broke down. Ultimately, progress proved too slow. On 7 June 1917, as the great Messines mines were detonated simultaneously in the opening act of the Battle of Messines, the Spoilbank mine gallery remained a long way from completion. Its mines were never laid and the project was abandoned.

Neither mechanical tunnelling machine had lived up to expectation and the British never used these machines again during the war. The Spoilbank engine room was not wasted, however. The generators were used to provide power for dugout lighting that extended over a large frontage from White Chateau, which was taken by the British in the opening days of the Battle of Messines, to Lankhof Farm behind the canal spoil banks and as far back towards Ypres along the canal as Lock 8, a coverage of almost 3.2 kilometres. The engine room remained in operation until April 1918 and a total of 750 lighting points were installed and connected back to the engine room via 24.5 kilometres of cabling.

St Eloi
Company Tour of Duty: St Eloi

One and a half kilometres south of the Ypres–Comines Canal and the next settlement situated atop the same low-lying ridge on which the Bluff and Hill 60 rested, was a collection of houses and outbuildings that comprised the hamlet of St Eloi. Like the nearby battle sites along the ridge, St Eloi emerged from the early years of the war with a bloody reputation. What made it the subject of fierce contention however, was another man-made spoil bank that had been piled on the apex of the ridgeline just outside the village. Known as the Mound, this spoil bank provided an observation advantage for its occupier over the adversary. The front lines were close and the Mound was regarded as a strategic prize worth committing many lives to win. And so it was that St Eloi became another Hill

60, the target of intense and protracted mining and artillery attacks, making the prospect of a long and healthy life in the vicinity distinctly uncertain.

The Germans had won the Mound after blowing a series of mines on 14 March 1915, despite a British counter-attack that cost 500 British casualties. Evelyn Fryer, who later served as an officer with the Grenadier Guards, but in March 1915 was serving with the Honorable Artillery Company, 7th Brigade, recalled arriving at St Eloi in late March 1915, soon after the Mound had been lost:

> The position of St. Eloi was this, the actual village, which was only a few houses, was in No Man's Land; the famous mound, a tumulus of earth, was held by the Germans, and overlooked our lines, although a constant target for our artillery; the village and the mound had been in our hands before the 15th. One curious feature of No Man's Land was a derelict London motor bus which had been used to rush up reinforcements and had fallen a victim to a German shell.
>
> We got in for a good deal of shelling, a new and very small type making its first appearance.
>
> We held the village of Voormezeele, 1,000 yards behind, and our reserves were billeted there in cellars. The village was a complete wreck, and I remember going over the churchyard there and being disgusted by seeing the tombs all blown up and bones lying about everywhere.[18]

The duel for St Eloi had begun. In addition to the constant barrage of artillery from both sides which pummelled the position, the British had detonated 13 mines and 29 camouflets during 1915 and the Germans 20 mines and two camouflets.

Following the successful German mining attack at the nearby Bluff in February 1916, the British Second Army commander, General Herbert Plumer, was eager to retaliate and St Eloi was chosen, the Mound once again the object of desire. The British 172nd Tunnelling Company embarked on a deep tunnelling program to place six mines below the contested no man's land and, in the usual program of the time, the mines would be blown at the launch of an attack, the craters overrun and the forward crater lips (the side facing the enemy) consolidated as elevated defensive positions. The six mines totalled 33.5 tonnes of high explosives, of which the four innermost mines contained the bulk of the charges, mine No. 2 alone being 14 tonnes and the largest of the war to that time. The mines were detonated on the morning of 27 March 1916, with some 300 Germans reportedly killed or buried in the explosion.[19] Over the following two weeks the British and Germans attacked and counter-attacked in a desperate bid to gain the ascendancy and take control of the mine craters. The British *Official History* describes the scene of the fighting:

> The front line was found in a deplorable condition, barely distinguishable as a line indeed after the mine explosions, continuous shelling, fighting and bad weather from which it had suffered. The parapets were broken down and there was no wire. The trenches, even where revetted and shored up, had collapsed, and were little better than a series of shallow untraversed ditches; at best captured trenches facing the wrong way, splashed with shell holes and without drainage. For dugouts there were only a few shelters, scarcely splinter proof and full of water like every other excavation; no communication trenches worthy of the name existed; whilst the four large craters formed a continuous and almost impassable obstacle, so that all traffic had to pass round the flanks; even carrying parties had to be roped together to afford a means of rescuing the men who stepped or fell into the water filled shell holes. With the wounded and dead, both British and German, lying half buried in the mud, the area was a depressing sight for any relieving division.[20]

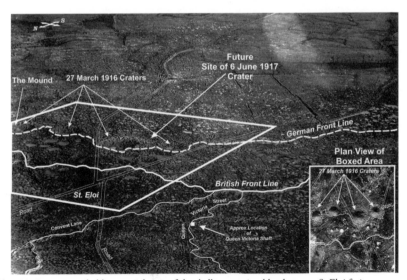

Plate 32. An annotated oblique aerial view of the shell crater-pitted landscape at St Eloi facing east towards the German lines. The mine crater field is evident in the centre left of the photograph. Bus House, where the Alphabet Company operated its engine room, is located just below the vantage point of the photograph. The infamous Mound is near the large crater on the left of the scene. The rubble of St Eloi village lies at the crossroads (McMaster University, Lloyd Reeds Library).

Despite these conditions, the 2nd Canadian Division relived the British 3rd Division during the struggle but was ultimately forced to relinquish control of the craters and the height advantages they offered. By the end of fighting, the Canadian division alone had suffered 1370 casualties. This was the situation at St Eloi until 7 June 1917.

With planning in progress to place the series of massive mines under and along the Messines Ridge to herald the start of the Battle of Messines, the old nemesis of St Eloi was an obvious choice. And so it was that in August 1916, the 1st Canadian Tunnelling Company commenced a new shaft for a new mine — the Queen Victoria shaft, named after the communication trench which accessed it. The shaft was sunk to a depth of 30 metres before the main mine gallery headed off in the direction of the German lines, to skirt the old March 1916 mine craters, then angle between the old Nos. 2 and 3 craters and ultimately also between craters 4 and 5. A chamber was constructed from a stairway landing at a depth of 10 metres in the Queen Victoria shaft to house a power plant, which was installed in October. The Alphabet Company was tasked to provide the power supply which duly arrived at St Eloi on 28 September 1916. The unit arrived with a 3.7-kilowatt electric generator and an electric dewatering pump. The pump was a crucial addition to the mining process. The Canadian mine gallery joined one of the old British mine galleries which had since flooded. The pump was used to dewater the gallery, allowing it to be cleaned before extension of the mine gallery proceeded. By May 1917, the mine chamber behind the old 1916 Nos. 2 and 3 craters had been completed and packed with 43.3 tonnes of high explosive, the biggest British mine load of the war. Time ran out for a proposed second chamber to be dug and charged, but as history has since testified, it was not needed. The St Eloi mine chamber was successfully detonated along with the other 18 massive Messines mines in the dawn light of 7 June 1917 at which time the Mound was finally secured.

In addition to assisting with underground workings, the Alphabet Company ran electric cables 100 metres across the surface of the ground from the power room in the Queen Victoria shaft to the front line to provide lighting and pumping to dugouts and other mining saps. Cables were also run 300 metres behind the shaft to provide lighting to a dugout system at Bus House, situated on the Voormezeele Road. The generator from the mine shaft was later moved back to Bus House dugouts since hostile shelling often made it almost impossible to move supplies and stores to the shaft. In total, the company installed and maintained 118 lighting points and 4470 metres of heavy and light-gauge electric cabling at St Eloi between 28 September 1916 and 19 June 1917.

Following the Battle of Messines, the generator at St Eloi was removed and the electrical system was centralised in an engine room at Voormezeele, one kilometre behind the front and west of St Eloi where a 6-kilowatt generator was established. This generator also supplied dugouts and a medical dressing station in cellars with an additional 148 lighting points. Running the generator and maintaining the 9.6 kilometres of electric cabling and 266 lights that had been installed between the two nearby locations kept an Alphabet Company team of one NCO and five other ranks constantly busy.

In the build-up to the Battle of Messines, the company suffered two fatalities close to Voormezeele, where customised infantry headquarters and medical dugouts had been constructed. Artillery fire that peppered the village in the days prior to the battle wreaked havoc with the exposed power cables in the area. In the course of repairing the wiring, two men from the Alphabet Company, No. 1026 Corporal Frank Hawtin, a recipient of the Italian Bronze Medal of Valour, and No. 804 Sapper Percy Baker, were killed by a random shell.[21] Alphabet Company CO, Victor Morse, described Frank Hawtin as a one of his 'medal' men, 'a great man as rough as you could make them', who would 'coolly go out in the thickest to benefit his mates regardless of all danger'. The same shell badly wounded Percy Baker in the torso and thigh. He managed to make his way to an aid post, where he collapsed and, when lifted inside, unaware that Frank Hawtin was already dead, asked his helpers to go and rescue his mate instead. Sapper Baker died of his wounds the following day. The two men are buried in adjacent graves in the La Clytte Military Cemetery in Belgium.

In the sector immediately to the south of Hill 60, No. 2348 Sergeant Alan Denton and No. 4154 Lance Corporal Charles Scorgie had been stationed in the St Eloi and the Bluff sectors since October 1916, their task the provision of lighting, ventilation and pumping. In February 1917, as more dugouts were being built along and in the vicinity of the western spoil bank on the southern side of the Ypres–Comines Canal opposite the Bluff, the men installed three power plants capable of generating 45 kilowatts for lighting and ventilation.

Hill 63: The Catacombs
Company Tour of Duty: Hill 63

Facing the southern end of the string of massive and deep mine chambers that stretched down the western slope of the Messines Ridge, packed ready for detonation on 7 June 1917, lies Hill 63, a well-known topographical feature to those soldiers whose sector included Ploegsteert Wood — more commonly known as 'Plug Street'. The hill possessed two very useful features: it was close to the front line and it was one of the few high points in the vicinity of the front that was not controlled by the Germans. The view from its summit extended across the shallow valley on its north-east side towards the town of Messines. The southern slope of the hill was angled in such a way that it could not be observed directly from the front line and the lower portion was covered in forest, part of Ploegsteert Wood. It was the ideal location to accommodate large numbers of men in relative safety close to the front.

By late October, the Prowse Point dugout system under Hill 63 on the northern side of Ploegsteert Wood had been completed. Known to the tunnellers as the 'Wallangarra dugout', but more widely referred to as 'the Catacombs', the system was completed by No. 2 Section of the 1st Australian Tunnelling Company following initial work by British and Canadian tunnellers. The shelter was massive in comparison to the size of the normal dugout. Three large entrances were tunnelled eight metres into the side of the hill and the huge dugout was then excavated in the heart of the hill. It measured 135 metres in length, 25 metres in width and 2.1 metres from floor to ceiling and was fitted with 18 rows of double-tiered wooden bunks, each row 4.9 metres wide and 19.5 metres long and separated from its neighbour by a 2.4-metre-wide corridor. The dugout was equipped with three vertical ventilation shafts at intervals along the innermost wall. Importantly, these shafts also served as auxiliary exits and extended vertically to the top of the hill for around 22 metres.

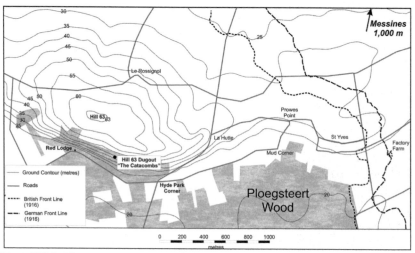

Map 8. Hill 63, Ploegsteert.

Plate 33. Entrance to the Catacombs at Hill 63, Ploegsteert (AMW E04486).

The system took the Australian tunnellers two months to complete. During that time they excavated almost 5500 cubic metres of soil from the hill. The central dugout was so large that its wooden bunking could accommodate 1200 men. The volume of timber used in its construction was such that, laid end to end, it would have stretched a distance of around 160 kilometres. Some of the excavated soil from inside the hill was dumped to fill the slope below the entrance of the dugout system and create a level platform. The soil-covered steel-framed dugouts provided additional accommodation for a further 150 men and 50 officers.

Such was the significance of the dugout that it was officially opened on 1 November 1916 with great pomp and ceremony by General Sir Herbert Plumer, GCB, KCMG, GCVO, ADC, Commander of the British Second Army. Also in attendance were five corps commanders, 14 divisional commanders and a score of brigadier generals. Given its proximity to the front line, such a gathering of important military software was almost unprecedented and presented a substantial risk. A few strategically aimed German howitzer shells could have wiped out 25% of the British senior army field commanders on that day.

The Alphabet Company arrived at Hill 63 on 28 October 1916, tasked with providing power for both lighting and ventilation, not only at the Catacombs, but other dugout systems, one located near Red Lodge, 500 metres west of the Catacombs. Initially an engine room was established at the Catacombs, but with a head covering of less than three metres of soil, it was considered too vulnerable to artillery. By January 1918 another engine room and quarters for the Alphabet Company maintenance crew had been constructed at Red Lodge and the 21-kilowatt supply from the two generators at the Catacombs engine room was replaced by two generators with a combined power output of 24 kilowatts. Duplicate sets of electrical cables were run from the engine room back to the Catacombs, one along the road and another through the woods, and to a third dugout system 800 metres beyond. Two large Sturtevant ventilating fans were installed at the Catacombs, capable of dual direction air flow — blowing air into or sucking air from the dugout system with through-flow via the ventilation shafts that rose to the surface at the heart of the hill. In total, 475 lighting points were installed across the three dugout systems and connected by 15.7 kilometres of electrical cabling.

By the time of the Battle of Messines in June 1917, the Alphabet Company had supplied all the necessary equipment and power generating plants for running over 1500 lights, 14 mine water pumps and 12 ventilation fans feeding into mines and dugouts extending from Hill 60 to the Catacombs Dugout at Hill 63 near Ploegsteert Wood. This represented an extraordinary achievement by a small group of men working in often dire conditions.

CHAPTER 5

GIVENCHY TO LENS

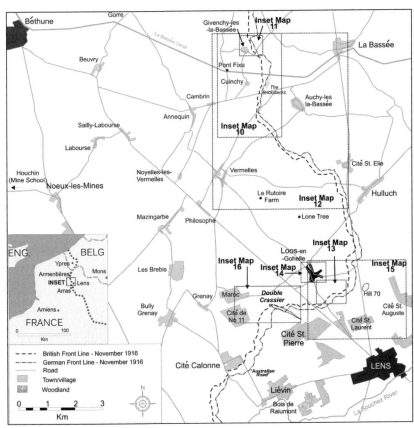

Map 9. Map showing the front lines between Lens and Givenchy to April 1917 and also the location of inset maps of key locations covered in this chapter.

Givenchy
Company Tour of Duty: Givenchy

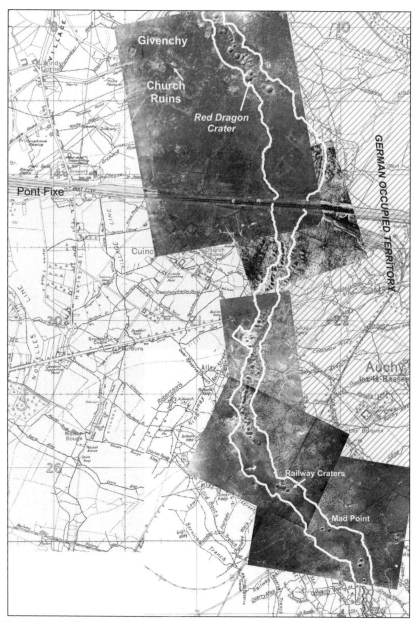

Map 10. Mosaic of aerial surveillance photographs overlying a 1917 trench map extending from
Givenchy to the Hohenzollern Redoubt south of Auchy les-la-Bassée showing the extent of mine crater
fields in no man's land in front of the shattered remains of the villages of Givenchy, Cuinchy and Auchy
les-la-Bassée.

These days, the name Givenchy is synonymous with one of the world's most famous fashion labels. Half a century ago, the same name would have brought recollections of horror to many thousands of British First World War veterans. The Givenchy front had been the scene of heavy fighting and mining activity since the arrival of the British in the sector in November 1914. Just east of the ruined village for a distance of 800 metres, no man's land was not much more than 100 metres wide and therefore ideal mining territory for both sides. By the end of the underground mining phase in mid-1917 an almost continuous line of connected mine craters stretched along the front, many of which were named. The biggest and arguably most infamous was the 'Red Dragon'.

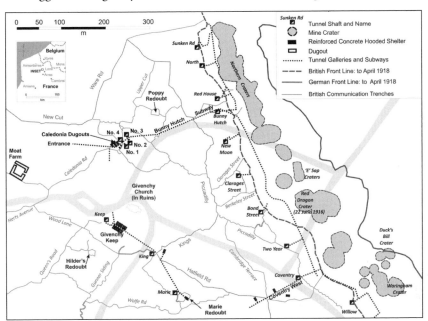

Map 11. The trench and tunnel system at Givenchy in 1918 showing subways and redoubts, the domain of No. 1306 Corporal Jack Nancarrow and his little band of men from the Alphabet Company from 1917 to 1918.

The mine which formed the Red Dragon crater was detonated by the Germans at 2.50 am on 22 June 1916, just six days after the arrival of the Alphabet Company. It was the largest mine of the war to that time. The explosion was followed by a firestorm of machine-gun and artillery fire aimed at covering a raid by some 150 Germans. The men of the 2nd Battalion, Royal Welsh Fusiliers, were in the trenches at the time and half of the unit's B Company perished. The crater was named in honour of those from the regiment who lost their lives that night. Among the dead were two subalterns, Lieutenants Pryce Edwards and Trevor Crosland. Nineteen-year-old Lieutenant Crosland had only just joined the company — that night was his first in the trenches. Both men were killed and their remains lost. In 1926, in a quirk of fate, a farmer ploughing over where the crater once lay uncovered a piece of wood which led to the discovery of the company's front-line headquarters within which lay the remains of the two young officers.[1]

Plate 34. The rabbit hole entrance to Engine Room 1, Givenchy (AWM H19521).

Plate 35. The entrance to Engine Room 2, Givenchy. The officer on the right is Lieutenant George Norfolk of the Alphabet Company (AWM H19520).

Plate 36. Two generating sets and switchboard in the cellar housing Engine Room 2, Givenchy (AWM H12183).

The blowing of the Red Dragon mine also trapped five tunnellers from the 254th Tunnelling Company underground, including No. 136414 Sapper William Hackett. His choice to stay with an injured tunneller, a decision that led to his death alongside the wounded man, won him a posthumous Victoria Cross. It was to be the only Victoria Cross won by Allied tunnellers during the war.

Such was its strategic importance that preparations for the defence of Givenchy had been made well in advance of any anticipated requirement. Key to its defence was a network of concrete machine-gun pillboxes and a long infantry subway and dugout system known as the Bunny Hutch subway. Bunny Hutch had been constructed from Moat Farm behind the British support line to the front-line mining system to ensure safe access for the infantry to the system even under the heaviest bombardment. A second deep dugout system had also been constructed between two strongholds, Givenchy Keep and Marie Redoubt. This dugout system extended for a distance of 300 metres, provided a head cover of at least 12 metres of earth and was capable of accommodating a garrison of two infantry battalions. Bore holes had been drilled down into the chalk aquifer from which drinking water was extracted. The system contained three steel-lined ventilation shafts, each fitted with a steel and concrete 'hood', the concrete in each hood alone weighing as much as 90 tonnes.[2]

The Alphabet Company arrived at Givenchy on 16 June 1916 and took over the running of two generators, 32-horsepower (24-kilowatt) Lister engines which provided power to the underground system and also, importantly, two water pumps. The mining systems and tunnel gallery systems at Givenchy were threatened by inflows of shallow groundwater and the continued operation of these first two dewatering pumps was crucial. Despite this, such was the extent of the underground labyrinth for conveying men to the front-line trenches and mining systems it was immediately recognised that a major expansion in dewatering operations was urgently required.

Plate 37. The entrance to Engine Room 3, Givenchy (AWM H19519).

Plate 38. The entrance to Engine Room 4 at Pont Fixe near Givenchy (AWM H19516).

Plate 39. The Pont Fixe bridge over the La Bassée Canal between Givenchy and Cuinchy (AMW H19531).

Plate 40. Captain George Norfolk (right) and two unidentified soldiers at the entrance to the Pont Fixe Engine Room (No. 5) (AMW H19517).

The two generators were almost worn out and were immediately overhauled. They were housed in the cellars of two bombed-out houses around 100 metres apart, close to what had been the Givenchy church, but by then was just a pile of shattered masonry and mortar, almost indistinguishable from other piles of pulverised masonry in what had been the village until November 1914. The two cellars were called Engine Room 1 and Engine Room 2. Engine Room

2 contained a second broken-down generator, a 10-horsepower (7.5 kilowatt) Unic, which was finally refurbished in 1918.

However the water pump and generators were not ideally matched and, when one of the water pumps stopped suddenly, either as a result of mechanical failure or, more often, due to shellfire cutting the leads, the generators suffered load shock which compromised their fragile condition. Two weeks later a third generator was delivered in a bid to solve the problem and was installed in what become known as Engine Room 3, a corrugated iron 'elephant shelter' located close to Engine Room 2. Given their proximity to the front line, the three engine rooms were soon targeted by German artillery and, as the emplacements began to suffer damage, the decision was made to relocate to a less exposed site, albeit only slightly further from the front. Engine Rooms 4 and 5 were selected, again in the cellars of former houses, 600 metres behind the village centre. No. 4 was established in the reinforced cellar of a former château while No. 5 was in a cellar located adjacent to the La Bassée Canal. The contents of Engine Room 4 were then relocated for the last time, to a new engine room on the opposite side of the La Bassée Canal to Engine Room 5, to form Engine Room 6. These two engine rooms adjacent to the canal were then able to draw cooling water for their engines directly from the canal. The cables from Engine Room 6 were laid above ground and entered the nearby Old Kent Road tunnel system to join and augment the Hulluch (Wings Way) engine room electricity supply.

Plate 41. A 50-horsepower De Dion belt-driven power generation set and three 40-horsepower Austin engines in the Pont Fixe engine room No. 4. They were later used in Pont Fixe engine room No. 6 to augment the Wings Way power station (AWM H12180).

By November the water-pumping facility at Givenchy had been expanded to nine pumps and, at the peak of pumping, 17 pumps were in operation, removing an estimated 1.4 to 1.8 million litres per day from underground workings. By the time the Alphabet Company wound up its operations at Givenchy in late 1918, a total of 41 water pumps had pumped hundreds of millions of litres of water from the underground workings. This total also included a water pump which supplied drinking and ablution water from a shaft in the underlying chalk aquifer to the front-line troops.

But the mainstay of the company's work was power supply and, more importantly, the provision of a reliable power supply. Following the battles of Arras and Messines, the activity of the resident tunnelling company, the British 172nd, turned from offensive mining to improving defences, namely the infantry subways and heavily defended redoubts (such as Bunny Hutch, Moat Farm and Marie). Loss of power supply to the front-line positions through breakages from shellfire was a constant problem that could occur at any time of the day or night. Breakages were unavoidable due to the sheer destructive power of the shells, but steps were taken to reduce the number of breakages and the time taken to repair these. The heavy twin core cables used to run 440-volt power supplies were particularly problematic. These cables were not favoured by the company because of the weight of the cable; laying it was a struggle compared to the single core cables which were used for 220 volt supplies. The dual core cabling was also susceptible to breakages caused by splinters of shells or debris thrown up by nearby explosions which could lodge between the wires, causing a short circuit. This type of damage was more problematic than a clean break because it was far more difficult to detect. The leads had to be followed and the entire length inspected until the damaged sections were located. In the dark, over muddy terrain, it was tedious and frustrating for the hapless men on shift whose job it was to make sure any disruptions to the front-line troops were as brief as possible. Furthermore, the 440-volt generators which provided the power operated at high speed and were more prone to failure than the 220-volt generating sets. Given the extra workload imposed on his men through the use of the 440-volt generators, Victor Morse argued with his seniors that these systems of generators and cables should be phased out. But he failed to convince headquarters and so was compelled to maintain the capability to provide both voltage supplies everywhere his company was required to supply power.

The Alphabet Company sought to improve the supply of power by running duplicate sets of both heavy and light power cabling to the forward positions.

The cable network was progressively extended, both to above and below-ground systems.

The Pont Fixe power station was, in the words of the Alphabet Company war diary, 'one of the largest and most important of forward stations on the front ... in one of the worst shelled areas of the front.'[3] The power cables from Pont Fixe entered the tunnel system at the Moat Farm dugouts close to the Caledonian dugouts. The cables lay in the open for 1550 metres, dangerously vulnerable to shellfire. Duplicate cables, spaced some 100 metres apart, were laid to reduce the possibility of total power loss due to breakages, in the hope that the power supply would continue via the undamaged cable while the breakage was mended. In February 1918, four sets of power lines were eventually buried to a depth of two metres, a move that paid dividends in April 1918 when the position was almost overrun and three of the four cables were broken during the intense artillery barrage of 17 and 18 April. One crucial power line remained intact, and continued to supply power to the Bunny Hutch redoubt.

Plate 42. A closer view of a complex electricity switch-board built, installed and operated by the Alphabet Company. This one belonged to the Pont Fixe engine room (Engine Room No. 6) (AWM J03025).

Plate 43. A power distribution point at Givenchy in 1918 showing the above-ground conditions. The cable from the nearby Pont Fixe engine room can be seen in the foreground. Visible also in the foreground is a grave containing the bodies of three unknown soldiers (AWM H12184).

It was around Givenchy that the Alphabet Company suffered its greatest number of casualties with four men killed in action or died of wounds while an unknown number were wounded. Nineteen-year-old No. 3807 Sapper Henry Ralph was killed by shellfire at Givenchy on 29 November 1917 as he emerged from a dugout. Three weeks later, on 18 December, 20-year-old No. 3961 Sapper Victor Thompson was killed in the same way close to the same place. Just across the La Bassée Canal at Cuinchy, No. 5144 Corporal Cyril 'Hobbie' Hobbs, MSM, was also killed by a shell close to one of the engine rooms on 9 May 1918. He had taken over operation of the power plant at Givenchy after the capture of Corporal Jack Nancarrow and his men during the German offensive a month earlier. Victor Morse described Cyril Hobbs as one of his best NCOs:

> … fine chap he was too, made good wherever he went, and this last job such a nerve test, took over and carried on when the majority of the previous party had gone west.[4]

Finally, No. 4509 2nd Corporal Arthur Wigzell was fatally wounded on 28 February 1918 as he walked along the tow path of the La Bassée Canal from Béthune on an inspection visit to the Pont Fixe power station. The concussion from a stray shell blew him into the water while a fragment of the shell hit him in the temple, penetrating his skull. The temperature of the water was close to freezing and, although his fall was witnessed by some

British soldiers who managed to pull his unconscious form from the water, the combined effects of his emersion and head wound finished him. He died on 8 March 1918.

Plate 44. The grave of 19-year-old Sapper Henry Ralph at Gorre Military Cemetery. This photograph was taken at the time of his burial by his CO, Major Victor Morse, DSO (NAA 10/75).

The company operated at Givenchy from 6 June 1916 to 29 October 1918, an unbroken period of 865 days. During that time it installed and operated 10 generating sets, which produced a maximum power output of 109 kilowatts. It also provided 41 water-pumping sets, seven air-ventilation sets and, when connected with the Hulluch (Wings Way) power system, covered a continuous frontage of tunnels, subways and galleries over a distance of almost five kilometres.

Hulluch–Wings Way Sector
Company Tour of Duty: Hulluch–Wings Way

On the southern side of the La Bassée Canal from Givenchy, the front lines snaked their way towards Loos and Hill 70, across ground made famous in the Battle of Loos in September 1915. The front formed a long arc around the village of Auchy-les-la-Bassée before resuming its southward track at a point known as the Hohenzollern Redoubt and reaching the village of Cité St Elie, yet another scene of intense underground warfare.

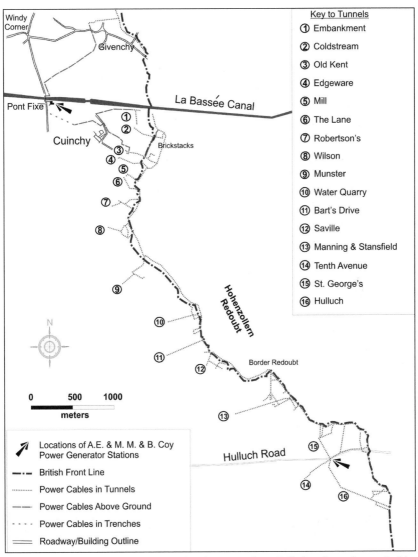

Map 12. The trench and tunnel system extending from Givenchy to Hulluch at the southern end of the Hohenzollern Redoubt. The lighting and power systems in the entire network were the domain of the Alphabet Company from mid-1916 to the end of 1918.

A particularly dreadful section of the front lay before the villages of Hulluch and Cité St Elie where the trench-lines had remained virtually unchanged since the Battle of Loos. This unusual state of stability allowed tunnellers the luxury of an almost unprecedented amount of time in which to create a labyrinth of connected underground infantry subways and galleries extending along the entire front and for a good distance behind the front lines. It was a front known as the Hulluch–St Elie or 'Wings Way' sector, previously the responsibility of the 170th Tunnelling Company until the arrival of the 3rd Australian Tunnelling Company in August 1917.

This subterranean system best illustrates the complexity and sheer size of the underground network created in the sector. The front lines along the Hulluch–St Elie sector were, like most, approached from below ground via a series of long tunnels which divided and multiplied, spreading like webs as they neared the front. They could be entered from multiple locations via shafts that connected with the surface communication trenches below which they passed. The area around the shaft entrances was characterised by large soil dumps from the excavated tunnels.

Between January and July 1917 a series of tunnels was constructed as feeder tunnels for infantry to access the front line from a distance of up to a kilometre to the rear. As each tunnel and associated dugouts were completed, they were fitted with electric lights, the tunnel lights 10 to 15 metres apart, and each dugout fitted with one to two lights. A small engine room was established along each tunnel and equipped with a 3-kilowatt engine and generator by the Alphabet Company. As more tunnels were completed, it became more difficult for the company to source and maintain generators given its small workforce, a situation that was to be rectified by the merging of the larger Pont Fixe and Wings Way engine rooms.

Situated at the approach to the underground systems facing Hulluch were the remains of the village of Vermelles. What little remained following the devastation of Loos — the skeletons of buildings and their cellars — were used as shelter. A large advanced dressing station was established with gallery connections to dugouts, and in the latter half of 1918 a system of 274 lights and two ventilation sets were fitted and operated by the Alphabet Company and powered from an engine room also fitted and maintained by the men of the company.

Among the longest approach tunnels to the Hulluch system from the direction of Vermelles was the Tenth Avenue Tunnel which was accessed from Tenth Avenue trench near Le Rutoire Farm a kilometre from the front line. Some 400 metres from Tenth Avenue trench, the tunnel forked. The southern fork became the Hulluch Tunnel which in turn further divided into northern and southern tunnels leading to the shallow Hulluch mining system and the Hulluch mine crater field. The northern fork became St George's Tunnel which led in turn to Grimwood Tunnel, leading to the trenches and mining galleries on the southern face of the Hohenzollern Redoubt. Originating from St George's Tunnel was another major branch tunnel, the St Elie Tunnel which, further on, separated into the Devon and Dudley tunnels and led to the St Elie trench and mining systems.

Where St George's and the St Elie tunnels forked, the Alphabet Company established an underground power station with generating sets capable of supplying 71.5 kilowatts. This power station, known at the Wings Way power station, was the second of two stations maintained and operated by the company, supplying power to all the front-line tunnels and their associated dugouts right along the Hohenzollern Redoubt, extending all the way from Coldstream Tunnel near the La Bassée Canal to the southern end of the Hulluch Tunnel system. The second, larger power plant was situated at Pont Fixe on the La Bassée Canal and also fed power to the Givenchy system.

Plate 45. Ruins housing the Vermelles dressing station and dugouts powered from the Vermelles engine room (AWM H19538).

With the removal of the German mining threat to the Hill 70 front as a result of the Allied advances during April and May, the 3rd Australian Tunnelling Company's sector was extended north from Loos. The vast and elaborate British mining systems that ran in an almost unbroken line to the north of Hill 70 as far as the La Bassée Canal desperately needed additional manpower — specifically tunnellers. In early August, sections from the company were allotted working sectors that extended from Hill 70 to the Hulluch–St Elie mining system, the next major mining system along the front, north of Hill 70.

Plate 46. Entrance to the Vermelles engine room operated by the Alphabet Company (AWM H19540).

The tunnels were fitted with dugouts of all description to enable men to live and move underground: cookhouses, aid posts, sleeping quarters, water supply wells, engine rooms for lighting and ventilation, machine-gun positions, trench mortar emplacements, artillery observation posts, and a range of infantry headquarters.

Plate 47. Entrance to the Wings Way engine room (AWM H19542).

Plate 48. The reinforced cellar at Wings Way which housed the engine room (AWM H19541).

At the northern end of the system on the heavily mine cratered Cuinchy–Auchy front, similar tunnel systems were well established and their names, Munster, Wilson, Robertson, Lane, Mill, Old Kent and Coldstream, would have been daily fare to the units that served on that front. Expanding and improving these massive and intricate tunnel systems was the bread and butter of the 3rd Australian Tunnelling Company during the latter part of 1917 and throughout 1918.

The 1/5th Leicestershires (138th Brigade, 46th North Midland Division) had been garrisoned in the sector just a few months before, in August 1917. The men described life in the extraordinary tunnel system that supported them:

> The various posts in 'Hairpin' were connected by an underground tunnel with four exits to the trench, while another with two exits did the same for 'Border Redoubt'. From each of these, a 300-yard tunnel ran westwards to what had been the old Support Line, where they were connected underground by another long passage - Feetham Tunnel. A branch of the Border Tunnel led to 'Rats Creek'. At various points along these tunnels exits were built up to fortified shell holes, occupied by Lewis gun teams; these were our only supports. Down below lived Company Headquarters,

the garrison, one or two tunnelling experts and the specialists, stokes mortars, machine gunners and others. It was a dreadful existence. The passages were damp and slippery, the walls covered in evil-looking red and yellow spongy fungus, the roof too low to allow one to walk upright, the ventilation practically non-existent, the atmosphere, always bad, became in the early mornings intolerable, all combined to ruin the health of those who had to live there. But not only was one's health ruined, one's 'nerves' were seriously impaired, and the tunnels had a bad effect on one's morale. Knowing we could always slip down a staircase to safety, we lost the art of walking on top, we fancied the dangers of the open air much greater than they really were, in every way we got into bad condition. The entrance to this tunnel system was at the end of our only communication trench, Stansfield Road, a deep well-gridded trench running all the way from Vermelles ... Battalion Headquarters had a private tunnel, part of the mining system, leading to Feetham, which could be used in emergency, but as this was unlit, it was quicker to use the trench. The main tunnel system was lit, or rather supposed to be lit, with electric light. This often failed, and produced of course indescribable chaos. Although the tunnels had all these disadvantages, it is only fair to say that they reduced our casualties enormously, for during the three months we lost only three officers slightly wounded and eighteen men; of these at least four were hit out on patrol. We also managed to live far more comfortably as regards food than we should otherwise have been able.[5]

No. 4209 Sergeant Edward 'Hughie' Dodd, a 21-year-old iron turner from Perth in Western Australia, was a member of the Alphabet Company who was embedded in a mining sector. Dodd left Australia with the 6th Australian Tunnelling Company but was transferred to the Alphabet Company in September 1916 and assigned to the Mechanical Section because of his skills as an ironworker. From there he journeyed south to maintain lighting and water-pumping equipment in the massive and complex tunnel systems along the front between Givenchy and Hulluch, close to one of the more hotly contested mining sections on the Western Front which included the Cuinchy and the Hohenzollern Redoubt mining systems.[6]

Dodd was to remain in this sector from the time of his arrival until the final retreat by the Germans in the latter part of 1918. He took with him a small party of Australian sappers from the Alphabet Company and also commanded a detachment of British sappers seconded from the 170th Company, the tunnelling company responsible for the mining system in same sector. Hughie

Dodd and his men were billeted with the 170th Company in their camp at Noeux-les-Mines south of Béthune and, during their war service, befriended more of their British tunnelling companions than their fellow Australians.[7] Hughie Dodd's situation was typical of the manner in which the men from the Alphabet Company were embedded within the units that defended the various front-line sectors along the British First and Second Army areas.

Plate 49. No. 4209 Sergeant Edward 'Hughie' Dodd (back left), No. 4509 2nd Corporal Arthur Wigzell (back right), No. 10 Corporal Thomas (Frank) Doyle (front left), No. 4212 Sergeant Hubert Marsh (front right) in winter woolskin jackets. Arthur Wigzell died of wounds in March 1918 and Hubert Marsh was awarded the Military Medal for his actions at Hill 60 (AWM J00231).

The Hulluch (Wings Way) power station was situated in a dugout below the Hulluch Road, around 300 metres behind the front line, and operated from 8 January 1917 until 13 November 1918. Between October 1917 and its closure in late 1918, it produced a peak continuous power output of 72 kilowatts, distributed through the underground tunnel and gallery systems between it and the Pont Fixe engine room 5.5 kilometres to its north-west, through a total of 73,000 metres of heavy and light gauge electric cabling. The engine room also housed an additional 15-kilowatt engine to power a large electric fan (14 inches or 356 millimetres in diameter) to provide rapid ventilation for the underground passages. The fan was used at times when no gas alerts were in force, with the air drawn from the surface and, as a precaution, passed through a large gas filter, also built and maintained by the Alphabet Company.

LENS FRONT LOOS: HILL 70 AND THE HYTHE TUNNEL
Company Tour of Duty – Hill 70 (Loos)

The next active fighting sector south along the front from Hulluch was one of the most famous of the war and it circled the small, shattered hamlet of Loos-en-Gohelle (Loos), the scene of Britain's first large-scale offensives in September 1915. The Battle of Loos, as it is known, was fought between 25 September and 16 October 1915 and ended in abject defeat for the British. During the three-week battle, British forces suffered over 61,000 casualties, of whom almost 7800 were killed. The battle was characterised by several notorious errors of judgement, not the least of which was the ill-advised order to release gas at the commencement of the opening assault when there was virtually no wind. In fact, the light breeze blowing at the time was just sufficient to blow the gas back across sections of the British assaulting troops who were equipped with inferior quality gas masks. The outcome of the battle precipitated the replacement of the British Supreme Commander, Field Marshal Sir John French. The new commander of the British forces on the Western Front was Sir Douglas Haig who, at the time of the battle, commanded the First Army, the army caught up in the debacle.

Prior to the battle, the partially damaged village of Loos and Hill 70 were held by the Germans. Hill 70 was a small but vital piece of elevated land just to the east of the village that overlooked Loos and the British defences behind and around it, and was one of the objectives of the assault. By battle's end, the village had been captured, albeit at great cost to the British. During the battle, Hill 70 had been taken and held tenuously by the British for a short period before being lost again following a German counter-attack. The 15th (Scottish) Division fought and suffered terribly at Loos. Over the course of the first two days of fighting, the 7th Cameron Highlanders, 9th Black Watch, 8th Seaforth Highlanders and the 10th Gordon Highlanders of the division's 44th Brigade suffered 2250 casualties.[8]

Following the battle, and once the new front lines re-emerged with the Germans still holding Hill 70, while Loos was in the hands of the British, a new mining war began under no man's land facing Hill 70. Several of the underground mining galleries which later extended towards Hill 70 from the British lines at Loos were named in honour of the Scottish regiments in recognition of their losses. The British mining galleries, commenced by the British 173rd and 258th tunnelling companies, were taken over by the 3rd Australian Tunnelling Company in the first weeks of November 1916. The Australian tunnelling company was to remain in this sector until the German retreat during the final days of the war. It was here that, just weeks after arriving, it suffered the greatest single loss to an Australian tunnelling company during the war when, on 27 November, 20 tunnellers were killed and nine others gassed following the detonation of a German camouflet deep below ground. Loos was also where the company lost its charismatic young CO, Major Leslie Coulter, DSO, killed in action in late June 1917.

When the men of the Australian tunnelling company arrived at Loos to take over the Hill 70 mining system from their British counterparts, they discovered their former comrades from the Australian Mining Corps in the newly named Alphabet Company already working there, having arrived three weeks earlier and having commenced what proved to be their own long association with Loos and its surroundings. Two landmarks dominated the village. The first was the steel, twin-towered coal mine pit head named Tower Bridge and situated at the western end of the second landmark, a long sloping pile of mine waste, the Loos Crassier, which tapered in the direction of Lens. Following the capture of Loos by the British in late 1915, the village was shelled relentlessly by the Germans. By late 1916, it had been all but levelled and Tower Bridge reduced to a tangle of shredded metal. The British front line lay at the eastern end of the Loos Crassier. North of the crassier was the three-levelled Hill 70 mine system taken over by the 3rd Australian Tunnelling Company. To the south of the crassier was the mining system known as the Copse and controlled by the 273rd Tunnelling Company.

Plate 50. Tower Bridge mine pit head at Loos-en-Gohelle with the Loos Crassier (the waste rock pile) extending towards the suburbs of Lens, a photograph taken prior to the Battle of Loos in 1915 showing the largely intact village from the British lines (photomerged images: IMW Q43113, Q43114, Q43115).

Plate 51. A view of the almost levelled village taken from a similar vantage point in 1916 once it was in British hands. By this time the front line had been pushed back beyond the far end of the Loos Crassier where the Loos (Hill 70) mining system extended below no man's land (AWM E01966).

The wreckage of the pit head buildings which backed onto the steep toe of the crassier, while not a luxurious setting with sweeping views over the village, was extremely well protected from German artillery and small arms fire. For that reason the Alphabet Company established an engine room for a 9-kilowatt petrol-driven generator among the ruins of Tower Bridge. The remains of the village, located close to the front line and offering some protection in the form of cellars and stone or brick walls, were far from deserted. Scattered throughout the place were aid posts, dressing stations, unit headquarters for the infantry units that manned the sector and accommodation dugouts. A lighting system was also extended into the village to service the many key locations.

Over the 19 months the unit supplied power from the Tower Bridge engine room, just over 18,280 metres of electric cabling were extended from the room to power lighting (210 lighting points and 500 electric lamps) to a range of dugouts and accommodation that had been established among the ruins of Loos, and to the Hill 70 and Copse mining systems. In the mining systems, four electric dewatering pumps were installed to control groundwater in the chalk aquifer in the deeper parts of the mine galleries and three air-ventilations sets were in operation. By July 1917, an improvised electric winch had been installed to haul chalk up the sloped inclines of mine shafts.

Plate 52. The wreckage of Tower Bridge and mine buildings at Loos, which housed the engine room that supplied power to Loos and the Hill 70 mining system (AWM E01634).

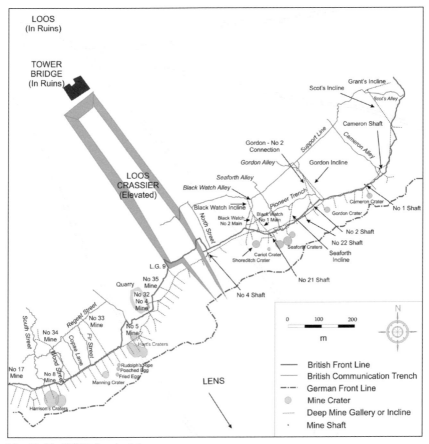

Map 13. The Hill 70 (Loos) mining systems.

As a result of the Battle of Arras in April 1917, British forces gained ground, pushing the German lines back eastwards from Arras and capturing Vimy Ridge. At the extreme northern end of the battle front, the western suburbs of Lens were secured from the Germans. By the end of that battle, the hinge point between the old and new British front line was in front of Loos. Part of the old German mining system, below what had been no man's land, was then controlled by the 3rd Australian Tunnelling Company. However one part of the old German mining system was not and this strange situation remained unresolved until the German front line was finally pushed back from the summit to the eastern side of Hill 70 by the Canadians in August 1917. It was only then that the mining war at Hill 70 finally drew to a close and many of the mining systems were stripped of their precious wooden props and cladding.

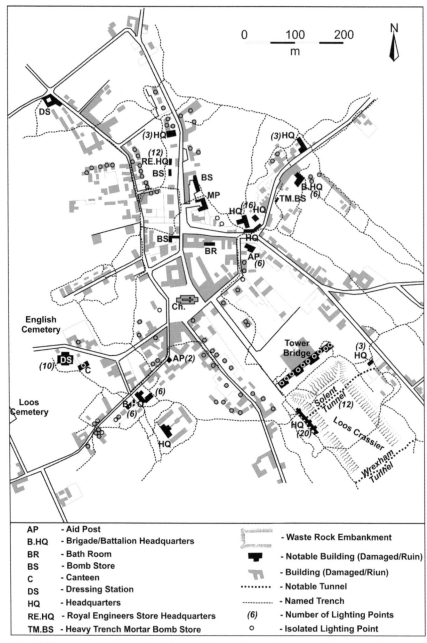

AP	- Aid Post
B.HQ	- Brigade/Battalion Headquarters
BR	- Bath Room
BS	- Bomb Store
C	- Canteen
DS	- Dressing Station
HQ	- Headquarters
RE.HQ	- Royal Engineers Store Headquarters
TM.BS	- Heavy Trench Mortar Bomb Store

	- Waste Rock Embankment
	- Notable Building (Damaged/Ruin)
	- Building (Damaged/Riun)
••••••••	- Notable Tunnel
-----------	- Named Trench
(6)	- Number of Lighting Points
o	- Isolated Lighting Point

Map 14. The proposed lighting scheme for Loos showing the trench system and locations of key positions in the ruins of the village in late 1916.

Following on from its success at Vimy Ridge during the Battle of Arras four months earlier, the Canadian Corps took the hill on 15 August 1917 at a cost of some 9000 casualties and consolidated in the days that followed. The new front line was established beyond the foot of the eastern slope of the hill. The ubiquitous Alphabet Company was not spared the ill effects of working in an active battle zone following the capture of Hill 70. On 21 August, during the early consolidation phase of the new front lines, the company lost No. 4356 Sapper James Hood, MM, killed in action. James Hood was one of the Alphabet Company's true quiet achievers and, had he lived, would surely have been awarded more accolades. Just five weeks before his own death, the dashing young CO of the 3rd Australian Tunnelling Company, Major Leslie Coulter, DSO, brought the actions of James Hood to the attention of Victor Morse with the result that Hood was awarded the Military Medal for gallantry in the field:

> I particularly wish to draw your attention to the conduct of the above-mentioned sapper under various trying circumstances. He first did good work on the occasion of a serious blow resulting in loss of life.[9] He assisted in the rescue of several gassed men from the workings and subsequently was able to start an electric fan, allowing rescue partiers to obtain access to the workings. He has repeatedly repaired electric leads under heavy shell fire, and is absolutely regardless of danger on such occasions. Recently under heavy rifle fire he went out with an officer and brought in a wounded man from an exposed position in Loos.[10]

After August 1917 the new British front line lay on the eastern slope of the hill. As a consequence, any movement over the crest of the hill towards the new front line along Hythe Alley communication trench exposed soldiers to observation and shellfire from the Germans. The solution was the construction of a tunnel below the hill, work undertaken by the resident tunnelling company, the 3rd Australian Tunnelling Company, which was not completed until mid-1918.

The completed tunnel was 1215 metres in length with two entrances. The first entrance was accessed via an incline from the Lens–La Bassée road and the second via an extension dug from the old German front line, 490 metres west of the road. At its far, eastern end, the tunnel branched and connected with another tunnel, Quarry Tunnel, which provided access to the front-line trench (Lynn Trench) and dugouts at the Quarry. At its deepest point, the tunnel provided 14 metres of head cover. Hythe Tunnel contained accommodation dugouts, a dressing station and provided access to four machine-gun emplacements. The tunnel and dugouts were fitted with a total of 120 electric lights supplied with power by an engine room constructed near the western entrance to the tunnel. Water for the tunnel and its dugout system was also provided by the Alphabet Company, pumped from a depth of 30 metres from old German mine workings in the underlying chalk aquifer and stored in a tank in a separate chamber.

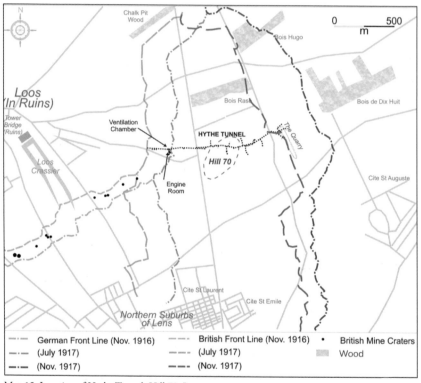

Map 15. Location of Hythe Tunnel, Hill 70, Loos.

In its workshop the Alphabet Company fashioned an improvised soil haulage set capable of being fitted with either hemp or wire rope and which featured specially made clips to attach haulage bags. The system was tested using both rope types and found to work well. Capable of hauling 1000 bags an hour, the system could remove between 32 and 45 tonnes of soil per hour. Two sets were eventually constructed and were in use as the tunnel and dugout systems below Hill 70 were expanded until finally abandoned in late October 1918 when the German front began its withdrawal east from the Lens front.

Plate 53. Hythe Tunnel entrance below Hill 70, Loos (AWM 19525).

Plate 54 (right). The view looking back to the entrance from inside the tunnel (AWM H19526).

When the Alphabet Company arrived at Hythe Tunnel on 7 June 1918, the engine room was fitted with two generators capable of supplying 6 kilowatts of power. Power generation was progressively increased over the following months until, by September, the engine room was generating 22 kilowatts. A fresh water supply was also pumped, via two electric pumps, from old German mine workings. Over 4500 metres of electric cabling was laid by the company at Hythe Tunnel. The engine room shut down permanently on 25 October 1918 and all equipment was withdrawn once the British front began its final move west in pursuit of the retreating German forces.

Double Crassier: Maroc
Company Tour of Duty: Maroc

The northern flank of the Battle of Arras, which included Vimy Ridge, extended as far north as Loos. North from the Souchez River, the front lines followed a broad arc around the western outskirts of Lens before resuming their northward meanderings from Loos. By 1916, active underground mining was in progress in the systems outside the coal mining villages at Calonne and Maroc. Between the village of Maroc (now incorporated into the settlement of Grenay) and the suburb of Cité St Pierre lay a unique and possibly one of the most recognisable landmarks on the British front — the Double Crassier, two mine waste rock piles from the Fosse 11 mine pit. The waste rock was delivered by rail and dumped at the railhead, with both the railway and rock piles progressively growing longer and higher as the piles were extended. By the outbreak of war, the two almost parallel waste rock piles were just over a kilometre long and rose to a height of around 15 metres above the surrounding landscape at their far (western) tip and were some eight metres wide along their flat tops.[11] The northern crassier was slightly shorter in length than its southern twin.[12] Their height afforded extensive views north and west across the flat plains which, prior to the Battle of Loos, were in German hands. The German front line, which ran around the toe of both crassiers, allowed the Germans access to those views from the top of the crassiers.

Plate 55. Looking east from Maroc towards the two ends of the Double Crassier, the waste piles from the Number 11 coal mine at Lens. The British front lines can be seen running across the view at the toe of the two soil piles with a trench running up the slope of the left (northern) toe-face known as Snow Hill. Photo dated July 1917 (IWM Q58148).

There was a shift in power during the Battle of Loos in late 1915, when the British 47th (2nd London) Division captured the German front line at the crassiers (Crassier Trench) and established the new British front from part way down the side slope of the northern crassier. The result was that from the north, the new German front line approached the northern crassier, to a point around halfway along its length, and crossed beneath the two crassiers via a tunnel, reappeared halfway along the southern crassier slope before following it for a few hundred metres then angling south towards the Calonne front. The western halves of both crassiers were technically in no man's land. However the British held the upper hand and accessed the western ends of the crassiers via a number of saps at what were known as Pultney and Snow Hills on the northern crassier and Ludgate Hill sap leading up the slope of the tip of the southern crassier. Access to the crassiers from the ruins of Maroc village was via a number of long communication trenches, primarily Seventh and Middle alleys.

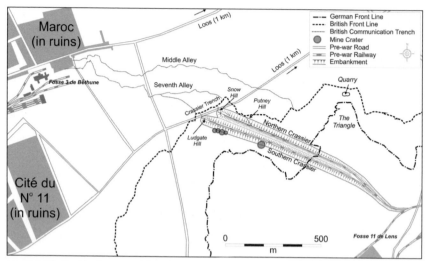

Map 16. The Double Crassier and front-line trenches from a Geographical Section, General Staff (GSGS) trench map dated February 1917, the period in which the Alphabet Company was supplying power to the British mine system below the southern crassier.

But it was activity below the crassiers that brought the Alphabet Company to the sector in August 1916. By mid-1916 the British 173rd Tunnelling Company had been defending the British front and, more importantly, preventing the Germans successfully using either crassier. Accessed from shafts and inclines in the front lines, the British mining system at the crassiers merged with the neighbouring mining system to the north and was known as the Copse. That system was in turn connected to the extensive system in front of Loos, between the village and Hill 60. Below the British front, out under no man's land, the mining system at the crassiers therefore extended below the northern crassier and, at a point almost 500 metres from their tip, the British tunnel galleries turned and ran parallel to the southern crassier and directly under it, to its western tip. The point where the German and British tunnels met lay just along the toe of the southern slope of the southern crassier and this was evidenced in the presence of a number of mine craters embedded into the toe of the slope, the aftermath of seven mines blown by the British on 16 March 1916. The British mining system at the crassiers therefore held the key to keeping the Germans at bay, and in this the British tunnellers were very successful, maintaining the status quo until the threat was removed following the Battle of Arras in April-May 1917 when the Germans were again pushed back to the southern and eastern suburbs of Lens.

Plate 56. The entrance to the Alphabet Company's engine room at Maroc (AWM H19529).

The Alphabet Company arrived to assist mining operations at the crassiers on 14 August 1916. A 12-kilowatt generator was installed in an engine room situated in the cellar of one of the shattered end houses on the Maroc–Loos road and just 550 metres from the front line. Electrical cabling was run along a communication trench (possibly Seventh Alley) to the Double Crassier and along its base to various mine entrances.

The Maroc mining system, which faced the Double Crassier coal mine slag heaps, was also prepared with power and lighting in readiness for the opening of the Battle of Arras on 7 April 1917. A key purpose, other than the provision of power for lighting the crassier mines, was power for ventilation of the mine systems occupied by the British 173rd Tunnelling Company. The exposed northern slope of the northern crassier was constantly shelled, closing mine entrances and damaging trenches. This forced relief squads of tunnellers to risk going over the top of the crassiers at night to reach undamaged and accessible mine entrances. With the number of useable mine entrances reduced, the quality of air in the tunnels deteriorated to the point at which, on occasions, the mine galleries could not be entered due to the foul air. The waste rock piles also contained slag, the rock-like residue of coal burning and steel production.

The slag generated heat in the body of the crassiers which permeated the ground and added to the discomfort of the tunnellers below. Consequently, powered air ventilators were essential. A total of seven air-blower ventilation sets were eventually supplied and installed in the mining systems by the Alphabet Company, two of which were destroyed by German shellfire. Electrical power and lighting to 170 lighting points was also supplied to several dugouts, a dressing station and front-line battalion unit headquarters situated in the ruins of Maroc.

The Alphabet Company withdrew its equipment from the Maroc front on 17 April 1917 following the movement of the front lines away from the Double Crassier and into the western suburbs of Lens — the achievement of the British 24th Division during the Battle of Arras.

CHAPTER 6

VIMY TO ARRAS

Vimy Ridge
Company Tour of Duty: Vimy Ridge

Vimy Ridge is, like the Somme and Passchendaele, a place name that is inextricably linked to the First World War. For some, it is familiar as the formidable ridge captured by the Canadians at great cost in April 1917 during the Battle of Arras. Such is the ridge's impact on Canadian consciousness that, on its summit, stands the largest monument to Canadian forces on the Western Front. This in itself is impressive as the Canadians participated in many of the bloodiest battles of the war in Picardy, Artois and Flanders. Likewise, Vimy Ridge and its approaches are, for the French, another testament to suffering and loss, like so many places along the front where Frenchmen were killed and wounded in appalling numbers. The French military cemetery of Ablain St.-Nazaire (also known as Notre Dame de Lorette), with its seemingly endless rows of crosses, its haunting basilica and ossuary, is a staggering reminder of the suffering of French soldiers in the area around Vimy before the sector was taken over by the British in early 1916. The horrific conditions endured by the common soldier are described in surviving accounts such as that of Louis Bathas, a corporal who served with the 296th Infantry Regiment and who kept a diary of his life in the trenches which was eventually published after his death.[1]

Vimy Ridge belongs firmly to the military histories of the Canadian, French, British and Germans. So where were the Australians? It will come as a surprise to many, none more so than Australians, that even today, on the western slope of the ridge, there is evidence of work completed by Australians in preparation for the capture of Vimy Ridge. Two craters lie almost lost in the crush of battle wounds that pockmark the ridge, one named after that sturdy Australian ground-burrowing marsupial, the wombat. The time-softened form of this crater lies at the end of a long, underground tunnel — formerly an infantry subway, Goodman subway — where no man's land once narrowly separated the British and German front lines. It was recently cleared of undergrowth after almost a century of lying forgotten, covered by a blanket of foliage. A second crater lies nearby, yet to be released from the vegetation that has reclaimed the hill over the decades since its formation.

It may also come as a surprise that several Australians were awarded medals in recognition of their actions in the lead-up to the taking of the ridge. One recipient was the CO of the Alphabet Company, Victor Morse, who was awarded the Distinguished Service Order (DSO) for his leadership and direction of his unit's works at Vimy Ridge.

The story of Vimy Ridge began long before the events of April 1917. It began when the Germans characteristically assumed strategic control of the high ground along the Western Front in late 1914 during the race to the sea. Vimy Ridge was a natural platform for the Germans to perch atop, offering stunning views for many tens of miles towards the west and over Allied lines. This was the prime motivation that drove the fierce and unrelenting battle to wrest the ridge from the Germans, a battle that was initiated by the French. The ridge, like all other vital high ground the Germans controlled from those early days of the war, had to be taken. And the fighting over Vimy Ridge was bitter and protracted.

Vimy Ridge is the topographical expression of a geological feature, a fault or crack formed across or between geological layers where one side of the crack is either pushed up or down in relation to the other side. In many places where this has occurred in recent geological history, a sharp ridgeline is formed along the face of the crack that has been pushed up. This is essentially how Vimy Ridge was created. The western side of the ridge was the up-thrust side of the Marquelles Fault, and on that side of the fault the ground surface slopes gently up towards the ridgeline, while just over the ridge, on the eastern side, the land falls dramatically away. In terms of what this meant strategically in the context of the war, if the Germans were to be pushed back from its summit and ridgeline it would be very difficult for them to take the ridge from the east due to the steeply sloping ground on that side. This was the Allied objective. However approaching the ridge from the west presented immense difficulties as all movement could be observed by those occupying the ridge. This explains why fighting to wrest the ridge from German hands was so desperate and bloody from early in the war, beginning with the French who fought there until March 1916, when the British took over the sector to relieve the French for the defence of Verdun. In many parts of the sector the front lines were very close and mining operations had been employed by the French before the British tunnelling companies arrived. In total, five British tunnelling companies served at Vimy Ridge: the 181st, 182nd, 185th, 175th and 176th.

The front along the western slope of the ridge was divided into a series of mining sectors, each under the control of a tunnelling company. The northernmost, where the ridge rose from the southern bank of the Souchez River, was the Carency sector, which faced a prominence called the 'Pimple'. Next to this was the La Volerie or Berthonval sector, followed by the La Folie sector. Heavy fighting and mining had occurred in the Souchez, Carency and La Volerie sectors before the British arrived and the French had almost reached the top of the ridge. However, in the La Volerie sector, a successful German attack on 21 May 1916 pushed the British front line back and some 500 metres down the slope. From that point until the capture of the ridge a year later, a tit-for-tat mining and counter-mining war was waged between the German and British tunnellers and no man's land along the ridge became a shattered wreck of mine craters, many of which can still be seen preserved in what is now the Vimy Memorial Site.

On the southern half of the ridge were more mining sectors: Neuville St Vaast, Ecurie North and Ecurie Central, which included an area known as the 'Labyrinth', so-named as a reflection of the mine and shell-devastated jumble of trenches which, in September 1915, had seen intense fighting between the French and Germans that resulted in 150,000 casualties. A former officer of the 185th Tunnelling Company who revisited the place 10 years after the war recounted that, on his company's front alone, there were over 100 mine craters and around 60,000 French and German dead lying unburied in no-man's land.[2] He referred to the place as 'Armageddon'.

Allied plans in early 1917 included a spring offensive against the Germans, spearheaded by the French on the Chemin des Dames front under the new leadership of the hero of Verdun, General Robert Nivelle. This led to a series of battles in the British sector of the front, collectively known as the Battle of Arras.

The genesis of the Battle of Arras lay in reform of the French military command following dissatisfaction with and criticism of the Commander-in-Chief, General Joffre, over the heavy losses at Verdun and on the Somme. Political pressure, both French and British, led to Joffre's resignation on Boxing Day 1916, two weeks after he had been replaced by General Nivelle as Commander-in-Chief of French forces. At the time of his ascendancy to the top job, General Nivelle was regarded by the French as a hero. Late in October 1916, Nivelle had succeeded in finally securing some reward for the vast quantity of French blood spilt on the altar of Verdun by recapturing Fort Douaumont on the Verdun battlefield, followed soon after by Fort Vaux. These were places of huge symbolic significance to the French psyche. His approach at Verdun was one of massed artillery bombardment followed by a swift attack, with artillery continuing to offer considerable close support to the attacking troops.

As he was being installed in his new position of supreme military command, Nivelle's plans to recapture the last remaining outposts at Verdun entered their final phase of preparation. Their realisation saw him hailed as the saviour of Verdun, a city which had endured 10 months of enemy occupation of the outpost forts and hills to its east. The lives of 162,000 French soldiers had been lost at Verdun, as had the lives of a similar number of Germans. The ultimate conclusion of that meat-grinding offensive resembled the lifting of a dark, heavy veil that had weighed on the French consciousness. Nivelle rode into his new role on a wave of victory, filled with confidence that he had the tactical answer to defeat the enemy.

Nivelle's grand scheme for defeating the Germans on the Western Front stemmed directly from his successes at Verdun. The difference in scale that greeted this new employment of his Verdun tactics against the prepared might of several German armies simultaneously did not cloud his belief that they would succeed. Even as the last of the French wounded were being recovered from the battlefields of Verdun, he met with his ally, Douglas Haig, and proposed a joint Franco-British assault against the Germans in the coming spring. In its simplest terms, the British would pursue an 'attack and hold' campaign on the Somme front between Bapaume and Arras with French forces replicating this action south of the British between the Arve and Oise rivers. Further south, Nivelle would break through the German front on the northern bank of the River Aisne. The French Aisne front was long, relatively straight and faced a strategically important ridge that mirrored the course of the river, known as the Chemin des Dames. The Aisne front lay to the south and at right angles to the fronts occupied by the British and the French Groupe d'armées du Nord (under General Franchet d'Espèrey). German resistance, he believed, would waver and collapse before the onslaught of his 'army of rupture'. The breach thus formed would facilitate the rapid advance of three French 'armies of exploitation'.

Nivelle predicted that the collapse of the German armies on the Aisne would precipitate the cumulative failure of the remaining German armies to fend off British attacks on the Somme front and a second French offensive to the south of the British. The two arms of the Allied offensives would then converge, having broken the back of the German forces on the Western Front.

Just as this plan was being sold, not only to the British High Command, but also to British politicians and, in particular, the new 'hands on' Prime Minister David Lloyd George however, the Germans retired to the Hindenburg Line on the Somme and on the Arve-Oise fronts where the Franco-British 'attack and hold' offensives were planned. But even this monumental repositioning failed to disrupt Nivelle's plans which were merely amended to take into consideration Haig's views on the best sector of the new front for the British to attack. These events sowed the seeds for what became known in the British sector as the Battle of Arras.

By late March, the date for the offensive had been set at 8 April. As the day approached, there came a dawning realisation that the German defences on the Aisne front were much stronger and constructed in greater depth than anticipated. Nivelle's assault was postponed until 12 April to allow more time for preparation. Later, the French offensive was again revised to 16 April. The British offensive was, however, delayed for just one day, from Easter Sunday to Easter Monday, 9 April.

Because of the German ability to observe Allied lines from the elevated positions along the crest of Vimy Ridge, any direct approach to the front in daylight by man or beast was extremely ill-advised. As a result, a series of long tunnels (infantry subways), their entrances in communication trenches set well back from the front lines, were dug and maintained by the tunnelling companies in each sector. These infantry subways were not only designed to allow access for mining but also general access for infantry to the front lines. The subways were dug into the western side of the sloping ground straight towards the ridge and were named, in order from north to south: Souchez, Coburg, Gobron, Blue Bell, Vincent, Tottenham, Cavalier, Grange, Goodman, Lichfield, Zivy, Bentata and Douai. They ranged in length from the shortest — Gobron at around 265 metres — to the longest, Goodman, at 1722 metres.

The *Official History of the Canadian Army in the First World War* was lavish in its praise of the subways:

> The protective tunneling constructed preparatory to the Battle of Arras, and especially Vimy Ridge, represented one of the greatest engineering achievements of the war, tunnelling companies excavated or extended eleven [sic] subways of a total length of almost four miles, leading to the Canadian front line. In these electrically lit subways, 25 feet or more underground, telephone cables and water mains found protection from enemy shelling. The subways provided a covered approach for troops moving up for the assault, or in relief, and they allowed a safe and speedy

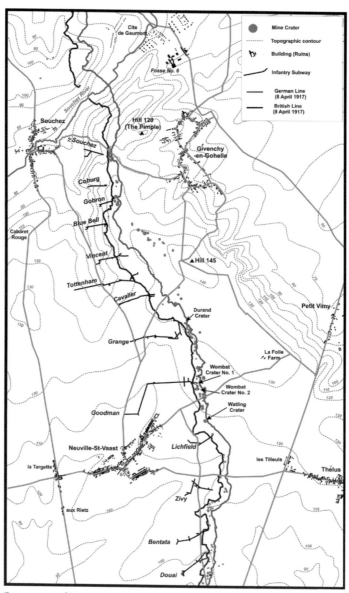

Map 17. Contour map of Vimy Ridge showing the British and German front lines prior to the capture of the ridge in April 1917. The Allied tunnel systems leading to the front are also shown. The installation and maintenance of the lighting systems in most of these tunnels was the work of the Alphabet Company. Mine craters scar no man's land along much of the front, testament to the ferocity of fighting in this sector up to April 1917. A total of 1125 lighting points and 12,500 metres of electrical cabling were installed by the company.

evacuation of the wounded. Chambers cut into their walls housed brigade and battalion headquarters, ammunition stores and dressing stations; while included in this underground accommodation were several deep caverns, left from chalk quarrying operations of an earlier day, the largest of which – Zivy cave – had room for an entire battalion.[3]

The central corridors were not spacious and, while the average man could stand, they were only just wide enough for two men to pass. They were, at best, snug, but safe and easily dug through chalk which was both dry and had sufficient intrinsic strength not to collapse unexpectedly.

The Alphabet Company's first introduction to Vimy Ridge and its workings came on 20 July 1916, during the period in which underground fighting between the British and German tunnellers below the ridge was most intense. A number of large mines had been blown by both sides in the Carency sector in front of the Pimple and a series of British mine galleries under the control of the 176th Tunnelling Company was located at the fighting end of the Souchez subway facing its German counterparts. Such was the severity of underground fighting that, during its time there, the British 176th Tunnelling Company alone lost two officers and 43 men killed or died of wounds, another 106 wounded and 36 men gassed though carbon monoxide poisoning.[4] Indeed it was because of the risks posed by the carbon monoxide accumulation in the underground British workings from a succession of mines and camouflets blown by both sides, that the Alphabet Company was initially called in to supply and power ventilation fans in the Z5 mine gallery in the Carency mining sector.

A 12-kilowatt electric generator was brought down from Hazebrouck, installed in an engine room dugout in the farm buildings known as Cabaret Rouge and, from there, 2400 metres of electric cables were extended via communication trenches to the front-line mining system. Two ventilation fans were installed and run continuously for five weeks and for 22 hours a day over the next seven months. One of the fans, which could supply 850 cubic metres of air per hour to the working mine faces through a flexible pipe 6 inches in diameter, was German, captured and salvaged during the battle then under way on the Somme to the south. Eventually seven fans were installed in the Vimy mining systems of which four were later destroyed by shellfire on 7 May 1917 during the lead-up to the Battle of Arras.

It was not until February 1917 that the Alphabet Company expanded operations fully across Vimy Ridge's subterranean systems. The infantry subways were to act as the means for attacking infantry — in this case, the men of the Canadian Corps — to launch their attack on the ridge at zero hour on 9 April

1917. In order to ensure the safe passage of a large concentration of officers and men and their equipment via the subways to positions as close as possible to the ridge, it was imperative that the subways were well lit and the lighting efficiently maintained both in the lead-up to and during the attack.

The Alphabet Company installed and operated a series of 220-volt, 2.2-kilowatt electric generators in small engine rooms excavated off each of the main subways along the ridge. This enabled them to supply power and lighting to the Blue Bell, Vincent, Tottenham, Cavalier, Grange, Goodman, Lichfield, Zivy, Bentata and Douai subways. Entire subway systems, including the main passages and ancillary dugouts, were wired and fitted with lighting. Electric lights, each with illumination of around 20 candlepower and fitted with thick wire guards, were hung at roughly 10-metre intervals down one side of the passage. This was designed to eliminate the necessity for leads to cross the roof where, as experience had shown, the leads were easily broken by the barrels of rifles slung over men's shoulders as they passed down the passages. In total, 10 power-generating sets were installed by the Alphabet Company in the 10 Vimy Ridge subways, powering 715 lights with a further 715 spare lights as back-up. They were installed progressively between early February and mid-May 1917. After the battle and with the movement of the front line further east, the subways were no longer needed, and the power plants were gradually withdrawn. The last of the plants were withdrawn from the two longest subways, Grange and Goodman, on 27 August 1917.

Plate 57. Entrance to Coburg subway on Vimy Ridge (NAA 9/92).

Plate 58. Entrance to Gobron subway on Vimy Ridge (the officer seated in both photographs is unidentified) (NAA 9/55).

As was the established pattern in previous battles during 1916 and 1917 in which sections of the battle fronts were separated by a narrow no man's land, mines had also been prepared at several points to be blown at zero hour, to add to the enemy's confusion in the opening minutes of a frontal attack. Three mines were blown by the 176th Tunnelling Company on the front facing the Pimple and two more on the southern end of the ridge where the charges were laid using the Australian-made Wombat borer. Both of the mines drilled by the Wombat borer were intended to create instantaneous communication trenches across no man's land, one from the end of Goodman subway, the second from a mine tunnel head that had been dug on the southern side of a mine crater known as the Chassery Crater. Both charges were blown by the British 172nd Tunnelling Company at 30 seconds after zero hour (5.30 am) on 9 April 1917.

The resulting craters were later measured at between 46 and 52 metres long, 10 metres wide and just under five metres deep. In the words of the Durand Group,[5] the two Wombat craters are 'unique features, not apparent anywhere else on the Western Front'.[6] Another hole was to be drilled by the Wombat borer from the end of Grange subway and directed just to the left of an existing crater known as the Durand Crater. A chamber to house a Wombat borer had been completed for this task but, on the night of 23 March 1917, the Germans, suspecting that plans were afoot for an offensive, detonated four massive mines in a line just north of the Durand Crater to form what were subsequently called the Longfellow Craters.[7] The mines destroyed the Wombat chamber and no further work was attempted before the attack on the ridge two weeks later.

Plate 59. The remains of the crater blown by the explosive charge placed using the Wombat borer at the ridge end of Goodman subway and detonated at the commencement of the Battle of Vimy Ridge (Institute of Royal Engineers).

Thus it was that Australians, specifically the men from the Alphabet Company, were not only below Vimy Ridge during the attack in April 1917, but had been at work there for nine months prior to the offensive. Indeed they played a vital role in ensuring that conditions below ground provided optimum support for what proved to be a monumental effort to capture the ridgeline at Vimy by the Allies, in particular the Canadians.

The Inspector of Mines at GHQ prepared a summary report following the battle, in which he wrote:

In both the First and Third Armies the majority of the subways were lit by electric light, and the experience gained shows that for any long system of tunnels, electric light is a necessity and not a luxury, for it provides an effectual remedy against confusion and congestion.

The value of these Subways has never been questioned. By their means it was possible to bring large numbers of men close up to their positions of assembly, and to retain them there in almost perfect security, until it was time to move out. It is not possible to say how many men were accommodated in the Tunnels, but, in the Arras Caves alone, the numbers amounted to 6,000.

By 12 April 1917, the ridge had been taken by the four divisions of the Canadian Corps at a cost of around 10,600 casualties, including some 3600 men killed. Unsurprisingly, this was the site chosen to commemorate the enormous Canadian sacrifice of World War I.

Alphabet Company men made an important contribution to the assault, ensuring that the attacking troops were sheltered safely in their underground marshalling points prior to zero hour. Indeed, between August 1916 and August 1917, along a front extending from the Vimy tunnel systems, the Alphabet Company installed and maintained some 800 lighting points connected to their respective engine rooms via networks of around 38,000 metres of heavy and light gauge electric cabling. This was no small feat and represents another of the extraordinary achievements of the small but highly skilled company.

Arras Caves
Company Tour of Duty: Arras Caves

The dawn that spread over northern France on Easter Monday 9 April 1917, the opening day of the Battle of Arras, should have held the promise of a pleasant mid-spring day. However, the winter of 1916–1917 was abnormally harsh and by April the winter chill clung tenaciously to northern France and Belgium. The opening of the British offensive was marred by squally rain, sleet and snow showers across a front that, for the following seven weeks, would absorb 33 British and Commonwealth divisions and 37 German divisions.[8]

While Vimy Ridge fell to the Canadian Corps during the first days of the Battle of Arras, their actions occurred on the northern flank of the much larger battle front, which eventually extended from Lens on the northern side of the Souchez River to Épehy in the south, a distance of 60 kilometres. The bulk of the British assault, however, was the responsibility of the Third Army's XVII, VI and VII Corps, centred to the east and south-east of the city of Arras.[9] The British Third Army would ultimately suffer some 82,000 casualties of the approximate 140,000 Allied losses during the course of the battle. Its sector extended from Roclincourt on the northern side of the River Scarpe to Croisilles in the south where it joined the northern flank of the British Fifth Army.

Plate 60. The war-ravaged shell of St Vaast Cathedral and cathedral buildings, central Arras. Note the lines of clothes drying in the cathedral grounds to the left of the photograph (Victor Morse collection).

Prior to the start of the battle, the front lines lay a mere 2500 metres from the heart of the ancient city of Arras which centred around the medieval abbey and cathedral of St Vaast. The city was at the mercy of German artillery and, during the course of the war, suffered accordingly, with three-quarters of its buildings damaged beyond repair. The city's defenders sheltered in the ruins which lay perilously close to the front and attracted intense shellfire. The only area of relative safety was below ground.

The construction of underground assembly points for the considerable number of men amassing for a major frontal attack was of paramount importance. Fortunately for the tunnellers tasked with their construction, Arras boasted several characteristics that assisted them in their work. The city is built on chalk, a material that, while hard, is not as hard as basalt or granite, allowing it to be excavated with relative ease. At the same time, chalk is sufficiently solid to support its own weight. Even before the war, many large cellars had been dug below the city as places of refuge during times of siege. Below two of the city's large squares, the Grande and Petit places, a number of cellars had been constructed for just such a purpose. When these were cleared for occupation by the military, they afforded space for some 13,000 men.[10]

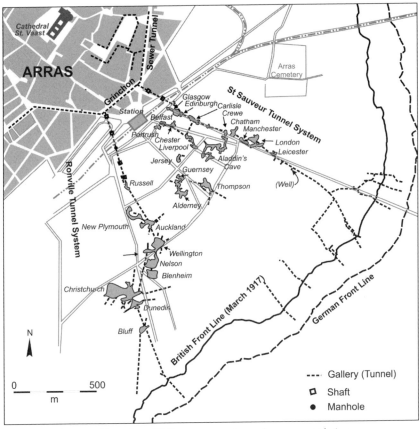

Map 18. The location of Ronville and St Sauveur cave and tunnel systems outside Arras.

More importantly, below the two suburbs that lay on the eastern outskirts of
Arras, Ronville to the south and St Sauveur to the north, lie a series of old chalk
caves, excavated in earlier times to supply building material to the city. The caves
were rediscovered in October 1916, and it was largely through the work of the
New Zealand tunnelling company that the caves were joined, like pearls on a
string, to form two massive cave and tunnel systems, the Ronville and St Sauveur
caves. Below Arras itself ran a sewer, the Crinchon sewer, which measured 2.5
metres in height and was two metres wide. The sewer could be accessed by
tunnels from numerous cellars along its length and was connected to the two
main tunnels that were driven out to form the Ronville and St Sauveur cave
systems. The tunnels opened at the British front lines and the St Sauveur system
could be exited from five shafts in no man's land. The caves in the Ronville

system were named after New Zealand cities and towns, and those in the St Sauveur systems bore the names of British cities. The caves and tunnel systems, both directly under Arras and those below Ronville and St Sauveur, in total afforded shelter to around 24,500 men and, more importantly, the network of tunnels allowed men to move to the front line from multiple entry points within Arras unobserved by enemy eyes. They were fitted with reticulated water pipes, telephones and, of course, electric power and lighting.

The two divisions that benefitted from the two tunnel systems at the opening of the Battle of Arras were the British 3rd and 12th divisions. In the words of the British official historian, 'No troops went into battle in a fresher state or had benefited more from the protection of the caves, cellars and tunnels.'

As the Battle of Arras continued through April, it became increasingly apparent that General Nivelle's ambitious plan for crushing the Germans on the Aisne front had failed. This realisation had well and truly dawned by dusk on 16 April, the first day of the main French attack. Although some ground was gained and there were local successes along the battle front, the anticipated rupture of the German line did not occur. French casualties in the nine days of fighting up to 25 April were estimated at 96,125, with just over 60,000 wounded, the remainder killed or missing.[11] More importantly, the repercussions of the failure on the Aisne were to heavily influence British offensives for the remainder of 1917 and, subsequently, the opinions of the British people for decades to come.

French hopes for an end to the war on the Western Front were shattered on the slopes of the Chemin des Dames. The French had suffered prodigiously in holding back the tide of German aggression on French soil over the previous two and a half years. However the former status quo was quickly re-established with little apparent impact on the German lines. The ferment of discontent within the French armies that had simmered below the surface prior to the Aisne and had been fanned by subversive elements within the ranks and in the civilian population, was given life by the collapse of French resolve as hope gave way to despondency.

By the end of the first week in May, the French offensive had all but petered out while the British and dominion divisions on the Arras front were still heavily engaged in battle. In mid-May, General Nivelle's command was rescinded and the new Commander-in-Chief was the highly talented General Henri-Phillipe Pétain, another hero of Verdun whose approach to warfare was more considered than Nivelle's. By the time of his appointment however, a crisis of confidence had begun rippling through the French infantry as morale plummeted and faith in their commanders and politicians waned. The gravity of the problem was such that it threatened the ability of the French military to defend its lines. Units refused to obey orders to return to the front, ill-discipline was rife and desertion rampant.

This was a massive problem for General Pétain to overcome and his highest priority immediately became the restoration of confidence in the senior leadership within his armies and the rebuilding of a credible fighting force. The process began in the bitter aftermath of the Aisne campaign, and it was some months before the French military regained that fighting quality that had characterised its campaigns prior to April 1917. The turbulence within the ranks of the French forces contributed significantly to events in the British sector, particularly in the Ypres salient, during the latter half of 1917.

The arrival of May brought a belated spring thaw across the Western Front and produced a transformation in the weather, with days alternating between a chilly dampness and an oppressive heat. While the British had just endured the brutal Battle of Arras, the parlous state of the French forces had exposed a glaring weakness in the Allied front that, if exploited by the Germans, had the potential to change the course of the war.

Unlike at Vimy Ridge, the Alphabet Company did not play a prominent role in the maintenance of the Arras Cave systems during the Battle of Arras. Indeed it was a full year after the battle that the company assumed control of the power and lighting systems in the vast network which was still being used to house troops. The enormous caves, illuminated with electric lighting through the efforts of the Alphabet Company, had a holding capacity of 10,000 men. One of the largest caves, Christchurch, in the Ronville system, was so large that it alone required 100 lights, or around 10% of the total number installed by the Alphabet Company.[12] The company used nine electrical generating sets in the caves, producing around 80 kilowatts of power, improving the original lighting by installing approximately 1000 lights. The men of the Alphabet Company also laid 38,715 metres of heavy and light gauge electrical cabling between the two cave systems.

At Vimy Ridge and in the cave systems at Arras, the Alphabet Company installed some 2000 lighting points and supplied and laid 70,000 metres of heavy core and light gauge electrical cabling. At the peak of its operations during the Battle of Arras, the company supplied and maintained 36 kilowatts of electrical power from the many small engine rooms along Vimy Ridge, followed by 80 kilowatts of electrical power in the Arras Caves during 1918. Once again, the company provided vital support during a crucial operation.

CHAPTER 7

FLANDERS

Ypres and Canal Bank
Company Tour of Duty: Ypres City

The regional city of Ypres (known in Belgium as Ieper) is one of the best known of all the towns associated with the Western Front. For those British Commonwealth countries that participated in the Great War, Ypres and the Ypres salient will rank alongside names such as the Somme and Passchendaele for the enormity of the bloodshed they witnessed. Ypres, the once majestic commercial centre in Flanders, Belgium, and famous for its linen trade, had developed since medieval times into a fortified city adorned with gilded buildings, dominated by the Cloth Hall and its neighbour, St Martin's Cathedral, and surrounded by thick rampart walls and a moat. Over the four years of the war, from 1914 to 1918, the city became the gateway to the Ypres salient and was slowly reduced to rubble. The eastern exit through the rampart walls, the Menin Gate, became for many hundreds of thousands of men, a march into hell.

A 'ridge' rising a mere 35 metres above the surrounding landscape would hardly be regarded as a feature of any great topographical significance anywhere else in the world. However Ypres lies just 25 metres above sea level and the countryside around the city is so flat and featureless that the Zandvoorde Ridge, the only elevated land in the area and which forms the horizon to the east of city, immediately appears remarkable. In a war in which the ability to see into and behind the enemy's lines meant crucial ascendancy, control of such a feature was a priceless strategic advantage which the Germans possessed, almost from the outbreak of war. They became comfortably entrenched along the ridge which angled from Hill 60, south of Ypres, to Passchendaele in the north-east. From there the ridge gently subsides into the landscape and the German front line swung back around the north of Ypres, almost to the Yser Canal which flows north from Ypres towards the Belgian coast at Nieuport.

The German front line thus formed a large arc around Ypres and, over much of its length, was elevated above that of their enemies, thereby affording a view not only of the land within the shallow arc (or salient), but into the settlements, including Ypres. The British, who held the salient for much of the war, could only look up towards the western slopes of the ridge which obscured their view beyond the ridgeline. It was only in the southern sector of the salient that the front lines faced each other close to the top of the ridge, with the British generally holding a footing below the ridgeline. The German artillery boasted an overwhelming observational advantage and it was this, and the regular concentration of British troops, that made daily existence in the salient a nightmare for those who were forced to endure it.

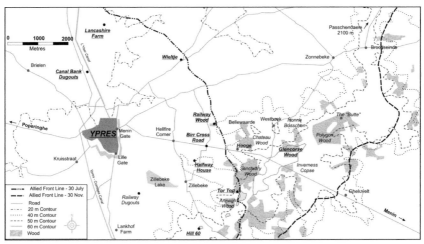

Map 19. British front line in the Ypres salient before and after the Third Battle of Ypres in 1917. Locations where the Alphabet Company served are underlined. They provided power, lighting and, in several locations, dewatering of mines or dugout systems.

The Ypres salient was one of the largest salients in the British-held sector of the Western Front. From the ridge, the Germans could see across to the city of Ypres and beyond for miles around. From that same ridge, they could shell the British in the salient from three sides with almost total impunity. This made the Ypres salient a dangerous place and was primarily the reason that such a large settlement could be all but levelled during the war. Almost all movement in the salient occurred at night to reduce the chances of being shelled, and even this was no insurance against death or wounding. The German artillery was registered on key locations with precision and could be fired at a moment's notice. The roads were obvious targets and crossroads, in particular, were relentlessly shelled day and night. Places named 'Hellfire Corner', located between Ypres and Hooge, 'Hellblast Corner' at Zillebeke, and 'Shrapnel Corner', 800 metres south of Ypres, were testament to the close attention of the German artillery.

The unique combination of topography, geology and artillery was to make the salient infamous for its mud. Years of shellfire had destroyed all semblance of the natural features that drained water from the ridge across the flat landscape and ultimately out to sea. The tight clay prevented water percolating into the substrata and rainwater simply had nowhere to go. Unless it evaporated, it remained in the myriad shell holes that carpeted the area. The deep pools of rainwater and sodden earth were repeatedly churned up by the relentless artillery and men unfortunate enough to fall in could sink and drown.

Plate 61. The view looking north along the western ramparts of Ypres showing the devastation of the township and the above-ground conditions in the area where the Alphabet Company's power station was located at the time. The station supplied power and lighting to dugouts, divisional and brigade headquarters and medical dressing stations scattered throughout the ruined township. All lighting and cabling was installed and maintained by the company for 870 days from early August 1916 to 27 December 1918 (AWM E01138).

Plate 62. A photograph taken by Major Victor Morse, DSO, of two soldiers, possibly from the Alphabet Company, near the ramparts in Ypres on 10 August 1917 (NAA: 9/68).

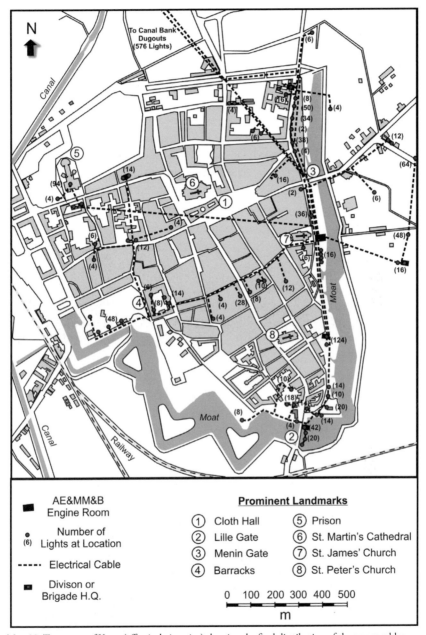

Map 20. Town map of Ypres (effectively in ruins) showing the final distribution of the power cables and lighting points supplied by the Alphabet Company from the power station in the western ramparts behind the ruins of St James's Church.

The salient itself was a place of notorious hardship and unmitigated misery for the British soldiers who existed there, some for almost four years. It is difficult to describe the distaste with which those men who had endured its discomforts greeted the name of this particular salient. By 1916, the salient resembled a lunar landscape, devoid of life or any sight pleasing to the human eye. There was virtually no safe shelter above ground; the landscape was swept by German machine-gun and artillery fire from the ridge that overlooked the salient and from which the Germans could observe every movement. Men could literally disappear in front of their mates under a direct hit from artillery shells. Like Dante's circles of hell, there were places within the salient where misery was piled upon misery.

The *Wipers Times*, the most widely read and eagerly awaited trench newspaper, published by soldiers for other soldiers to read and circulated from February 1916, printed a tongue-in-cheek soliloquy left by an unknown contributor as he departed the salient:

> I think that always I shall be glad to have seen the Salient. A month there holds more than a year elsewhere. 'Wipers! He's a strange man who can gaze on that unmoved. Who, that has known it, will forget the high strung tension of the Menin Road, who, unmoved, can pass those fields of crosses? The Menin Road and all it means. To know all the by-paths and alternate ways so as to dodge when shelling starts! To know all its holes and ditches when machine guns loose! Can there be any emotion equal to that of lying prone in a crump[1] hole with a machine gun ripping across your back? Hell Fire Corner! Aptly named. The span from there to Hooge, who that has slithered along it in gum boots high will ever forget. And now I no more to ponder as to which route to use. No longer the old question 'where are they putting 'em to-night?' For we're going back to rest!
>
> But not all – some of us remain. Poor lads: There they stay in the Salient and crosses mark the price they paid. Always, when the strain of the Salient may have left us, the memory of those crosses will remain, and those true hearts who sleep there may rest assured that we, who worked with them, fought with them and hoped with them, will exact the price.[2]

This lament was penned before the Third Battle of Ypres and the events of 1918 when the Germans won back ground lost in 1917 but were finally pushed into retreat. The crosses and fallen comrades referred to by this soldier were to be considerably outnumbered by new crosses.

The main entry and exit point to the salient was through the ancient city of Ypres (or 'Wipers' as it was more commonly known by the men who passed through it). Like Givenchy, Ypres was among the first places the Alphabet Company established itself and, from August 1916, it became part of the furniture, remaining there for the entire course of the war until the end of 1918.

An engine room was established in a dugout constructed in the eastern walls of the city ramparts. A large system of galleries connecting dugouts in the rampart had already been built when the company arrived, entirely lit by candles. In the words of the unit history, 'it was found that with improved lighting cleanliness followed' as did improved air quality in the confined underground systems. Given the extensive use of the city for troop billeting (in the cellars of shattered buildings), it was soon recognised that the power supply would have to be expanded throughout the city. The main engine room, located in the rampart wall behind St James's Church, and peripheral supplies were vastly expanded, so much so that, by April 1918, some 119 kilowatts of generating equipment were in use. With up to four generating engines running together, motor cooling became a major issue. This was solved by drilling a hole 18 metres long through the rampart wall behind the dugout, through four metres of concrete and three metres of brick, using a Wombat boring machine. Water from the rampart moat was then drawn via a 50-millimetre pipe to a number of cooling water tanks built inside the engine room. Water from the tanks, once heated by the engines, was then pumped out to separate bath tanks in a nearby dugout where it was used for bathing by the resident troops.

The engine room and its Alphabet Company staff were under the command of Sergeant Wilson, assisted by Staff Sergeants 2348 Alan Denton and 831 Fred Whitwell.[3] Cabling to the different dugout sites throughout the city was generally laid in trenches to minimise damage from artillery. However, feeder lines were run outside the city walls to the Canal Bank dugouts north of Ypres and other locations within a radius of a kilometre of the ramparts. These feeder lines were raised on poles to minimise damage from traffic.

During the Battle of Messines (June 1917), power was supplied to a dressing station at the Lille Gate, the southern entrance to Ypres through the rampart walls. Artillery shells constantly tore at the fragile wiring cables which, at that time, were not suspended on poles, but lay along the trenches and laneways of the destroyed city. Maintaining power supply to the dressing station and repairing the damaged wires was one of the responsibilities of No. 176 Sapper Harry Maxfield who carefully restored the power lines up to 40 times a day. His efforts were rewarded with the MSM.

In December 1917, following the end of the Third Battle of Ypres, the Alphabet Company had a brush with disaster. A fire started in an officers' dugout located just a few rooms away from the rampart engine room late one morning and quickly spread to the engine room. The engine room staff had just sufficient time to rescue the 200 gallons (1000 litres) of petrol from the fuel dugout adjacent to the engine room before the whole room was engulfed in flames. Eighty kilowatts of generating equipment and a cooling water pump engine were lost. An emergency engine was rushed forward and, by 6.00 pm that evening, a baseline supply of 6 kilowatts was being produced from another dugout 200 metres from the still burning engine room. A new, expanded room was then quickly built in place of the old, with room for more generators and an improved layout of cooling tanks and shut-down and connection boards.

The next threat to the Alphabet Company works at Ypres arrived in the form of the German spring offensive in April 1918. The Flanders assault, codenamed St George, rolled forward with such momentum that the defenders of the Ypres salient were pushed back over ground won at enormous cost during the previous summer and autumn. The loss of Ypres to the Germans loomed large and, as a precaution, between 15 and 27 April 1918, the generators sets were removed from the engine room and power across the city shut down. Ultimately Ypres did not fall into German hands, although by the time the German assault petered out, the front line at Ypres was just a few kilometres from the eastern ramparts. The Alphabet Company restarted the engine room on 22 May 1918 and it remained operating at a reduced level compared to pre-April 1918 levels, until it was finally closed and withdrawn from service on 27 December 1918.

Ypres is surrounded on three sides by a wide moat. The southern and eastern sides are water impoundments overlooked by the thick rampart walls of the city. On the western side of the city, the Ypres–Comines Canal flows north where it joins the Yser Canal outside the northern exits to the city.

Just outside the north-west corner of the city, the canal angles towards the north-east, beginning its progress towards the Belgian coast at Nieuport. The canal is partially man-made, and as such was constructed in straight lines, punctuated here and there with minor deviations and gentle corners to pass around villages. The canal forms a natural barrier and was used as such during the war. As a last, desperate measure to stem the German advance in October 1914, the sluice gates at Nieuport were opened and the Flemish lowlands between Dixmude (Diksmuide) and the Belgian coast, which are close to sea level, were flooded with seawater.

The first large village, five kilometres north of Ypres, is Boesinghe (Boezinge). Until the Third Battle of Ypres, the canal between Dixmude and Boesinghe marked the front line between the Germans and the Allies. The canal at Boesinghe marked the point at which the Ypres salient commenced its long, southwards curve around Ypres. For much of the war, the sector of the front north of Boesinghe was held by either French or Belgian forces.

The Yser Canal between Ypres and Boesinghe was thus an important defensive feature for Allied forces. The canal forms a large arc around and to the east of Boesinghe. The first of the canal's angled deviations occurs some 2500 metres north of Ypres in the section between Ypres and the bend, where the canal is around 30 metres wide. During its construction, the waste soil was dumped in a pile two to three metres high and 10 metres wide along the western bank. This became known as the Canal Bank and, like the rampart wall of Ypres, it offered excellent shelter and protection to troops on its western side.

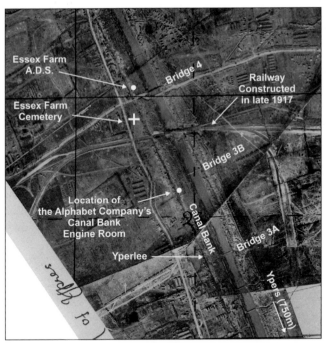

Plate 63. An aerial photo mosaic of the Canal Bank north of Ypres, compiled in February 1918, showing the location of the Alphabet Company engine room. The area at this time was heavily modified from pre-1918 conditions with the appearance of camps, railway sidings and transport depots following the Third Battle of Ypres. The black gridlines denote the British Geographical Section, General Staff (GSGS) square 25 from the Ypres map sheet 28 C (Photo part of composite image IWM P_0005280).

Not surprisingly therefore, the entire western side of the bank soon became crammed with dugouts and, over time, a line of neat, sandbagged dugout entrances appeared along the face of the bank. Set slightly back from the toe of the bank and flowing parallel to it, was a small, narrow rivulet, the Yserlee, which drained water from the western side of the canal embankment. A wooden duckboard path traversed the face of the dugouts and small wooden bridges crossed the rivulet at intervals. On the eastern side of the Canal Bank, the canal was crossed by a series of larger footbridges which appear on trench maps of the day and were referenced by a number.

Located beside Bridge 4 was an advanced dressing station known as Essex Farm and established during the Second Battle of Ypres in April 1915. Nearby was (and still is) the Essex Farm Cemetery. The dressing station, which started as an earthen dugout in the bank, was expanded and rebuilt in the side of the Canal Bank as a substantial concrete, multi-roomed structure. It was relocated in the early 1990s and has been refurbished by dedicated historians and made accessible to the public. The dressing station holds particular historical interest as, during the battle, it was used by Canadian Major John McCrea, a field surgeon with the Canadian artillery. It was during his time at Essex Farm that he penned his famous poem *In Flanders Fields* following the death of a friend and fellow officer who was buried in the vicinity of Essex Farm Cemetery.[4]

Given the number of dugouts and men accommodated along the Canal Bank by mid-1916, and the expectation that this situation would continue for some extended period of time, the Alphabet Company was tasked with expanding its works from Ypres to the Canal Bank. On 8 September 1916, a small (3 metres x 2 metres) engine room was established in the Canal Bank just south of Bridge 3B and equipped with a 9-kilowatt generator. The engine room remained in operation until 8 November 1918, supplying power to 590 lighting points along 1800 metres of the Canal Bank dugout systems. Some 20,300 metres of electrical cabling were laid and the power supply linked to the Ypres engine room which provided a considerable amount of power to the Canal Bank in its own right.

Power and lighting were also provided to a dressing station at 'Canal Dead End'. While the dressing station is not mentioned by name in the unit history, it was almost certainly the Essex Farm advanced dressing station which would have been powered by the Canal Bank engine room located just 350 metres north along the bank.

Cabling was initially run along the side of the bank on the ground but later buried and wired as circuits in series, parallel with a minimum of around

10 lights on each circuit. Lights inside dugouts and galleries were hung from their leads as high as possible and protected by wire mesh guards to prevent rifle or bayonet tips catching and shattering the glass light bulbs. The bulbs were hung away from the walls of dugouts or galleries as the ground vibration from shell explosions shattered light bulbs when the (usually wooden-clad) walls resonated against the glass. The provision of light switches to individual dugouts was not economical and all lights remained on until they were switched off from the engine room or another specially provided central switching board (such as for a dressing station or headquarters dugout). Given the quantity of tempting electrical cabling available, there was a certain amount of unauthorised 'tapping on' by individuals who sought to draw their own power for personal use. However this was usually exposed when the power series in question 'shorted out'. Power to a particular sector where this had been identified was then shut down for 24 hours and not re-established until a written note of cooperation from the officer in charge of the affected sector had been provided to the Alphabet Company NCO in charge of the engine room. It was a hard but fair solution and one that stood the test of time — a total of two years and two months.

The Canal Bank and ramparts power supplies at Ypres represented the Alphabet Company's longest period of service in one location during the war, lasting 870 days. In all, 20 power-generating sets were used between the two locations, powering a total of 1390 lighting points spread between numerous troop billets, dugouts, dressing stations and at least three divisional headquarters in and around Ypres. Life for troops stationed in Ypres between September 1916 and December 1918 would undoubtedly have been far less comfortable had the Alphabet Company not provided the basic creature comforts for which most soldiers yearned.

The Ypres salient

Prior to the Third Battle of Ypres (more familiarly and inaccurately known as the Battle of Passchendaele) the Alphabet Company's jobs became more widely spread across the salient and the company featured at several key locations in the heart of the salient.

The Third Battle of Ypres (July–November 1917)

The Third Battle of Ypres commenced on 31 July 1917. The objective was to push German forces off the ridge that formed the salient and continue eastwards towards Antwerp, joining a British assault driven in from the

Belgian coast and clear the submarine bases at Ostend and Zeebrugge. The secondary objective was to draw German divisions into the fight, destroy as many as possible and divert German attention from the French sector while French forces recovered from the impact of the Nivelle offensive along the Aisne in April and May.[5]

Following a localised attempt by two divisions from II Corps to attack Inverness Copse, Glencorse Wood and Westhoek Ridge on 10 August, the battle across the whole salient resumed on 16 August. In what is now known as the Battle of Langemarck, eight British divisions were tasked with advancing an average of 1500 yards (1.3 kilometres), with high hopes of gaining the crest of the Gheluvelt Plateau which gave rise to the salient and allowed German artillery unsurpassed observation across northern Flanders and into Ypres in particular.

When the battle drew to a close on 22 August, the only significant achievement was the capture of the village of Langemarck on the northern flank of the attack front. Such was the strength and doggedness of the German defence on the Gheluvelt Plateau that virtually no gains had been made apart from a small advance with the taking of Westhoek Ridge, the next spur to the east of Bellewaarde Ridge behind Hooge.

The failure to dislodge the Germans from the top and western side of the plateau after three weeks of heavy fighting was a serious disappointment to the British high command. With control of the plateau, the Germans retained their artillery superiority over the British, providing significant disruption to British movement and preparations in the salient despite British artillery successes in counter-battery fire. The failure to secure the plateau prompted a change in approach and tactics that were to have enormous ramifications for the Australians.

Sir Douglas Haig decided to call on the services of the ever-reliable General Sir Herbert Plumer whose Second Army was holding the Messines Ridge to the immediate south of the Ypres battle front. He asked General Plumer to extend his front to include that part of the Fifth Army (II Corps) sector facing the plateau. General Plumer assented, but asked for three weeks to prepare his army for the projected assaults. His request was granted. Haig also revised his tactic of attempting large-scale attacks with deep objectives to one of a succession of 'step by step' attacks with limited objectives. This was a revision he regarded as necessary until the plateau was taken.

The Battle of Menin Road commenced at 5.30 am on 20 September. It was preceded by seven days of preliminary bombardment from the artillery batteries of four British armies. Three and a half million artillery rounds had been allocated to the preliminary bombardment along the two army fronts, with the same number of shells used on the day of the attack. On the day itself, 3125 Allied artillery pieces were engaged. The effect was a wall of steel and a crescendo of noise both unbroken and overwhelming. The battle of the British and German artillery that day is a story in itself. As an indication of the magnitude of that 'battle within a battle', over 1300 Allied artillerymen were killed and over 2000 wounded on that one day, 20 September 1917.[6]

By the evening of 20 September, the brief but ferocious Battle of Menin Road was all but over, the objectives on the Allied front successfully gained. The next day was dominated by strong German counter-attacks and severe retaliatory artillery bombardments — but the line held. The British divisions fared well with all but a couple of the strongest positions taken. Although the fighting gradually abated over the next three days, this would prove merely a pause before the next step.[7] The war was far from over.

In the Ypres salient, 4 October dawned to reveal a sodden battlefield under a brooding sky. The Battle of Broodseinde was to be launched at 6.00 am, and was preceded by a terrific British-Australian artillery barrage from over 2300 guns. The Germans replied in kind, delivering a fierce counter-artillery and *minenwerfer* bombardment for 40 minutes before zero hour, targeting the thousands of packed troops of the two Australian corps who had assembled close to the jumping-off lines. The men could do little except pray for six o'clock and huddle together in whatever boggy shell holes they could find. The men of I Anzac suffered most during this 40-minute period of terror. According to later estimates, almost 15% of the I Anzac attacking force was killed or wounded in the German pre-attack bombardment — including 20 officers. The bodies of many of those who died during that terrible blitz disappeared without trace.[8]

In spite of this horrific setback, the survivors moved off and, by noon, all five army corps involved in the advance had prevailed, taking 90% of their objectives. The 2nd Australian Division captured the remainder of Zonnebeke and then Broodseinde in heavy fighting, while the 1st Australian Division captured Molenaarelsthoek. To the north, the New Zealand and 3rd Australian divisions took the St Gravenstafel spur and the village after which the small ridge was named. Further north, in the XVIII Corps sector, the British 18th Division moved into the village of Poelcappelle.

One of the toughest days of fighting in the Third Battle of Ypres fell on 4 October. The ground over which the men fought was thickly populated with pillboxes which had to be rushed and taken one by one.[9] The defending

Germans countered bravely, but the impact of the day on the German psyche was profound:

> In the opinion of officers of long experience on the Western front, the number of dead Germans seen on the battlefield exceeded that observed in any previous British assault of the war.[10]

That day was described as a 'black day' in the German *Official History* with almost 5000 German prisoners taken. The two German divisions that bore the brunt of the attack by the 1st and 2nd Australian divisions (I Anzac), the *45th Reserve* and *4th Guard Divisions*, suffered almost 5700 casualties.[11]

The weather, which since the end of July had vacillated between periods of heavy rain and hot sunny days, began its inevitable transformation into winter at the beginning of October. The days were frequently cold and wet, and the battlefield — difficult to negotiate during August and September — now assumed the nightmarish characteristics for which the Battle of Passchendaele is historically renowned. The weather finally broke on 4 October during the Battle of Broodseinde. It rained solidly for two days and the battlefield became a muddy morass that refused to solidify until the freezing temperatures of deep winter arrived two months later. In a meeting on the evening of 7 October, both General Plumer (Second Army) and General Gough (Fifth Army) told Douglas Haig that they would be happy to close down the offensive; Haig, however, was determined to secure a greater portion of the ridge.

Thus the battle continued despite the marked deterioration in the weather. As the Allied front line continued its eastward push, the forward movement of artillery and troops to support the advance towards the village of Passchendaele likewise continued. The lighter field artillery required to complete the offensive had to be sited as far forward as Zonnebeke and gun platforms had to be constructed and stabilised so that the guns would not sink into the mud as soon as they were fired. Roads had to be constructed and dugouts built to accommodate the large number of men in the forward areas. With the rain and badly churned-up ground, conditions were almost intolerable and every task strained the bounds of possibility. Much of the work was thrust on the engineering units of the armies involved, with battalions of infantry ordered to assist. In General Plumer's Second Army alone, an average of two infantry battalions, seven pioneer battalions, 10 field companies of engineers, seven tunnelling companies, four army troop companies and two labour companies were employed each day in this work.[12] In the I Anzac sector, almost 17 kilometres of plank roads and a similar length of crushed rock roads were constructed over a 27-day period.[13]

On 9 October, fighting again erupted as a precursor to the main assaults leading to the capture of the village of Passchendaele. With the French First Army on the extreme left of a 12.3-kilometre battle front, eight divisions of the British Fifth and Second armies attempted to advance almost a kilometre towards the ridgeline between the villages of Passchendaele and Westrozebeke. Most of the troops involved were completely exhausted and, by nightfall, only the British Guards Division and the French on the left flank of the attack had attained the day's objectives.[14]

On the right flank, the two Australian corps advanced a mere 500 metres from their starting positions to their intermediate objective — a paltry advance that cost 6957 casualties, most incurred by the two British Divisions, the 66th (East Lancashire) and 49th (1st West Riding) Divisions of II Anzac. With the close of fighting for the day, the exhausted divisions were replaced by the support divisions in their respective corps and the new divisions readied themselves for the next assault. On the evening of 11 October, the 3rd Australian and New Zealand divisions relieved the British 66th and 49th divisions on the II Anzac front which stretched 2750 metres along the face of the slope of Passchendaele Ridge leading to Passchendaele village, which was built at its highest point. Only one corps from the Second Army — II Anzac — would be engaged in the next phase of the battle, although the 12th Brigade of the 4th Australian Division (I Anzac) was part of a flanking operation with the 3rd Australian Division. The Fifth Army's XVIII and XIV Corps entered the fray north of II Anzac.

The battle that became known as First Passchendaele opened at 5.25 am on 12 October under a leaden sky cursed with rain and a chill wind. The conditions on the battlefield were, by now, appalling beyond comprehension. The Allied artillery pieces had been moved forward and placed in their positions only through superhuman feats of strength and endurance. At midnight, just hours before the attack was to begin, General Gough, Commander of the British Fifth Army, rang General Plumer's Second Army headquarters asking whether the attack should be called off. It wasn't. The mud and rain were so effective in slowing the movement of men, laden with their packs, rifles and entrenching tools, that elements of the 3rd Australian Division could not reach the jumping-off lines by zero hour. Many of the heavy howitzer shells failed to explode in the sodden ground causing no damage other than sending up great showers of mud. Artillery shells became so covered in mud during transportation to their batteries that they were unusable until they had been cleaned — a difficult and time-consuming process in the heat of battle.

The II Anzac divisions faced manned and readied German pillboxes and belts of unbroken wire.[15] Both British and Anzac divisions struggled on with little real momentum. Only the northernmost British corps in the attack, XIV Corps, succeeded in securing any measurable gains. The following day, the British high command decided to delay the battle until conditions improved and the roads forward could be reinforced to allow the most effective use of artillery. Douglas Haig also decided to bring a 'fresh' corps of infantry into the attack. The Canadian Corps moved north from the Lens-Loos front, relieving II Anzac on 18 October, and preparing to take on the most difficult part of the final assault to Passchendaele.

On 22 October a massive artillery barrage opened up along the entire British Second and Fifth Army front in an attempt to persuade the Germans that a major attack was taking place. Four days later, at 5.40 am on 26 October, the last great push in the Third Battle of Ypres, known as the Second Battle of Passchendaele, commenced. This now infamous battle, in which the Canadian Corps took the leading role and suffered the most, took the form of a series of assaults with short objectives fought over a front that was half under water, requiring the corps to attack along two smaller, discrete fronts. The assault was followed by another on 30 October, and yet another on 6 November, before the Passchendaele Ridge and its village were finally taken on 10 November. This last dogged fight for the tiny shattered village is now viewed as somehow representative of all the battles fought across the Ypres salient in the second half of 1917. The month-long, frenetic tour of duty in almost unbelievably appalling conditions in the salient cost the Canadian Corps 15,654 battle casualties.[16] Following its harrowing ordeal at Passchendaele, the Canadian divisions returned to the Lens-Vimy front.[17]

Thus, the Third Battle of Ypres finally ground to an exhausted conclusion on 10 November 1917. By then winter gripped the countryside and Allied soldiers were forced to hunker down surrounded by mud and cold, sheltering among the desolate ruins of the villages they had fought so desperately to win across the pulverised salient leading to Passchendaele. Debate will continue among military historians for many more decades concerning the merits or otherwise of the series of battles waged over that nightmarish period of some three and a half months. The combined battles of Third Ypres from 31 July to 10 November 1917 officially resulted in 238,313 British casualties, of whom 2118 officers and 33,713 other ranks were killed.[18] German casualties have been estimated at around 400,000.[19]

Operations — Ypres Salient: North

Wieltje
Company Tour of Duty: Wieltje

Place names from the northern quadrant of the Ypres salient will feature in Belgian, French, Canadian and British military history, but until the writing of this book, the sleepy villages and towns that dotted the flat plains of Flanders to the north-east of Ypres in the pre-war period did not appear in Australian texts. Thus few Australians will have heard of Wieltje, a tiny cluster of farmhouses hugging the road between Saint Jean (Sint Jen) and Poelcappelle (Poelkapelle) via Saint Julien (Sint Juliaan). By 1917 the village had been erased from the map and the British front line ran right through what had been its centre. All that marked its place at that point was the faint tracing of the main road which split on the village's eastern fringe, and the colour of the ground, which was lighter than the surrounding earth, presumably from the white plaster walls of the houses which had been long blown inside out and pulverised to dust.

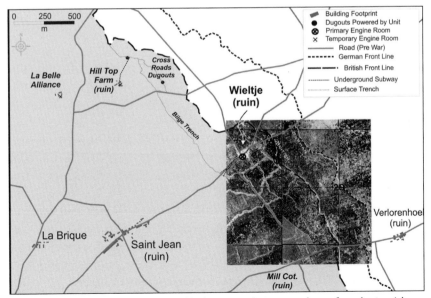

Map 21. The Wieltje front-line sector in early July 1917 overlaying a trench map from the time (photo part of a composite image, IWM P_0005283).

The Alphabet Company arrived on 5 July 1917 to assist with preparations for the Third Battle of Ypres. The engine room was situated just 100 metres from the front line and, due to its vulnerability to shellfire, was the smallest structure possible, measuring just 4.2 metres x 2.4 metres. As a result it was extremely uncomfortable, hot and cramped for the company's staff of one NCO and six other ranks who operated there until February 1918 when a larger engine room dugout was constructed by the resident British tunnelling company, the 171st.

On 31 July 1917, the opening day of the Third Battle of Ypres, Wieltje was the jumping-off sector for the British 55th (West Lancashire) Division for what became known as the Battle of Pilckem Ridge. On that first day, the front line was pushed west by almost two kilometres. It then took another 13 weeks to slog the same distance further west before the Third Battle of Ypres concluded. By then, Wieltje was well behind the new front and the area had become a staging ground for winter accommodation for reserve troops. Support depots now began to litter the landscape between the little village and the Ypres Canal. Railway lines were pushed across the canal into the area and Wieltje became a railhead for a light railway.

Power and lighting were supplied by the Alphabet Company and, until the front lines were pushed back, the men also provided ventilation for the mining system. Water pumping was essential to keep the underground galleries and tunnels clear of water. The area was plagued by water inflow problems, with anywhere between 225,000 and 450,000 litres of water removed daily. Six water pumps were eventually used in the sector before the locality was abandoned in June 1918.

The front-line galleries and mining system were accessed by an underground subway 300 metres long which could be entered via Bilge Trench, 500 metres behind the old (31 July) front line. The subway also contained an advanced dressing station. The engine room itself was located in a dugout in the subway below the former village square, within 100 metres of the old front line.

The engine room served as a base either to provide power directly to, or to support other dugout systems in the area, namely Hill Top Farm (1000 metres north-west of Wieltje), Mill Cot (750 metres south of Wieltje) and La Belle Alliance (500 metres west of Hill Top Farm). All of these dugouts were equipped with 3-kilowatt power plants for varying periods of time.

In total, 373 lighting points were installed and maintained at Wieltje and the surrounding dugout systems, along with 6000 metres of heavy and light electric cabling, with cabling to distant supply points hung from overhead lines. Up to 51 kilowatts of power was supplied to the system in February 1918 from four generators at a new, centralised power station at Wieltje. The system was eventually connected to the Railway Wood engine room. On 26 June 1918, after almost a year, the company ceased its operation at Wieltje.

Lancashire Farm
Company Tour of Duty: Lancashire Farm

Over a month before the Alphabet Company established power operations at Wieltje, it began to assist with works at the Lancashire Farm dugout system, located close to where the northern flank of the Ypres salient defensive line ceased its arc at the Yser Canal, 4500 metres to the north of Ypres. The position was 2750 metres north-west of Wieltje and the remains of the farm were just 350 metres behind the front line. The British 179th and 255th tunnelling companies were working in the area and, in preparation for the opening of the Third Battle of Ypres, were expanding the forward dugout system to connect it with a battle headquarters.

The main problem with this location was flooding, and proofing the dugout systems against the shallow groundwater inflow was a constant battle. On 26 May 1917, the Alphabet Company supplied the first electric water pump to Lancashire Farm. As the dugouts expanded, a second pump was supplied on 6 June and then, on 20 July, the company arrived to construct a 7.5-kilowatt engine room and added another two water pumps to the two already in use.

The British 51st (Highland) Division held the line in the Lancashire Farm sector in the days leading to the opening of the Third Battle of Ypres. On 31 July 1917, the 51st swept forward to push the front line 3000 metres back towards the town of Langemarck.

The dugouts at Lancashire Farm continued to be used throughout the months of the battle. As conditions deteriorated and the area became saturated, a further two water pumps were added to the four in use. A total of 50 lights were also installed in the dugout systems, although once the battle ceased, the company withdrew its pumps and generator.

Operations — Ypres salient: Central

Railway Wood
Company Tour of Duty: Railway Wood

The Alphabet Company's long association with the salient proper began at Railway Wood. Situated on the front line at the heart of the salient, Railway Wood was an extensive and heavily contested subterranean mining and dugout system north of the infamous Menin Road. The company arrived there on 15 November 1916 and remained until 16 April 1918. The NCO in charge of the company's plant and equipment was No. 831 Sergeant Fred Whitwell.

The system was plagued by a variety of problems, all requiring power to resolve, in particular the provision of ventilation and the pumping of water. By the time of the Third Battle of Ypres, the crater field in no man's land represented an impressive monument to the underground battles waged by British and German miners. Above ground, the shell-pitted landscape was likewise testament to the almost three-year war waged between British and German artillery batteries and which would only worsen once Third Ypres commenced.

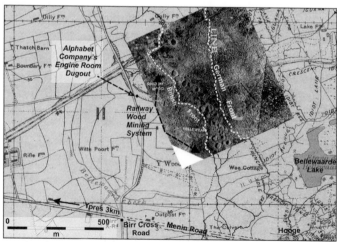

Plate 64. The Railway Wood front-line sector in mid-1916 overlaying a trench map from prior to the Third Battle of Ypres in 1917 (sometimes referred to as the Battle of Passchendaele) showing the proliferation of shell and mine craters (several of which were named). The location of the dugout containing the Alphabet Company's engine room is also shown (photo part of composite image, IWM P_0005280).

204

The engine room was located 200 metres to the rear of the front lines in a dugout 10 metres below ground level. The waterlogging of the ground, exacerbated by the water-filled shell holes, caused excessive inflows of water to the underground mining systems and dugouts. Shallow sumps were dug at intervals throughout the underground system to collect the drained water. Electric pumps placed in the sumps then pumped the water from below the ground. Over the period the company spent at Railway Wood, 12 pumping sets were used, although only two or three were in simultaneous use at any one time. Around 270,000 litres of water per day were pumped from the workings to maintain the viability of the system. During the early stages of pumping, the pump impellors (blades inside the pump housing that push the water) constantly clogged with hairs from the thousands of sandbags used as retaining walls throughout the system and with silt and sand washed from the muddy soil that surrounded them. While the problem was never resolved, its severity was reduced somewhat by the digging of silt traps in the galleries and covering pump intakes with charcoal strainers. In gassed sections of the mines, Sergeant Whitwell installed an electric-powered portable compressor with fans which ventilated the workings until they were clear of gas. In all these areas, he was forced to work while wearing the bulky proto breathing apparatus.

In July 1917, just as the mining war was ending, the Alphabet Company supplied an electric winch to haul excavated soil from mining systems to the surface along an inclined shaft. However its use was short-lived as it was, in the vernacular of the tunnellers, 'crumped' (destroyed by shellfire).

Over time the engine room at Railway Wood was gradually expanded to provide power to the numerous pumps, ventilators and lights (244 lighting points were installed in the underground galleries and dugout systems). It achieved a maximum power output of 24 kilowatts and, once the front lines had been pushed further to the east at the end of the Third Battle of Ypres, the power supply was connected to augment nearby dugout systems. Over 3700 metres of heavy and 6800 metres of light electric cabling were laid and maintained by the company at Railway Wood.

Tor Top
Company Tour of Duty: Tor Top

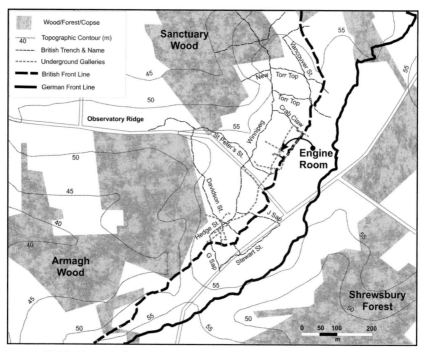

Map 22. The Tor Top sector showing lines, communication trenches and part of the underground system of tunnels and dugouts which were served by the Alphabet Company's engine room.

Until July 1917, when the Third Battle of Ypres commenced, the Railway Wood and Tor Top mining sectors were at the leading edge of the Ypres salient. In this area the shelling was relentless and nowhere was safe from enemy observation posts along the top of the Gheluvelt Plateau which ringed the southern and eastern fringe of the salient. However the Tor Top mining sector was slightly better matched with its German counterparts compared to the nearby Hill 60 and Mount Sorrel mining sectors. At Tor Top the British front line lay abreast of a short section of the plateau and, in that respect, shared the same height advantage as the Germans. Despite this, however, it was not a pleasant place to reside and mining was fierce due to the narrowness of no man's land.

The gas filter at Tor Top was installed by the Alphabet Company on 27 November 1917 and was capable of supplying 20,400 cubic metres of filtered air per day to dugouts located along the system tunnel galleries through pipes that measured 150 millimetres (6 inches) in diameter.

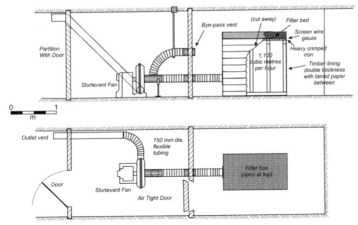

Diagram 4. The design of an Alphabet Company dugout gas filter as used at the Tor Top and Hulluch dugout systems. It was effectively a super-sized box respirator.

Birr Cross Road
Company Tour of Duty: Birr Cross Road

Plate 65. 'Our Gas Experiments Prove a Complete Success (for Germany)' by Hugh Thurlow. A less than complimentary depiction of the testing procedure used for an Alphabet Company dugout gas filter. This was the process used at the Tor Top and Hulluch dugout systems. (AWM 3DRL/4059).

The Birr Cross Road dugout on the Menin Road just south of Railway Wood was controlled by the British 177th Tunnelling Company. This was a two-level dugout system, the first level at around 10 metres below ground and the deeper system, at 14 metres, which accommodated corps and divisional signalmen. During the battles, the dugout was used as battle headquarters and an advanced dressing station.

The Alphabet Company arrived at the dugout and installed the first of two 4-kilowatt electric generators on 18 July 1917, two weeks before the start of the Third Battle of Ypres. The engine room was located in the lower level of the dugout and exhaust from the engine room petrol generators was directed up a pipe that rose to the surface via an old disused mining shaft.

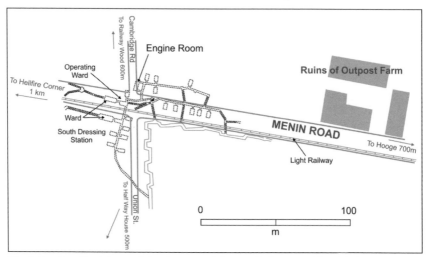

Plan 1. Birr Cross Road dugouts below Menin Road showing the location of the Alphabet Company engine room.

A slight hiccup occurred on the morning of the opening day of the battle, 31 July, when a road gang attempting to keep the Menin Road repaired and open to traffic, unwittingly covered the mine shaft. The shaft soon filled with exhaust fumes which diffused through gaps in the wood-lined shaft, and the toxic gas entered sleeping quarters in the upper level of the dugout. Several men were badly gassed before the cause of the problem was identified. There is no record of any man dying as a result of being gassed.

By mid-October 1917, the appalling weather conditions that have become synonymous with the Battle of Passchendaele reached their nadir, and the struggles of men above the ground were little better than those below. In an attempt to manage this, water entering the system was permitted to flow into the central mine shaft where the level was maintained by both electric and man-powered pumps. There the water level in the shaft would be maintained at the same level as the lower dugout system. Water was then pumped back to the surface. Rainwater ponding beside the Menin Road backed up and flowed into the dugout entrances, probably supplemented by water already pumped from the dugout. In addition to five electric water pumps supplied by the Alphabet Company, 32 tunnellers were needed to man hand-pumps in an attempt to free the system of water.

Once the battle had moved into its last phase during the assault on Passchendaele on 30 October, the company shut down the engine room and power for lighting was then sourced from the larger Railway Wood engine room via a cable run above ground between the two dugout systems.

Halfway House
Company Tour of Duty: Halfway House Dugout

The Halfway House dugout, located at the intersection of Ritz and Oxford Street communication trenches between Hellfire Corner and Birr Cross Road, 500 metres south of the Menin Road, was constructed by the ubiquitous 171st Tunnelling Company which undertook much of its work in and around the Ypres salient in preparation for the Third Battle of Ypres. On 7 September the 1st Australian Tunnelling Company replaced the 171st Tunnelling Company, assuming responsibility for maintaining and extending the system.

Like the Birr Cross Road dugout, the Halfway House dugout was extensive and, during the battle, housed an advanced dressing station, brigade and battalion headquarters and accommodation for tunnellers, signallers and around 1000 infantrymen. It also housed units from the British 8th Division in the days leading up to the start of the battle.

On 15 October, the Inspector of Mines, General Robert Harvey, sent an envoy to inspect the work of the tunnelling companies in the Second Army area. Lieutenant Donald Yates from the 1st Australian Tunnelling Company acted as a guide for the envoy, conducting him around the dugout systems on which the company was working. One was Halfway House. Not surprisingly, the horrendously wet conditions for which the Third Battle of Ypres is now famous, were a recurring theme in the envoy's report of his visit. In one corner of the Halfway House dugout system, the floor was flooded to a depth of 60 centimetres where water had poured into the dugout through the entrances via the trenches at the top of the dugout steps. Squatting close to the dugout was a disabled tank mounted with a 60-pounder artillery gun which was being repaired by a salvage team.

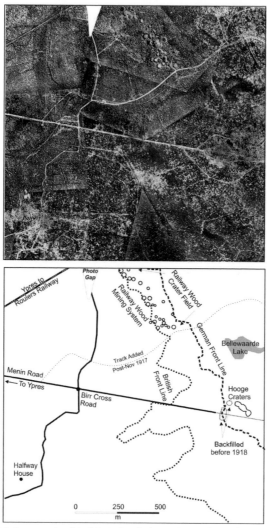

Plate 66 (top). Aerial photo mosaic of the Menin Road taken in August-September 1918. Note the heavily shell cratered landscape and the size difference between artillery shell and mine craters (IWM P005326).

Map 23 (bottom). A map covering the photo mosaic area, highlighting points of interest to this book.

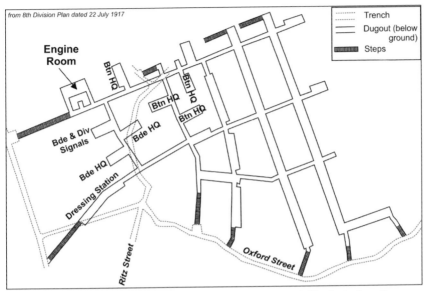

Plan 2. Halfway House dugouts on 22 July 1917 before they were expanded by the 1st Australian Tunnelling Company and showing the location of the Alphabet Company engine room.

On 31 October, No. 3607 Sergeant Alexander Hood of the 1st Australian Tunnelling Company, who had been photographed by an Australian war photographer at the Hooge Crater dugout just one month earlier, was killed when a long-range, high-explosive shell hit the unit's forward cookhouse at Halfway House. Killed also were Sappers No. 3563 Joseph Bailey, No. 145 Archie Ivall and No. 5579 Roy Mason of the same company.

Hooge Crater
Company Tour of Duty: Hooge Crater Dugout

Hooge Crater was another notorious location in the Ypres salient and would have been known to all men who passed along the Menin Road. Until the Third Battle of Ypres, Hooge village and the remains of its château lay on the front line, on the northern side of the Menin Road at the western end of what was once the village (see Plate 66 and Map 23).[20]

The crater (actually the conjoined remains of a group of mine craters) was formed by Lieutenant Geoffrey Cassels of the 175th Tunnelling Company in July

1915, with the first experimental use of what became the tunneller's explosive of choice — ammonal. This explosion involved the largest mine charge laid by the British tunnellers to that time. The resulting craters become a landmark feature as a large, bean-shaped depression that spilled into the old Menin Road. Indeed, during the Third Battle of Ypres, a deviation had to be made around its southern end by road repair gangs from the engineers. Even today, a large part of the crater complex still exists, forming what is now the tranquil, tree-lined pond beside the entrance and car park of the Kasteelhof't Hooghe (hotel and restaurant). The craters are horrific scars wrought on the landscape, a sobering reminder that men were killed in their formation. Yet, after their creation, they became places of refuge for those who sought shelter from shellfire at a time when such places were in desperately short supply.

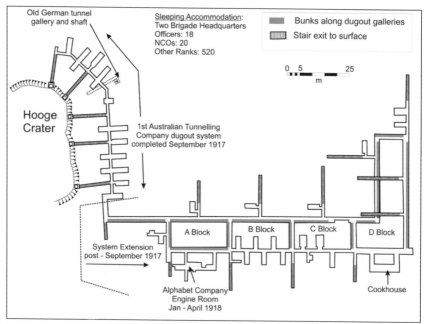

Plan 3. Hooge Crater dugouts in April 1918 after being expanded by Australian and Canadian tunnelling companies in late 1917, showing the location of the Alphabet Company's engine room.

On 6 September 1917 the first contingent of tunnellers from the 1st Australian Tunnelling Company was ordered to proceed to the Ypres salient from the Messines Ridge around Wytschaete to assist in preparations for the forthcoming attack in what was to become known as the Battle of Menin Road. The tunnellers were to complete the construction of an advanced brigade headquarters in the

Hooge Crater and assist with the construction of plank roads to the front.[21] The Australian tunnellers embarked on the construction of a series of dugouts extending either side of a 51-metre-long central gallery running below the eastern side of the Hooge Crater at around 25 feet (7.5 metres) underground. The main gallery was accessed by five inclined stairways, the sandbagged entrances to which punctuated the side and northern end of the crater. As with many other underground dugout systems in the heart of the salient, the inflow of water from rain, which either flowed directly into the workings, or indirectly seeped through the shell-churned soil above, ensured that the miners worked in mud and stinking water, which had to be continuously pumped out by hand. The miners took it in their stride, referring to the slop as 'hero juice', as they envisaged the water seeping into the workings from above and passing through layers of corpses from the succession of battles fought there since late 1914.[22]

Plate 67. Members of the 1st Australian Tunnelling Company excavating at Hooge, in the Ypres sector, September 1917. Work on these dugouts constituted a record for tunnelling companies employed under such conditions, as the ground, in close proximity to the famous Hooge Crater, was a shell-churned marsh and soakage was heavy. Accommodation was dug for two brigades and the headquarters of a machine-gun company. Commenced on 5 June 1917, the task was completed and dugouts handed over to the 2nd and 3rd infantry brigades on 19 September for the use of troops engaged in the operation the following day. Identified, foreground, left to right: two unidentified members of the 56th Battalion; No. 5488 Sapper C.G. Allcock (third from left, looking at camera); unidentified member of the 56th Battalion (working with Allcock). Background, left to right: No. 5529 Sapper H.J. Edmonds; No. 5374 2nd Corporal E.S. Sherrin (resting against sandbags); No. 3688 Sapper J. Tither; No. 3363 Sapper J.E. Rimmer (pushing upright cart); No. 5380 Sapper J.W. Mcdonough (second from right); No. 5555 Sapper J.J. Horne (extreme right) (AWM E01396).

Following the Battle of Menin Road, the 3rd Canadian Tunnelling Company took over and considerably expanded the Hooge Crater dugout system from the southern end of the existing system, adding 12 more entrances and vastly increasing its accommodation capacity. When complete it could comfortably house some 560 men and included two infantry brigade headquarters and a dressing station. Like other major dugout systems such as the nearby Halfway House, it had its own cookhouse and, importantly, its own power supply from an engine room which was occupied by a squad from the Alphabet Company on 25 January 1918. They brought with them a 6-kilowatt engine and generator connected to 90 lighting points distributed thought the dugout system via 1435 metres of electrical cabling. The wooden interior of the dugout was painted white to increase the lighting efficiency of the electric lamps. Water, which continually seeped into the dugout, was drained through a sump fitted with a petrol-driven (J.A. Prestwich) water pump, the water removed to the surface.

Glencorse Wood
Company Tour of Duty: Glencorse Wood Dugouts

Glencorse Wood was one of the collection of famous woods in the heart of the Ypres salient scattered across the slopes straddling the Menin Road leading to the ridgeline of the Gheluvelt Plateau. Like Sanctuary Wood, Chateau Wood, Inverness Corpse, Nonne Bosschen, Shrewsbury Forest and Polygon Wood, Glencorse Wood bristled with concrete pillboxes equipped with machine-guns that could only be captured or incapacitated by men on the ground fighting their way through them. Through August, September and October 1917, the woods were taken one after another. Glencorse Wood was taken by the 1st Australian Division on the first day of the Battle of Menin Road on 20 September and the torn stumps that marked the place were soon left behind as the British divisions pushed east to the top of the ridge that had confined the Ypres salient since late 1914. By the time the Third Battle of Ypres concluded in November, the wood was around 2000 metres behind the new front line and was consolidated to accommodate front-line reserve troops through the winter of 1917–1918.

The Alphabet Company did not arrive in Glencorse Wood until 25 March 1918 when the British 49th (1st West Riding) Division was in control of the sector. When the company arrived, it established an engine room equipped with a 9-kilowatt generator. It installed 92 lighting points across a series of dugouts which, in total, accommodated eight officers, 28 NCOs and 288 other ranks. The dugouts, constructed by the 3rd Canadian Tunnelling Company, followed a standardised design which included the whitewashing of the internal wooden cladding to further enhance the limited lighting arrangements. Glencorse Wood represented the Alphabet Company's most easterly location in the Ypres salient during the war.

The unit's sojourn was brief however, as, just three weeks after establishing itself, the position was overrun and had to be abandoned as the British divisions fell back to safeguard Ypres. Consequently, the engine room and its switchboards were destroyed.

Belgian Coast Operations 1917
Company Tour of Duty: Belgian Coast

The Belgian coast, where the front lines disappeared into the North Sea in a tangle of rusting rows of barbed wire, may appear remote from the Ypres salient, but was planned as an integral element of operations for the Third Battle of Ypres in 1917. As a consequence it is useful to include some discussion of the small role of the Alphabet Company on that particular stage.

Until mid-1917 the Western Front sector extending from just north of Ypres to the Belgian coast where the Yser River discharges into the North Sea at Nieuport Bains had been held by the Belgian Army with support from the French. Belgian neutral territory had been violated in the opening days of the war when the Germans attempted to encircle Paris from the north and take control of strategic ports along the English Channel. They were only partially successful, capturing Zeebrugge and Ostend, which were later used with devastating success as bases for German U-boats. In those desperate early months of the war, the Belgians, under King Albert I, resorted to using the power of nature to impose a water 'barrier' to literally bog down German lines of supply across northern Flanders. Sluice gates at Nieuport were opened, allowing seawater to inundate the low lands originally reclaimed from the sea (known as 'polders'), to the town of Dixmude, some 12 kilometres to the south-east.

With the stemming of the German advance in late October 1914, the Belgians and French faced the Germans across the Yser Canal and exchanged artillery fire, gradually laying waste to everything within the built or natural landscape for a kilometre either side of the canal, while the full fury of the war turned to more highly prized sectors of the front much further south. In June 1917, however, attention focused once more on the northern sector.

As plans were being developed for the British offensives of 1917, a scheme to envelop the Germans in a pincer movement through Flanders was proposed. This would involve an eastern thrust from the Ypres salient to take the high ground surrounding the city. A simultaneous thrust down and east from the Belgian coast would merge with the attack front from Ypres. The proposed northern flank for the pincer movement, which would require a beach landing behind the German front lines on the coast, was called Operation Hush.

On 20 June, the 1st and 32nd British divisions (XV Corps) relieved the French in the Nieuport sector. The 1st Division took over the former seaside holiday village of Nieuport Bains from the French 29th Division. The British artillery batteries immediately set about registering on the opposing Germans.

The push was part of Field Marshal Sir Douglas Haig's Flanders Plan to clear the Germans from the Belgian coast and remove the formidable submarine threat to British shipping in the English Channel from the ports at Zeebrugge and Ostend. Following the invasion of Belgium and the German occupation of these two important ports so close to the English Channel and the North Sea, the British Admiralty immediately recognised the threat to the shipping of troops and materiel for military operations on the Western Front. By early 1917, shipping losses inflicted by German submarines were jeopardising British lines of supply. With each passing month these losses ground deeper into the Allied shipping capability.

The British had been planning an offensive to clear the Germans from the captured Belgian ports since late 1915 and these plans were well advanced prior to the Somme campaign in the summer of 1916. The capture of the Messines Ridge in June 1917 opened the way to focus on two other main thrusts for operations in 1917 — Operation Hush, the coastal attack at Nieuport, and the drive east from the Ypres salient, in what has become known as the Third Battle of Ypres.

The attack and landings along the coast at Nieuport Bains were to be launched by five British divisions once the main British offensive in the Ypres salient had pushed the Germans back to Cortemarck, 12 kilometres east of Dixmude. The British coastal assault was to take the form of a three-pronged beach landing centring on the village of Middelkerke Bains, 2500 metres north-east of the Yser Canal. The assault would be conducted by landing parties of the British 1st Division comprising infantry, artillery, medical and machine-gun support, and tanks. The landing parties were to be transported to the beaches in three massive, low-draught pontoons, each almost 170 metres in length. Operation Hush was initially scheduled for 8 August 1917, to take maximum advantage of high tide for the beachhead landings.

The arrival of the British and their artillery produced a rapid and commensurate change in attitude from the Germans and counter-bombardment recommenced in earnest, making movement to the front very difficult. A zone of sand dunes stretches along the coast, making transportation problematic, with vehicular access to the forward areas largely confined to the pre-war roads which could easily be seen by German artillery spotters from their observation balloons. The roads were systematically shelled day and night. Travel from Coxyde Bains to Nieuport Bains during the day required courage, cunning and a speedy vehicle to avoid shellfire from 77-millimetre field artillery shells, called 'whizz bangs' by British soldiers after the sound of the approaching shells.

When the British took over from the French, the Allied front line opposite Nieuport Bains lay around 650 metres from the eastern side of the Yser Canal. The eastern side was less developed than the western side and a series of sand dunes ran parallel to the coast. One dune, known as the 'Grande Dune', ran through both the Allied and German front lines. Another dune, known as the 'Black Dune', cut into no man's land. Between the two dunes was a flat stretch of sand that had previously been part of a golf course.[23] Close to the dunes the front lines were less than 80 metres apart and therefore afforded an obvious target for tunnelling to mine below the German lines. As part of the proposed British offensive at Nieuport Bains, mines were to be detonated below the German front line where it crossed the Grande and Black dunes. Three tunnelling companies had arrived with the infantry divisions, the 2nd Australian Tunnelling Company and the British 256th and 257th tunnelling companies. Mining operations at Grande and Black dunes represented the principal reason for the transfer of the 2nd Australian Tunnelling Company to the sector. Mine chambers below the dunes would be packed with several tons of ammonal and, on the launch of the British attack, the charges would be detonated. The 257th Tunnelling Company was given the task of constructing infantry subways at the township of Nieuport, just inland from the coast, while the 256th was assigned duties that included the construction of shelters in the dunes along the coast behind Nieuport Bains and the sinking of drinking wells, also in the dunes. Access to the Allied side of the canal was via three pontoon bridges that had been constructed at intervals over the Yser between the railway station and the foot of the breakwater.

The build-up of British divisions and the completion of preparatory works for the operation were supposedly secret. However, in the words of Garnet Adcock, an officer who served with the 2nd Australian Tunnelling Company:

> ... the idea of the push was perfectly well known to everybody ... everyone knew that a division was being trained in great secrecy in a closed area near Dunquerque [sic] in embarking and disembarking from rafts. It was to be a well advertised Gallipoli over again.[24]

British warships scheduled to take part in the offensive were clearly visible off the coast. They further advertised the impending British offensive in spectacular fashion with the nightly shelling of selected points behind the German lines. Artillery observation posts and machine-gun posts were to be constructed with underground access while large underground dugouts and infantry subways of sufficient size to allow the concentration and traffic of a substantial body of infantry were also to be completed prior to the advance.

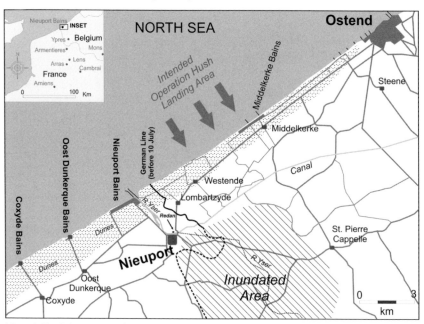

Map 24. The Belgian coast, where preparations for the foiled British Operation Hush were in progress when the Alphabet Company arrived in mid-1917.

By early July, British preparations for Operation Hush were well advanced. However, Admiral Ludwig von Schroeder, commander of the elite *MarinesKorps Flandern,* the German corps responsible for defending the valuable naval bases along the coast, was aware of the arrival of the British in his sector and foresaw an imminent attack. On 10 July, he pre-empted the attack with what proved to be a highly successful surprise attack of his own, codenamed *Strandfest* (Beach Party). On 6 July the Germans commenced a slow, low-intensity preliminary artillery bombardment of Nieuport Bains. In the days leading up to the surprise German attack, low cloud and poor visibility hampered British aerial observation of German positions. Furthermore, local operations of the Royal Flying Corps had been severely curtailed after a German air raid on the nearby British aerodrome at Bray Dunes on the night of 6 July in which 12 British aircraft had been damaged.[25] Consequently, the British did not suspect an imminent German attack.

However, at dawn on 10 July, the Germans commenced shelling the entire British front from Nieuport Bains to Nieuport, the intensity of shelling increasing throughout the morning. The British 1st Division was holding the front at Nieuport Bains. The 2nd King's Royal Rifle Corps and the 1st Northamptonshire (1st Brigade) were garrisoning the front line on the eastern side of the Yser Canal. With them were 47 men from the 2nd Australian Tunnelling Company and a similar number of attached infantry from the 1st Black Watch and 1st South Wales Borderers who were acting as labour for the Australian tunnellers. The second of the XV Corps' three divisions in the Nieuport sector, the 66th (2nd East Lancashire) Division, was in support of the 1st Division when the German attack commenced. At the time, Private George Brame was serving with the 66th Division's 2/5th East Lancs (198th Brigade) and had been detailed to a working party assisting the Royal Engineers at Nieuport Bains.[26] He described the artillery bombardment that unexpectedly descended on 10 July:

> I shall never forget that terrible bombardment. I never experienced anything like it before or since. The shells were flying in all directions, heavies, lights, high explosives, armour piercing shells of all calibers, some whistling overhead, to burst as far away as La Panne, others dropping in the village with a roar that shook the foundations of the earth ... Hour after hour the awful bombardment raged. To venture out was certain death, for the enemy aircraft were dropping bombs and training their machine guns on the cellars.[27]

By late morning, the three pontoon bridges at the mouth of the Yser and all telephone communications to the detachment on the front line side of the Yser Canal had been destroyed. During the afternoon the Germans started shelling using a new type of gas shell, 'Yellow Cross' or, as it was more commonly known, mustard gas. The German attack on 10 July 1917 marked the first reported use of mustard gas in the war.

The three pontoons close to the mouth of the Yser Canal were the only means of escape for the men on the northern shore. Once they were destroyed there was no way back other than by plunging into the water and swimming. During that night and into the early morning of the next day, some stragglers managed to swim across the canal under cover of darkness, but the vast majority of British and Australians on the northern side of the canal were either killed or captured. The British 1st Brigade on the northern side of the Yser Canal lost 50 officers and 1253 other ranks captured at Nieuport Bains that day.[28] Three officers and 52 other ranks from the 2nd King's Royal Rifle Corps and one sergeant and eight other ranks from the 1st Northamptonshire managed to escape. Both of the front-line battalions were, in the words of the British Official Historian, 'practically annihilated' and the British front was pushed back to the western side of the Yser Canal. Two days later, the 1st Division was relieved by the 66th Division.

However this setback in preparations for Operation Hush on the Belgian coast did not significantly alter plans for the commencement of Sir Douglas Haig's offensive at Ypres. On 16 July the British commenced the preliminary artillery bombardment for the impending battle. A total of 717 artillery batteries (some 2300 guns) were employed for this task at the start of a long and difficult operation for the Allied artillery brigades. This bombardment continued, day and night, for two weeks. During this preliminary phase alone, the British fired over 4.3 million artillery shells into the German front line and support positions in the Ypres salient.

At 3.50 am on 31 July 1917, the Third Battle of Ypres commenced. The major attack front extended from the village of Steenstraat in the French-held sector north of Ypres, to the Ypres–Comines Canal south of Ypres. Four British infantry corps (from north to south: XIV, XVIII, XIX and II) of General Sir Hubert Gough's Fifth Army launched the assault, supported by 132 tanks.

The Alphabet Company arrived in support of what ultimately became holding operations by the British on the coastal sector in the third week of June.[29] The tunnelling companies commenced a period of consolidation, strengthening defences along the Yser Canal between Nieuport and Nieuport Bains. The concentration of thousands of men into a relatively narrow defensive area also prompted the construction of shelters and a series of machine-gun posts in the dunes between Nieuport Bains and Oost-Dunkerque, the next settlement south-west along the coast. Further south along the beachfront was

Coxyde Bains. It was here that the unit installed a generating set to power a sawmill, which in turn supplied sawn timber to the 2nd Australian Tunnelling Company for its tunnelling operations in the dunes.

At Oost Dunkerque the 256th Tunnelling Company sank a series of water supply wells in the dunes by hand. The provision of water was a serious planning issue as the British preparations for Operation Hush occurred during summer. Because rainfall on the dunes immediately disappeared into the sand, securing drinking water for men and horses was a major concern. However fresh water could be obtained from beach dunes close to the sea, as fresh water is less dense than seawater and 'floats' as a thin layer on the surface of the seawater which saturates the adjacent dunes below sea level. If extracted carefully, this fresh water could be used for the troops. The tunnellers had to be wary of over-pumping the water from a well or borehole to avoid drawing the salty water that lay below the fresh water into the pump.

The method used for digging wells was highly manpower intensive. Metal tubing was pushed down with weights and sand removed from inside the tubing. As the sand was removed, the weight forced the tubing further into the sand. However, once water was reached, at between 1.5 and 2.5 metres below the surface, it began to enter the base of the open tubing rapidly and had to be pumped out to allow more sand to be excavated and the tubing gradually deepened. This pumping was initially done by hand and had to be continuous, otherwise the well would fill with water-saturated sand. Up to eight or more hand-pumps were needed, each of which took eight men to operate over a 24-hour period. The Alphabet Company installed a generating set, using the generator captured from the Germans during the Battle of Messines earlier in June, which was located centrally, some 800 metres from the proposed location of a series of wells in the dunes, with cables run along the ground to power electric water pumps. Two pumps per well could both dewater the tubing during well installation and also remove sand by stirring the saturated sand to make a slurry which was then pumped, although the pump impellors lasted just a few days before they had to be replaced. This considerably reduced the number of men required during the well-sinking process.

At both Nieuport and Nieuport Bains, the Alphabet Company supplied power and lighting for many of the underground infantry subways connected between house cellars, which represented the only safe way to approach the Yser Canal, and isolated cellars which were being used for forward accommodation. At Nieuport Bains, the previous French garrison had been running a small 4-kilowatt generator supplying lighting to 70 lights, in cellars and the lower floors of buildings along the beach, with power backed up by a battery. By the time the Australians handed the sector back to the French in December, they had installed 340 lighting points powered by a 10-kilowatt generator.

Plate 68. The Yser Canal at Nieuport, with houses from the town silhouetted on the horizon (left). The entrance to the Redan is below the trees to the right, and one of the small wooden bridges crossing the canal is also visible (author collection).

At Nieuport township, which suffered badly from German artillery shelling and was the primary target in the sector, the British 257th Tunnelling Company worked to significantly extend the tunnel systems below the town, installing a network of infantry subways and connections to cellars which were extensively used for troop accommodation. A 12-kilowatt generator was installed in an engine room manned by an NCO and six other ranks. In total, 292 lighting points and a series of ventilation fans capable of circulating 850 cubic metres of air per hour and connected by 6500 metres of cabling were distributed between 2.5 kilometres of underground tunnels and cellar accommodation. The first generator was destroyed by fire on 3 October, and the artillery that registered on the smoke emanating from engine room fire made the room impossible to use. So a new engine room with generator was established away from the former location. When the system was handed back to the French in December, the captured German generator from Messines had replaced the unit's own generator.

On the opposite (northern) side of the Yser Canal was a forward position known as the Redan, constructed within earthen embankments made of soil excavated from the canal and a series of ponds which acted as water obstacles, similar to a moat. The embankments were used for shelter and forward observation posts for the infantry garrison on duty despite the fact that it was in a salient, exposed to concentrated artillery and machine-gun fire. Access was via two small wooden bridges named Putney and Crowder by the British, and fitted with narrow gauge railway tracks to facilitate the transport of supplies across the canal. The spoil bank and the reinforced structures it contained offered some protection for its defenders and the men from the Alphabet Company, with between 1.5 and 3 metres of soil cover. But the position was frequently hit by shells, some from a 15-inch naval gun. In order to reduce the possibility of its destruction, the size of the engine room was kept to an absolute minimum — a mere 1.5 metres x 2.5 metres wide and 1.7 metres high. So difficult were the conditions for the men from the Alphabet Company working at the Redan to maintain 108 lights and an air ventilator below the soil bank in support of the infantry garrison, that a program of short-shift and relief from the company's Nieuport contingent was soon devised.

Several attempts were made to connect the system across the canal to the main engine room in Nieuport, with cables both over and under the water. However the shellfire was so destructive that, on every occasion this was attempted, the cables lasted no longer than three hours before being cut. The position therefore remained an isolated outpost with its own small power supply. The company installed equipment it considered of least value, in the expectation that it would not remain in working condition for long.

During September a specialist squad of men with drilling experience from the 2nd Australian Tunnelling Company was assembled to undertake investigative drilling in the town of Nieuport. Construction of an infantry subway under the Yser Canal at Nieuport had been proposed as a means to connect both sides of the Yser Canal and avoid using the exposed and vulnerable bridges. A short drilling program was completed to assess the feasibility of constructing a subway. This work was close to the embankments of the canal and dangerously exposed, and the drilling proved difficult. The drilling arrangement, which consisted of a wash boring system designed to excavate a hole using high-pressure water, had to be moved five times before the first hole could be completed successfully. In the sixth hole, the men discovered that the top of the Ypresian Clay, the blue clay that was ideal for tunnelling, lay 27 metres below grass root level. The rig then shifted to the northern side of the canal close to the Redan, where another hole confirmed the depth to the top of the clay. Lieutenant Loftus Hills, the Alphabet Company's geologist, was present throughout the drilling, taking notes.

During August it had become increasingly apparent to the British high command that the succession of battles taking place in the Ypres salient was unlikely to result in a British breakthrough on the coast as had been hoped earlier in the year. Any breakthrough in central Flanders would certainly not occur in time to combine with a successful assault on the Flemish coast, if such a success were still possible in September. As the weeks of September passed, the likelihood diminished further. When the weather in Flanders finally broke during the first week of October, Operation Hush was consigned to history and with it went the need to develop an infantry subway below the Yser Canal at Nieuport. The drilling program that had been completed at great risk to those men involved had come to naught.

In November, as winter again closed in, military operations in Flanders ground to an exhausted halt. There was no further need to keep British forces on the Belgian coast, so the British divisions and, by association, the Alphabet Company, withdrew and the Nieuport sector was handed back to the French. In the Ypres salient, a relative calm descended and the British defenders of the ground recently won at such great cost, hunkered down in their dugouts to await the coming of what they knew from experience would be a new killing season, with the advent of spring 1918. Scattered across the salient, in some of the larger dugout systems, the Alphabet Company remained with them, keeping the lights burning, the clear air flowing and diverting the water from the men's feet as much as possible, while also awaiting their fate in 1918.

In Memoriam

The fire in the ramparts dugouts on 13 December 1917 referred to on Page 192 started in a corridor of the dugout system at the opposite end from where the Alphabet Company's engine room was situated. The dugout housed men from a number of units including the headquarters of the British 33rd Division and the 77 Heavy Artillery Group (Royal Garrison Artillery – RGA). Many men managed to escape the blaze, some in their pyjamas, including Major General Reginald Pinney, the GOC 33rd Division. The fire was so intense it burned for over three days. Tragically it claimed the lives of 10 men: Capt. Herbert Spoor MC (Royal Army Medical Corps), Lt George Isaac (RGA), 2nd Lt Richard Huitt (RGA), 253169 Sgt Charles Smalley (Royal Engineers),115989 Cpl George Gray (RGA),89222 Gnr William Le Noury (Royal Field Artillery), 618 RSM Walter Gubby (RGA), L/6356 Bmbdr Alfred Taylor (Royal Field Artillery), 90248 Gnr George Pavitt (Royal Field Artillery), 70936 Pte Lawrence Turner (Machine-gun Corps).

May they like so many others, Rest in Peace.

CHAPTER 8

OTHER ARROWS TO ITS BOW

Geological Investigation

At the outbreak of war in August 1914, British military strategists had little idea that geology and its related cousin geomorphology would dictate how troops on the ground lived and survived the war. The impact of sub-surface conditions on trench warfare had not been considered and, even as the front lines solidified across the map of France and Belgium, the nature of the ground on and under which men would live and die was barely understood — until the first mines were blown. Even at that point, it was the engineers who were called on to provide engineering solutions.

The first British geologist did not arrive in France until June 1915 in the solitary form of Lieutenant (later Captain) William Bernard King.[1] GHQ had requested the services of a geologist to advise on water supplies, particularly groundwater, across the areas occupied by the BEF and in German-held territory in the event of a breakthrough. King was the only serving British geologist in France until the arrival of the Australians 13 months later. From that time on, the nature of geological works evolved to full-scale investigations initiated for a wide range of reasons. The Australians brought with them the men and equipment to change the face and the pace of geological investigations across the British-held sector of the Western Front.

With the arrival of the Australian Mining Corps came Major William Edgeworth David, and the appearance at the front of such an experienced and internationally renowned geologist was to prove serendipitous. Once in France, and having quickly assessed the British military establishment's parlous understanding of the local geology and related issues facing the armies on the various fronts, he ascertained exactly what had to be done and where, commencing his geological investigation work on the First Army front. In the words of Brigadier General Robert Harvey, BEF Inspector of Mines:

> ... before I took over the appointment of Inspector of Mines, I did not realise that geology has anything to do with military mining. At the time of the advent of the Australian Mining Corps and Colonel David

in March 1916 I was actually Inspector of Mines and we were just beginning to think of mining deep, that is, mining between depths of 75 and 120 feet. Just after Colonel David came he got busy at once on the 1st Army front and put them right on many matters to do with the level of water in chalk and I began to believe there was something of value in geological information. That belief culminated when Colonel David fell down a well and very nearly killed himself. Then I was determined that the geological information should not disappear with Colonel David, so I called him back to G.H.Q. where I kept him there.[2]

While King and Edgeworth David were, by definition, working on different aspects of geological investigation during the war, their offices at GHQ were located in close proximity and they were able to liaise regularly, developing a close and mutually respectful working relationship. They also developed a sound working relationship with French and Belgian civilian geologists. The war machine sought simple answers for simple questions that affected the course of the war. The geologists were scientists at heart and they had to temper their scientific interests with the clinical task they had been given. Somehow they still managed to do both and took delight in advancing the understanding of the near-surface geology of Picardy and Flanders.

'Old Prof' Edgeworth David had been at the front less than two months when he presented a lecture entitled 'The geological strata of the British front with reference to military mining and boring' at the First Army Mine School located in the village of Houchin, south-west of Béthune. To be able to speak with authority on a subject of such significance and in such detail so soon after arriving at the front was an impressive achievement. The lecture was attended by most of the senior officers from the Australian, British and Canadian tunnelling companies.

By early September 1916, Edgeworth David was doing what he loved best: conducting scientific measurements in the field. One piece of information vital to tunnelling operations was the depth of groundwater below surface level along the front — particularly the variations in groundwater levels between winter and summer. Equipped with this information, the tunnelling companies could avoid tunnelling to depths that would see the shafts flooded during the winter months as the groundwater levels rose, swollen by the rain and snowmelt that percolated through the soil. Edgeworth David was in the Hulluch mining sector, two kilometres north-east of Loos and under the control of the 258th Tunnelling Company. There he had been overseeing the sinking of investigation boreholes to determine groundwater levels in the chalk substrata through which the mine galleries in that part of the Western Front were dug. While he was there, he was taking great interest not only in the information he was collecting from the drilling, but also in data on groundwater levels collected from tunnelling company mine shafts in the sector over a number of months. He concluded at the time that, in the Hulluch area, the groundwater level in the chalk fluctuated over three metres between the summer and winter months.

Edgeworth David's military work never overrode his love of geology. Since chalk is produced by the skeletal remains of marine creatures, mostly microscopic in size, it invariably contains the fossilised remains of larger, long-extinct animals. On one occasion he was notified that some fossils had been unearthed in the chalk of the nearby mine system at Loos. In one of his notes to the commander of the local tunnelling company which discussed military matters concerning his investigations, he could not resist asking that some fossils be kept for him before lavishing pre-emptive gratitude on the officer and his subordinates.

On 25 September the incident which almost killed Edgeworth David and to which the BEF's Inspector of Mines, Brigadier General Harvey referred, occurred close to Vimy Ridge. Edgeworth David was engaged in measuring groundwater levels and, on this occasion, he was being lowered down a disused shaft near Vimy Ridge. His means of accessing the lower levels was to sit astride a bucket, which was then lowered down the shaft. The bucket was attached to a rope and windlass which was hand-cranked from above by some assistants. Halfway down the shaft, his plans suddenly —and quite literally — fell apart when the windlass at the surface collapsed. Both bucket and rider fell over 20 metres down the shaft, bouncing off the sides as they descended. By some miracle, the tough old geologist survived and was hauled up by the same means. But the fall had taken its toll and, in spite of forced jocularity, he was in pain. Among some superficial scrapes he was found to have suffered a ruptured and bruised urethra and a fractured rib. He spent a week in a casualty clearing station before being shipped to England to recover.

As he noted earlier, when he heard of the incident, Harvey decided that Edgeworth David was far too valuable a resource to lose through such foolhardiness and seconded him to the staff at GHQ — then located at Montreuil — where he could keep a more careful eye on him. Thus, on 11 November, Edgeworth David assumed the very important and privileged role of geological technical adviser to the entire British front, reporting directly to the Inspector of Mines.

However his new role at GHQ now meant reduced contact with the Australian tunnelling companies as his work took him to all parts of the front gathering data and giving lectures. His direct link with the Alphabet Company likewise was broken and, although Edgeworth David continued to take great interest in the activities and experiences of his former comrades, he was now separated from their day-to-day lives.

Edgeworth David's achievements on the Western Front were many and varied. As the senior geological adviser to the British in France and Flanders, he and his assistant, the Tasmanian geologist Loftus Hills, were responsible for planning, collecting and interpreting geological data from a total of over 8500 linear metres of investigation boreholes along the front.[3]

Many of the major dugout systems constructed along the British front by tunnelling companies after mid-1916, particularly those in the Ypres salient, were situated and built according to detailed sets of geological maps and cross-sections developed by Edgeworth David. These were based on data collected by Loftus Hills and his teams of drillers.

Plate 69. Lieutenant Loftus Hills, MBE, of the 1st Australian Tunnelling Company. Hills was attached to the Alphabet Company for most of his service and was one of the five 'British' geologists at the front (image courtesy of Mineral Resources Tasmania).

Edgeworth David possessed an extraordinary level of technical skill, a fact that was demonstrated frequently as he worked his way along the front. In September 1917, he and his close geological associate, Captain William 'Bill' King who, in his previous life as a civilian had worked for the British Geological Survey, were examining captured German pillboxes on Vimy Ridge. From the fragments of crushed rock within the concrete of the pillboxes, the two men recognised the presence of a rare rock found only in one location — near Cologne along the Rhine River. They concluded that this rock must have been transported to the Western Front through neutral Holland. Dutch authorities were alerted and transportation of the rock through Holland — shipped under the guise of 'civil material for use in Belgium' — ceased forthwith. Lieutenant Loftus Hills was later appointed an MBE for his crucial assistance to Edgeworth David in supervising the drilling and in the interpretation of borehole data returned from men in the field from the many hundreds of investigative holes.

Geological Boring Sets

The most widely used geological testing units were the truly portable boring sets that could be operated by teams of two to three men. Because of their portability, these boring sets could be used in front-line trenches, almost under the eyes of the enemy. The simplest set was brought to France by the Australian Mining Corps and consisted of 3-foot (91-centimetre) lengths of steel drill pipe, half an inch (12.5 millimetres) in diameter, threaded at both ends. The drill pipes could be fitted with augers that were one or two inches (25 or 50 millimetres) in diameter, and driven into the ground using a 'T' piece turning handle. The 50-millimetre auger was used to drill down to a depth of around five metres, then withdrawn and a pipe 32 millimetres in diameter, known as a 'casing', was inserted to the bottom of the hole. The smaller 25-millimetre auger and drill pipe were then introduced down through the casing and drilling continued until a bottom depth of around 12.5 metres was achieved. This unit, with all its parts and tools, weighed a mere 42 kilograms. It was usual for two 40-foot (12-metre) holes to be bored in one day by a team of four men. While a single man could turn the drill rods during drilling, it took four men to overcome the suction forces when pulling the rods back from the hole. The Australian boring set was fairly rudimentary and an alternative set, known as the Acme boring set, and later the Modified Acme boring set, was sourced from England and employed widely for geological testing works.[4]

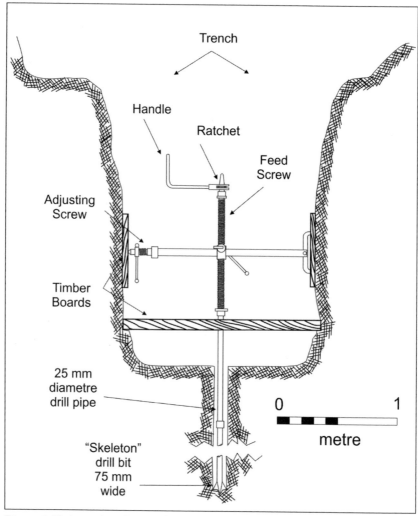

Diagram 5. The key working elements of an Acme boring set which relied on a ratchet-driven feed screw to drive a drill bit measuring 75 millimetres in diameter into the ground. The drill pipe was 25 millimetres in diameter and was fitted in 91-centimetre lengths.

These sets, like the Australian set, used small-diameter drilling pipe, but employed a threaded 'feed screw' to drive and rotate the drilling rods into the ground using a ratchet handle. Water was introduced down the drill hole until a slurry of water and drilling material made movement of the drill too difficult. The drill rods were then removed and the slurry was pumped from the bottom of the hole by a 'sand pump' which was a length of pipe with a one-way valve at the bottom. This was agitated in the slurry, the slurry would move up into the pipe, but not back down due to the valve, allowing the slurry to be removed. Drilling would then continue until the bottom depth was reached at around 12 metres. A two-man team could drill a 12-metre hole in eight hours.[5] A complete set of gear for one of these units, with all parts and tools, weighed around 70 kilograms and was easily transported by two men, who could then set it up quickly and begin operations almost immediately.

While geological investigations for suitable dugout sites began in earnest in May 1916 after the arrival of the Alphabet company, they did not reach their peak until the end of 1917. Boring work was performed by men from the tunnelling companies whose area of operation covered the investigation site. The boring sets were supplied from Alphabet Company stores with the number of sets gradually increased as demand rose. When the Alphabet Company arrived in France there were only 10 sets. By the end of 1917 there were around 110 sets and over 100 holes being drilled per week.[6]

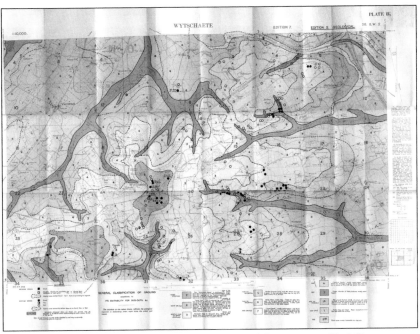

Plate 70. A Dugout Suitability Map, the result of investigative drilling using portable drilling sets supplied by the Alphabet Company and prepared by Major Edgeworth David. The maps were based on geological interpretation of bored lithology by Lieutenant Loftus Hills of the Alphabet Company (Institute of Royal Engineers).

The type of soil and its moisture content (dry, moist, wet) from each drilled hole was noted by the men operating the drilling sets and passed to Loftus Hills who drew up a vertical lithological representation of the stratigraphy at each hole. Based on this data he assessed whether a drilled site was suitable for dugout construction. These records were forwarded to Major Edgeworth David at GHQ who developed detailed geological maps, modified from existing French and Belgian geological maps, to show the suitability of ground for dugout construction. The maps were then issued to both the Chief Engineer and Controller of Mines in the army areas covered by the maps, primarily the Second and Fifth armies. Twelve maps were produced and printed by the British Ordnance Survey at Southampton.

Hill 60 at the northern end of the Messines Ridge where it overlooked Ypres from the south was an early target for Major Edgeworth David. Working tirelessly with boring equipment and men from the Alphabet Company, he soon established the geological stratigraphy of the hill. He also collected data on the groundwater level and established the variation between summer and winter groundwater levels. This knowledge allowed the tunnellers to drive their mine galleries to depths that avoided, as much as possible, the groundwater-bearing zones.

The Wombat borer

One of the most innovative pieces of equipment that arrived from Australia with the Mining Corps was the portable drilling unit known as the 'Wombat' borer. Weighing around 163 kilograms, it was not as portable as the lighter Acme-style borers, but was much sturdier and could drill a hole with a far larger diameter and tunnel over greater distances. Thirty-six of these machines left Australia with the corps.[7]

The Wombat borer was designed in Australia by Stanley Hunter and was intended for use at Gallipoli. However, by the time the machines, and for that matter, the Australian Mining Corps, was ready to embark for the front, the Allies had withdrawn from the Gallipoli peninsula. Once the borers arrived and their use under fighting conditions was observed at first hand, the machines were adopted by the British Army for use on the Western Front and used extensively, not only by the Alphabet Company, but by most of the British and Commonwealth tunnelling companies until the end of the war. In addition to the original 36, a further 50 machines were manufactured, bringing the total number employed on the Western Front to 86.

The primary purpose of these machines was the drilling of dugout ventilation holes, usually vertically through the ceiling of dugouts. However the machines were also used for demolition, for creating an instantaneous trench as was the case at Vimy Ridge, or for charging camouflets in deep mine systems. Occasionally they were also employed for boring water supply wells from the confines of a dugout.

Each unit could be fitted with auger blades or coring barrels up to six inches (150 millimetres) in diameter which could drill through the clay and sandy soils or chalk at any angle from the vertical through to the horizontal plane. The borer was designed to be either hand-operated or powered by a 12 or 16-horsepower electric motor.[8] Most operations were performed manually using detachable drive handles, one fitted to either side of a small gearbox at the centre of the machine. The drive handles were long enough for two men to work each handle if necessary, for example when boring through tight clay or hard chalk.

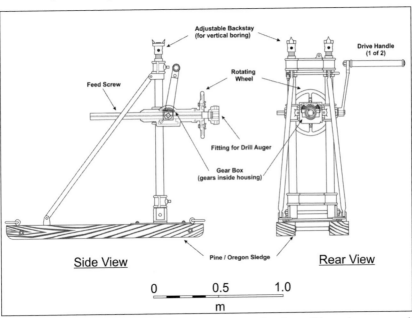

Diagram 6. Main working elements of the Wombat borer. Internal workings of the gearbox are exposed in this diagram but were enclosed in the operational units. This diagram is based on blueprints dated February 1916, and thus the machines featured in Plates 71 to 73 vary slightly.

The most ingenious design element of the unit was the central feed screw, a long, threaded steel cylinder which was driven forward or backwards by the turning of the drive handles. Drilling extension rods were progressively connected to the end of the drive screw and its rate of forward movement was governed by what was called the 'sleeve feed nut' which was controlled in turn by a rotating wheel. When the wheel was fixed, every rotation of the driving handles would progress the drilling rods around six millimetres, but if the rotating wheel was turned in either the same or opposite direction to the feed screw during drilling, the rate of progress could be increased or decreased to suit the drilling conditions.

Plate 71. A Wombat borer being used in the horizontal position to drill a hole through an earthen embankment by two unnamed Alphabet Company sergeants (AWM H12773). The feed screw, to which the auger drilling rod is connected, is rotated and driven forward by the turning of drive handles that are connected in turn to a small gearbox at the centre of the unit (AWM H12773).

Plate 72. The Wombat borer fitted with a six-inch diameter 'calyx' cutting head and core barrel, used for drilling through hard chalk containing flint fragments (courtesy Phillip Robinson).

Plate 73. A Wombat borer in the vertical position boring a ventilation hole in a dugout at the headquarters of No. 2 Section, 3rd Australian Tunnelling Company, in the Cité St Laurent, January 1918. The adjustable backstays have been extended to the dugout wall behind the two men, while the sledge is supported against a vertical wooden beam at the left of the photograph. The feed screw is in its starting position as drilling has not commenced. Note the candle on the rotation wheel, which is unlikely to remain alight since this is the only place for chalk to fall from the hole above. This suggests the photograph was staged to show how the Wombat machine was used in a dugout. Shown are Lieutenant James Robertson (left) and No. 4368 Sapper Cyril Jolley of the 3rd Australian Tunnelling Company (part of AWM E01689).

Plate 71 shows the key elements of the Wombat borer in action. The bemused sergeant on the left is in the act of cranking a drive handle while the sergeant at the front of the machine is adjusting the rotating wheel. Part of the threaded central feed screw can be observed projecting towards the drilling auger. The auger blade entering the embankment has its forward cutting edge buried in the soil. Resting against the rear of the boring machine is another length of auger which will be connected to the end of the drilling auger and driven forward in turn. Dislodged soil at the cutting face is fed back and out of the borehole by the auger's screwing movement. This process can be repeated so that the borehole is driven in some considerable distance while the turning of the drive handles becomes progressively more difficult as friction increases and the weight of the steel auger lengths accumulates.

A full boring squad for one machine consisted of eight men — one NCO and seven other ranks. The basic unit, without powered motors, drilling rods or tools, weighed around 165 kilograms and could be moved by two men. The machine was used for a wide range of purposes, from water supply boring, geological testing, dugout and tunnel ventilation, burying signal wires, draining trenches and demolition.

Between Nieuport, just inland from the Belgian coast, and the village of Wulpen, four kilometres south-west along the Nieuport–Dunkirk Canal, over 600 metres of signal wire were buried in horizontal bores drilled by the Wombat borer some 2.5 metres below ground level at intervals along the bank of the canal.[9]

Water Supply and Deep Geological Exploration Drilling

The largest boring units were the motor-driven drilling rigs, the most notable the American-built Star and Keystone rigs. These types of rig are known as cable-tool or percussion drilling rigs. The drilling tool is a solid steel rod with a sharpened end which breaks up material at the bottom of the hole. The other end of the rod is attached to a cable which allows the steel rod to be lifted and dropped into the hole, progressively pulverising the material at the base of the hole. The broken material is removed by a hollow steel tube with a non-return valve at its end, which allows the broken material at the bottom of the drill hole to be collected while preventing it spilling out the end of the tube. The drilling rods and tubes are lowered down through an outer steel pipe known as a casing, which prevents the drilled hole from collapsing and provides space for water to eventually escape from the hole. As drilling progresses, the casing is hammered downwards into the deepening hole and continually extended at the surface. All these actions are performed by an actuating arm on the drilling rig. In the cable-tool rigs used at the turn of the century, the actuating arm was powered by steam. This method of drilling is slow by today's standards, but was used widely around the world until the mid-twentieth century when the increasing power of rotary drilling methods quickly outstripped the older style. Although slow, the technique boasts a significant advantage over other techniques in that it allows drillers and geologists to clearly see the material through which the drilling occurs, record the depths at which the materials change and recognise when zones bearing a high volume of water are encountered. For this reason, cable-tool rigs are still used occasionally, even today.

Plate 74. Two of the unit's Star cable-tool drilling rigs used for drilling deep water supply boreholes in chalk (NAA 10/58).

Plate 75. 'The Latest Thing in Wombats going to the Front', a satirical cartoon by Hugh Thurlow poking fun at his comrades in the drilling section with Captain Stanley Hunter leading a band of men. Hunter's panache for inventing his own drilling equipment is being satirised — there was never a drilling rig that resembled this contraption (AWM 3DRL/4059).

Plate 76. Four Alphabet Company soldiers in front of one of the company's cable-tool drilling rigs. A drilling tool can be seen at the end of the steel cable. The men are standing on a working deck — the borehole is drilled through the centre of the deck (NAA 9/71).

Plate 77. Alphabet Company drillers in action during cable-tool drilling of a water bore. The men are wearing their steel helmets. The bore is being drilled through chalk as shown by the white slurry on the ground which is removed using the metal tubing which is fitted with a one-way hinged flap at the lower end (AWM H09559).

During the war, the cable-tool rigs used were kept busy drilling water supply bores in rear areas. There were six boring sections, five British and the Alphabet Company section. Each of the British sections was attached to one of the army areas. The British sections operated under the auspices of the Engineer-in-Chief, but under the day-to-day direction of Captain King, while the Australians operated under the Inspector of Mines. During the course of the war, the six water-boring sections drilled around 500 water boreholes with average depths of 100 to 120 metres.

Once the bores were drilled and cased with steel casing, water was obtained by blowing compressed air below the water level via a pipe. As the air rises up the enclosed casing it lifts the groundwater up through the borehole — a technique called 'air-lifting'. This is not a particularly efficient method of pumping water from a bore, but it is effective and very simple. Air-lift yields from bores installed in the chalk aquifers which lay below much of the British-held sector could yield water at rates of up to 15 litres per second, enough to fill an Olympic-size swimming pool in two days. During the swift advance of the British forces during the final months of the war, the rapid securing of reliable water supplies for hundreds of thousands of men and tens of thousands of horses was critical and was accomplished with great skill by the British and Australian boring sections.

Works at Bailleul
Company Tout of Duty: Bailleul

On 23 July 1916 the company opened a battery-charging station for miners' lamps using a 10-kilowatt gas-powered generator in part of the Second Army's timber workshops in Bailleul. Their rationale was that the local tunnelling companies, which sourced mine timber from the workshop, would also deposit and collect recharged miners' lamps from the same location at the same time.

Soon after the station was established, reports of its success reached the Inspector of Mines and the unit was given responsibility for charging the many thousands of portable miners' lamps from all the tunnelling companies across all the army areas. As lamps were received at the station they were cleaned, repaired if required and the batteries removed and recharged, with charging taking between 12 and 36 hours to complete. With the expansion in intake, recharged lamps were also delivered to the Army Mine Schools on a weekly basis for collection by the tunnelling companies. This operation continued 24 hours a day, seven days a week, with an average of around 2000 lamps a month recharged, up to a maximum of 1000 a week in times of peak demand. The electric miners' lamps used by the tunnellers at the time were the same models used in coal mines in England and included CEAG or Oldham lamps.

Plate 78. An electric CEAG miners' lamp , one of several models of lamp used at the front by British tunnellers. (author collection).

Plate 79. The lamp's accumulator (battery). The accumulator was fitted in the cylinder below the bulb and handle (author collection).

The lamps could comfortably supply a solid eight hours of light, enough for one underground shift. However, during transportation, which inevitably occurred in daylight hours, the lamps were almost always inadvertently knocked to the 'on' position and run down, the glowing lamps difficult to detect in the bright daylight. Miners also tended to exhaust their additional battery power by forgetting to turn their lamps off when they returned to the surface during daytime, again when the light from their lamps was not easily detected. The charging station operated from 23 July 1917 until 12 April 1918.

In addition to the timber workshop at Bailleul, the company also operated a 6-kilowatt generating plant for a short period at Béthune to power a mining timber-cutting workshop for the 254th Tunnelling Company.

Army Mine Schools

The British First and Second armies established mine schools in their army areas to provide specialist training facilities for tunnellers, engineering troops and officers who were required to perform tunnelling work in various forms. The First Army Mine School was located at Houchin, three kilometres south of Béthune in France, and the Second Army Mine School was located at Proven, four kilometres north-west of Poperinghe in western Flanders.

The installation of a 9-kilowatt engine and generator at the Second Army Mine School on 20 May 1916 was among the first technical tasks of the Alphabet Company. This task was completed during the period in which the unit was still attempting to understand its role following the disbandment of the Australian Mining Corps. The generator was used to power Wombat boring machines used by the school for training. Mock underground mine galleries and chambers were constructed by the British 177th Tunnelling Company, and the Wombat borers were used for vertical and horizontal boring underground, completed under the supervision of an NCO from the Alphabet Company and the CO of the school, former Australian Mining Corps headquarters officer Major James Pollock.

A slightly larger 10.5-kilowatt generator was supplied and operated by the unit at the First Army Mine School for the same purpose on 12 July 1917. The power generated was then used for lighting nearby camps. The generator remained at the school until April 1917.

CHAPTER 9

THE LAST GASPS — 1918

While the winter of 1917–1918 conformed to the established pattern of a weather-induced cessation of large-scale hostilities, it also heralded the beginning of the end of the war, although the protagonists remained unaware of this. General Erich Ludendorff, chief strategist of the German forces on the Western Front, recognised that it was imperative his armies launch a massive and decisive assault against the Allies. Part of his reasoning lay in the fact that, almost one year earlier, in April 1917, America had reluctantly entered the war. Since October 1917, every month had seen around 50,000 American troops arriving in France. By early 1918, this figure had escalated to some 250,000 a month.

For three years, the Germans, French and British had been pounding one another in a war of attrition until everyone was desperately weary and reserves of men, particularly for the German forces, were becoming more difficult to procure as war weariness also bit deep on the home fronts. In November 1917, following the October Russian Revolution, the war with Russia on the Eastern Front had ended, freeing battle-hardened German reserves from that theatre. With each passing month however, Allied strength on the Western Front increased, albeit with officers and men inexperienced in the peculiarities of trench warfare. In stark contrast to Germany and its flagging allies, American involvement threatened the German high command with a virtually limitless supply of fresh and eager men, and a vast influx of equipment and supplies. Ludendorff, the Quartermaster General behind the German war effort, was a meticulous strategist and planner. He realised that the Germans had to break through the Allied lines before the sheer number of men and machines opposing them became overwhelming. He planned a calculated gamble based on the belief that, by focussing a series of battering-ram assaults on the British front, he could break through the British line. With the British defeated, the whole Western Front would crumble and the war would be won before the American presence was fully established.

Ludendorff developed precise and detailed plans for moving huge numbers of men and supplies behind the German lines in preparation for his assaults and for maintaining an unbroken momentum once these assaults were launched.

The first of the assaults, codenamed 'St Michael', commenced on 21 March and took place over a 96-kilometre front between the River Oise in the south and Arras in the north.

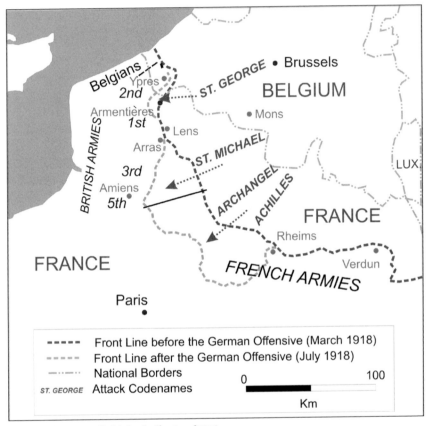

Map 25. The German 'St Michael' offensive of 1918.

On the southern flank of the British sector, into which the assault crashed, the British Fifth and Third armies were holding the line. The signs of an impending German attack had been building throughout February 1918 and into early March as German artillery action escalated and the use of gas shells increased in a bid to weaken the British defenders. At the time, the 2nd Australian Tunnelling Company was constructing dugouts along the British V Corps front facing Cambrai. During the first few days of March, the company lost 67 men through gas poisoning. The unit war diary records the estimated number of gas shells fired into its corps area between 12 and 15 March as a staggering 110,000.

The German offensive hit the British Third and Fifth Armies like a runaway truck. The British staggered under the sustained momentum of the attacks. Ground that had been won at bitter cost to the British, Canadian and Australians over the two preceding years was lost in a matter of days as the Allied divisions retired in leaps and bounds under the relentless pressure of the German onslaught. The men struggled back as best they could with what equipment and stores they could gather. Pockets of defenders were marshalled to offer some form of precarious and highly fluid rearguard protection in an attempt to slow the tide. Gradually, as the German front moved westward, the lines of supply lengthened dangerously and the German attacking forces grew increasingly exhausted. By 26 March, the British VII Corps had been reduced to three divisions, and its GOC, Lieutenant General Walter Congreve, VC, was instructed to form a line of resistance across the peninsula formed by the confluence of the Ancre and Somme rivers, from the city of Albert on the Ancre River to the village of Bray-sur-Somme (Bray) on the northern bank of the Somme.

By the time the so-called GHQ Defence Line had been established by the British to protect the vital communication and transport hub of Amiens, the German St Michael offensive had all but spent its energy and lost its sting. Massive damage had been inflicted on both sides. The St Michael attack drew to a close on 5 April, by which time 220,000 Allied troops had been killed, wounded or captured along with an estimated 1500 artillery pieces and 100 tanks. The Germans had lost some 240,000 men, their highly trained storm-trooper units decimated.

But the tail of the German scorpion was quickly redirected towards another part of the British line. As the tension that had gripped the British forces in the region of the old Somme battlefield began to subside, the second, northern prong of the German spring offensive commenced — on 9 April, the anniversary of the opening of the Battle of Arras by the British a year earlier. Codenamed 'St George' but now more commonly referred to in British history as the Battle of the Lys, the offensive targeted the front between Givenchy and the Messines Ridge outside the township of Wytschaete. The German objective was the high ground between Bailleul and Ypres, the Mont des Cats and Mont Kemmel. The British Second Army under General Plumer, the hero of the Battle of Messines in June 1917, faced this new onslaught. Among the hundreds of thousands of men who would eventually be caught up in the events of 9 April, were those of the Alphabet Company.

The offensive was launched at 8.45 am following a four-hour bombardment with phosgene and high explosives shells. Eight front-line German divisions attacked the line between the La Bassée Canal (at Givenchy) in the south and Armentières in the north, a further six divisions supporting them in reserve. The front was covered by just four Allied divisions, from south to north, the 55th (West Lancashire), 2nd Portuguese, 40th and 34th divisions. The Portuguese Division, (referred to as the 'Pork and Beans' by Tommy soldiers) was the weakest division in the line, stretched over a nine-kilometre front at the centre of the German attack. It was hammered by four German divisions. The British 55th Division to the south of the Portuguese was in the line at Givenchy where the Alphabet Company had been operating since July 1916.

The Portuguese division collapsed and set in motion a cascading withdrawal combined with a desperate rearguard action by the British forces in the region that was to last two weeks. As the centre of the line was overrun, the Germans turned and began to roll back the flanks of the British lines to their north and south while at the same time pushing on to cross the River Lys.

Such was the pressure on the British during this battle that Field Marshal Sir Douglas Haig issued the now famous Special Order of the Day on 11 April to all British troops in France and Flanders. Haig wrote:

> Many amongst us are now tired. To those I would say that Victory will belong to the side which holds out the longest. The French Army is moving rapidly and in great force to our support.

> There is no other course open to us but to fight it out. Every position must be held to the last man: there must be no retirement. With our backs to the wall and believing in the justice of our cause each one of us must fight on to the end. The safety of our homes and the freedom of mankind alike depend upon the conduct of each one of us at this critical moment.[1]

The 1st Australian Division had arrived in Hazebrouck the previous day (10 April) and was later credited with having 'saved the situation' by the XV Corps Commander, Lieutenant General Sir Henry de Lisle.[2] The division had been in transit from Messines to join the other Australian divisions defending Amiens, which was under threat from the St Michael front of the German offensive. The first of its brigades had already arrived at Amiens and was moving into a series of positions in the forward areas when, at the last minute, it was hastily redirected north. On 11 April the division turned tail, reboarded trains and hurried back to join XV Corps in the defence of Hazebrouck.

While conditions at Armentières during April were tense, at Givenchy on the extreme southern flank of the St George front, the situation had become critical as the position at Givenchy was vitally important for the protection of the Béthune coalfields to the south and west of the La Bassée Canal.

On 16 April, while the fight for Givenchy had yet to be won, the CO of the Alphabet Company, Victor Morse, wrote to his wife expressing his pride in his men during such a tense period:

> …you cannot imagine the work done by my chaps the last week, a good percentage haven't had any sleep, except a snatch between spasms. The hun is getting it pretty warm, the 1st Div. have done great work already.

The British 55th (West Lancashire) Division bore the initial brunt of the onslaught at Givenchy and was relieved by the British 1st Division on 15/16 April. Lance Corporal Thomas Owen of the 1st South Wales Borderers, 1st Division, was a member of a machine-gun section that relieved a section of the 1/10th (Liverpool Scottish) Battalion during a brief lull in the battle. He described his new position in the front-line trench:

> Dead men lay about here and there; the communication trench to Headquarters – a small pillbox in the centre of the square – had partly collapsed at the sides and was sickeningly yielding underfoot with the bodies of buried men. Here and there a leg or an arm protruded from the trench sides. The wire was cut in places and the gaps in the trenches, caused by mortar attacks, were staringly open and dangerous.[3]

The offensive resumed in its full fury on 18 April. At 8.10 am, after seven hours of intense bombardment, three German divisions concentrated their attack on Givenchy. Two companies of the 1st Black Watch Battalion were overrun as the German infantry targeted the exits of the complex of tunnel systems in the front-line trenches, trapping the men before they could emerge to counter-attack. In spite of the overwhelming numbers opposing them, the defenders held firm, fending off waves of attacks, particularly against such fortified strongholds as Givenchy Keep and Marie Redoubt. At one point, the garrison at Givenchy Keep was reduced from two officers and 40 other ranks to one office and eight other ranks.[4] Thomas Owen described the events from his advanced position in the front line:

Looking over the top I saw the long grey lines sweeping along four hundred yards away. They were marching shoulder to shoulder, heavily weighted with picks, ammunition and rations. We scrambled to the fire step. We fired madly and recklessly. The Lewis gun rattled and the two magazine fillers worked with feverish haste. It should have been horrid slaughter at the distance, for the Germans seemed to huddle together like sheep as they lurched over No Man's Land. But there were thousands of them and our aim was hurried and bad. We fired in abandonment rather than by design. Still the grey hordes advanced.

A hoarse voice shouted at the back of us. It was Sergeant Winnford: God knows how he got through to us; and he yelled 'Retreat back to support line; you corporal, see them all out.' He made for a gap in the trench. The survivors followed him. As he reached the open a stray shot, or splinter, splattered his brains out and he fell without a sound. Stupefied, the others crept through and got clear, and raced across the open land with the enemy in full cry behind. Barker was the last to crawl out. I howled at him to hurry but he was tall and lanky and dead beat. I raced at his side. 'Slip off your pack' I shouted, as I got out of my own trappings. He did so, but he was ashen and panting. I felt a smart above my elbow and there was blood trickling from the tips of my fingers. 'Barker, Barker!' I screamed. 'Hurry up chum for God's sake!' I might have saved my breath. As I turned my head to him, and as he made a supreme effort to hasten, I saw the bullet hit the back of his tin helmet and spurt out at the front. I ran a dozen steps further. Something hit my other elbow, searing hot and smashing through, and I spun round like a top and lay once more in the slime. I thought my arm had gone. If it was death I was numb, careless and content. I sank into a dull stupor and the hordes of grey uniforms trampled over me, round me and by me, and forgot me in their own terror.[5]

The battle descended into chaos and soon became a desperate fight to the death. But, while the British defenders were forced to concede ground, they did not lose Givenchy. Every available man was thrown into its defence.

The British 251st Tunnelling Company was the tunnelling company in residence at Givenchy and, since the opening of the German offensive on 9 April, both infantry and tunnellers had been at the mercy of heavy shelling. The Moat Farm and Bunny Hutch subway entrances were captured and, over the next few days, the tunnellers fought alongside the infantry, becoming infantry soldiers themselves. Some were captured and others died with their infantry comrades.

But the line at Givenchy held, just as it had when the 55th Division was battered during the opening days of the offensive. Some ground had been lost, but the position was maintained, albeit at tremendous cost. Losses among the defenders (55th and 1st divisions) during the attacks on Givenchy in April 1918 totalled 5243 men killed, wounded and missing.

The little band of men from the Alphabet Company under Jack Nancarrow — Sappers No. 374 Charles Calf (a plumber in his civilian profession), No. 8037 Cyril Hylton (an electrician who had transferred from the 5th Field Company of Engineers, AIF), No. 6112 Frederick Gaydon (also an electrician) and No. 7244 William Patrick (a turner in his civilian life) — were in the wrong place as they worked to keep the underground power supplies, lighting and water pumps operating. The Germans overran their positions that day and, the following day, once the fighting had abated and those lost positions had been regained, there was no sign of the men. The Australians, like Thomas Owen and hundreds of others, had been taken prisoner at Givenchy. This was not immediately apparent to their CO, nor to anyone else in the company for quite some time afterwards. Ultimately, however, all returned to Australia at the end of the war.

Hughie Dodd, at the company's Wings Way sector on the other side of the La Bassée Canal, recalled events that swept up his friends, events which filtered down to where he and his men were working:

April 6: Johnny opened up with barrage this morning, up around Givenchy

April 7: Repeat

April 8: The bombardment died down a little this morning

April 10: Knocked Marlybone [sic] Tunnel in Givenchy. Engines have not been on for a few days past

April 15-23: Been some heavy fighting up around Givenchy

April 24: We lost eight plants up north. Nancarrow, Geydon [sic] and Charlie Calf are missing from Givenchy job, so they have new personnel.

Over the following months, word reached Alphabet Company headquarters that its men had been taken prisoner at Givenchy and were alive and well, albeit living in camps in Germany. Charlie Calf managed to write to his CO to reassure him that he and the others were indeed alive and to pass on their best wishes to their mates.

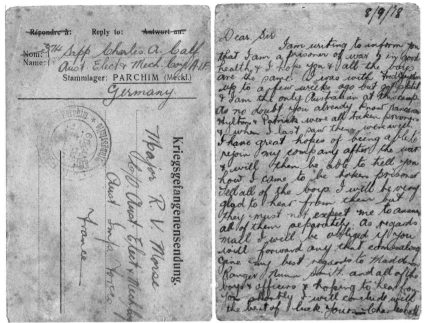

Plate 80. A postcard sent to Victor Morse from the Parchim prisoner-of-war camp dated September 1918, advising the unit that the card's author, Charlie Calf, and other men captured at Givenchy are alive and well (Victor Morse collection).

For his courageous conduct during the German attack at Givenchy and his calm direction as his little band of men worked desperately to maintain power to the underground system, Jack Nancarrow was awarded a Bar to his DCM. His first medal had been recommended by his CO, Victor Morse, just one month earlier, during the general artillery softening-up along the Allied front lines which heralded the build-up to the German offensive. Givenchy was a natural target and, as a consequence, two of three electric generators used for powering pumps to keep the underground galleries clear of water were smashed. With the power failure, water began to fill the underground galleries vital for the safe passage of men and supplies. Over a period of two and a half days, Jack Nancarrow remained at his post, supervising the installation of a new generator and keeping both it and the remaining generator operating despite being subject to heavy shellfire the entire time. Although both generators were operating at dangerous levels, the underground galleries remained relatively free of water, the level never exceeding two feet in depth. No. 229 Sapper John 'Scotty' Parker, who provided invaluable assistance to Nancarrow during the crisis in March, was awarded the MSM. Nancarrow became one of only 88 Australians in the war to receive the DCM and Bar and one of only three recipients who served in a unit of Australian Engineers.

In September 1919, the Hobart Mercury reported an unusual follow-up to the Jack Nancarrow story:

> At Rawlinna a little station 230 miles east of Kalgoorlie, and on the edge of Nullarbor Plains the Prime Minister (Hon W. M. Hughes) while en route to Melbourne presented to Lance Corporal Nancarrow the Distinguished Conduct Medal which was won by him in France. He showed conspicuous gallantry and devotion by operating an electric power station, and repairing a cable under heavy machine-gun fire. All the residents had assembled from far and near, and by the light of a lantern dimly burning Mr. Hughes pinned the decoration so gallantly won. Mr. Hughes said that Lance Corporal Nancarrow was one of those to whom his fellow citizens owed everything which they possessed. Mr. Hughes added that the D.C.M. with a bar was rarely conferred.

When the situation at Givenchy resumed some semblance of calm after the storm, the First Army Controller of Mines, Lieutenant Colonel Robert Stokes, wrote a letter of appreciation to Victor Morse for the efforts of his men. In his letter he expressed sentiments that exemplified the regard the British high command had developed for this unit:

> With reference to the excellent work done by your Detachment at Givenchy during the recent operations, regarding which you have received messages of appreciation from the Army Commander, GOC I Corps and COC 55th Division.
>
> I would like to put on record my appreciation of the continuously valuable services you have rendered in the defence of the Givenchy Sector throughout the last two years. Before you took over the pumping of the Givenchy Mines, extreme difficulties were encountered in this sector owing to the excessive water. Progress was slow and in some areas impossible. The enemy took advantage of these difficulties when he blew the Red Dragon Crater under our lines on May [sic] 22, 1916.
>
> Gradually, the work done by your Company in co-operation with the 254th Tun. Coy. R.E. and later the 251st Tun. Coy. R.E. resulted in establishing a mining and dugout system, in which pumping and lighting arrangements were unfailing, giving absolute confidence

to the Infantry and completely removing the mining danger. The reliability of the power service has been remarkable and the courage and promptitude with which breaks in the overland cables have been made good by your staff, in all circumstances, have won wide appreciation.

The degree of efficiency has been largely due to the skillful attention of Lieut. Piper and to the gallantry and devotion to duty displayed throughout by Corp. Nancarrow.

The way in which your whole detachment have stuck to their post at Givenchy and Pont Fixe for so many months with little rest has been a striking example of the invariable custom of the Aust. E. and M.M. Coy to 'make good' in all tasks they have undertaken.[6]

At the same time, the St George offensive was winning ground along the frontage of the Lys River between Armentières and Givenchy. Ground won at enormous cost over the previous three years was also being yielded further north across the Ypres salient. Power supply engine rooms established during the previous summer and expanded over the winter in the large dugout systems in the salient and further afield along the Messines Ridge were abandoned by the company's operating squads on 15 and 16 April. In most places, the engines and generators were shut down and withdrawn before the positions were overrun. Generating equipment was salvaged in the engine rooms located at Railway Wood, Tor Top, Glencorse Wood, Wieltje and Halfway House.

On 15 April at the Hooge Crater dugout located next to the Menin Road, the Gardiner engine and generator and a dewatering pump were destroyed by their operators and the system was left to flood. That same day, the local squad of Alphabet Company operators at nearby Hill 60 received secret instructions to destroy the unit's two Coventry Simplex engines and generators and a dewatering pump at noon the next day and withdraw. The machinery had to be destroyed without the use of explosives or by any means that might signal to the Germans that the British were withdrawing from the position. At the appointed hour the equipment was smashed with hammers and the men withdrew without incident.

Further south from the salient, positions along the Messines Ridge were also abandoned. The first to go, on 12 April, was the charging station at Bailleul followed by Hill 63, Wulverghem and finally, on 25 April, the engine room supplying power to the dugout systems and an advanced dressing station at Voormezeele near St Eloi.

Further north, at the centre of the St Michael attack front, the capture of Armentières and the forced withdrawal of the British on the Second Army front heralded a real threat that Hazebrouck, the township that had served as the base for the Alphabet Company since its arrival two years earlier, would be overrun. The company was ordered to pack its huge collection of stores and equipment — amounting to some 270 tonnes — and retreat west.

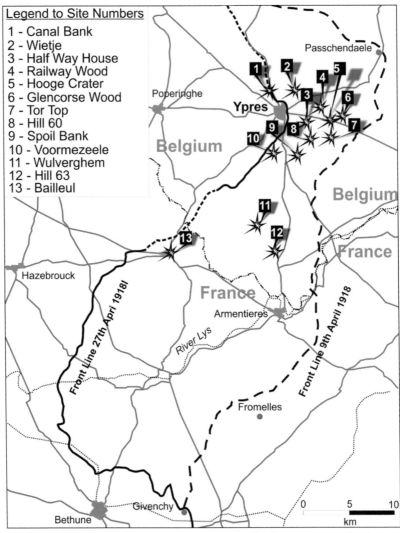

Legend to Site Numbers
1 - Canal Bank
2 - Wietje
3 - Half Way House
4 - Railway Wood
5 - Hooge Crater
6 - Glencorse Wood
7 - Tor Top
8 - Hill 60
9 - Spoil Bank
10 - Voormezeele
11 - Wulverghem
12 - Hill 63
13 - Bailleul

Map 26. The German spring offensive 1918: sites at which the Alphabet Company was forced to abandon its works and in some cases destroy its equipment to avoid salvage by the Germans.

The Alphabet Company's withdrawal from its headquarters at Hazebrouck was duly effected with neither panic nor casualties. While Hazebrouck did not fall into German hands, the precautionary principle prevailed. The company benefitted from its retirement to the tiny village of Assinghem-sur-l'Aa, 10 kilometres south-west of St Omer, where it quickly re-established its workshops in a paper mill. On 28 April Victor Morse wrote to his wife:

> Have just arrived at a pretty little village … am sent to a place by the powers that be, so that my men can be rested more effectively after their 2 years continuous period in the line … our strenuous time has been recognized, and the last few weeks have not by any means been the slowest, and we've still got plenty to do yet in the thick of things. Have had a lively time moving shop, getting a couple of hundred tons of it away the hun shelling his damnest … The taking of Kemmel hill by him had me busy getting some of my staff out, 'twas an observation post.[7]

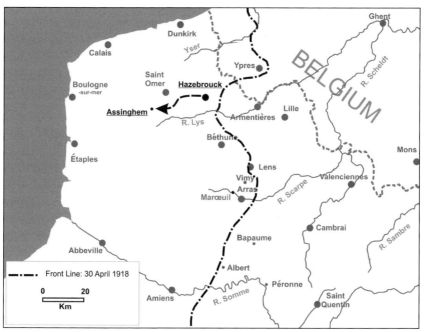

Map 27. The move to the tiny village of Assinghem-sur-L'Aa on the River Aa occurred during the last week of April 1918 in response to the German threat to Hazebrouck where the Alphabet Company's workshop was relocated.

The men made the most of the more relaxed atmosphere at Assinghem and of surroundings virtually unaffected by the war:

> At present I'm in my newly fitted up office neatly lined with scrim and paneling whilst from above, the waft and strains of the banjo, a couple of my Staff Sgts, practicing for a concert, from their sanctum up aloft, which with a few idle hours and a little loot in timber and scrim they've made it the envy of a first class householder. The last few days we've had it uncomfortably hot for trench trampling, so you can imagine what it's been like for the water, the lads in their spare time have made all sorts and conditions of boats and rafts, one a very fine little racing canoe which I indulge in early mornings.

> 'Tis wonderful to see the beneficial change already in the mess, most of whom have had little or no rest from the line for a couple of years. Yesterday ... 'twas a hot Sunday ... in the afternoon, the near-by C.C.S played us water polo which we won easily, the whole crowd of a couple of hundred lining the bank, many of which tried the water voluntary and otherwise ... an English Col. brought along and introduced me to an immaculately dressed French Col, me in nature's robes and panting after strenuously ducking my Sgt Major and polo playing.[8]

The unit played cricket and held water polo and rugby matches with the French while the officers escorted nurses from the nearly No. 2 Australian Casualty Clearing Station to divisional concerts and tea parties. The Matron of the clearing station was none other than Sister Constance Keys, who had sailed with the Mining Corps in the *Ulysses* in 1916. On one occasion, a party of nurses and officers attended a concert show given by the 49th Division, only to learn an hour after leaving that the venue had been 'knocked' (hit by German artillery). Men who had spent months in front-line positions were rotated through the camp and enjoyed a welcome respite from danger and endless routine.

In early June, ensconced in the verdant setting of his new headquarters in a peaceful village nestled beside a pleasant little river with summer in evidence all around, Victor Morse mused on the effect of his new surroundings and the welcome change in routine:

> 'Tis a glorious day with only the hum of aeroplanes and the crump of long distance shells to allow one to realize that the war is on. I'm in the same old groove here, to be amongst my own here, one with them in their sport and work, and am so proud acting as host to the many little

entertainments and visitations we've been able to undertake these last couple of weeks. I'm only too glad to find duty up the line and send my other officers. I've just realized 'tis my first week in France that has passed without actually being in the trenches ...[9]

During the spring and early summer of 1918 the German offensives had pushed the Allies to the limits of their defensive powers on the Western Front. Despite this, and although battered and bruised, the Allied forces not only prevailed, but drew strength from their success in withstanding the onslaught. As summer took hold across the front, the Allied forces had time to draw breath and prepare for their own assault, what was to be the last great push before the end. Like many units along the front, the men of the Alphabet Company also took time over the summer to enjoy the respite from the fighting before they were to be drawn into the next and final phase of their wartime commitment.

With the coming of summer along the British-held sector of the Western Front the ferocious German offensives appeared to stall and were replaced by a return to the old routine of desultory shelling, raking of machine-gun fire, sniping and raiding which re-established itself along the new line extending from the Somme to the considerably depleted Ypres salient. But by July 1918 there was a growing sense of optimism among the Allied troops at all levels — they had withstood the test and were growing stronger with every passing day. The great German offensive had dented the line but it had held and the eye of the storm was, for the time being, deflected elsewhere. During the first week in June, a massive battle was fought, but this was many kilometres to the south of the British sector. The opening of General Erich Ludendorff's offensive against the French on the Aisne front saw hostilities return to the already blood-soaked ridge north of the Aisne River between Soissons and Reims, the Chemin des Dames. The battering ram Erich Ludendorff had unleashed against the British between 22 March and 29 April was now hammering the French.

The offensive opened on 27 May and involved the German *Seventh* and part of the *First armies*. As was the case with the British, the relentless charge of the German forces in the opening days overwhelmed the opposing French Sixth, Fourth and Tenth armies, forcing a hasty retirement. By 30 May, 50,000 men and around 800 artillery pieces had been captured. Like the British before them, the French defenders now found themselves in a perilous situation. The Aisne River had been crossed and the city of Soissons lost. By 13 June the front line was pushed back almost 50 kilometres to Chateau Thierry on the Marne River. But, while the offensive had succeeded in achieving Ludendorff's aim of pulling French divisions back from the British front in Flanders, it had cost the German high command more than it could afford to lose. Around 170,000 of its officers and men had been lost. The price paid by the Germans in the offensive ended Erich Ludendorff's plan for a renewed assault against what he believed would now be a weakened British Army in Flanders.

Although wary of further attacks during June, the British forces had time to regroup and regain their composure as the Aisne offensive raged. Even as the Germans were unleashing their forces against the French, British supplies of men and ammunition in France had been replenished and were now regarded by the high command as 'entirely satisfactory'. During May, a vast number of American troops had arrived in France. The addition of eight American divisions (4th, 27th, 28th, 30th, 33rd, 35th, 80th and 82nd) brought the number of American troops in France to just over 650,000, some 221,000 more than the previous month. Although these forces were severely handicapped by their lack of battle experience, this injection of new blood and enthusiasm into the conflict could not be matched by the Germans.

During June the first tendrils of the global influenza epidemic also began to emerge on the Western Front. However the increasingly warm, dry days of April and May meant that, by June, the men were reasonably fit and healthy and, as illness took hold among the troops its effects were rarely fatal. This situation would change later in the year with the arrival of the colder weather and the intense, stressful weeks of the final battles.

By the beginning of July, the wave of German offensives across all fronts was almost spent. On 17 July the German tide reached its high mark in the Second Battle of the Marne and, the next day, it finally turned.[10] On 24 July, General Foch, the supreme Allied commander on the Western Front, wrote in a memorandum to his Allied commanders-in-chief: 'The moment has arrived to abandon the generally defensive attitude forced on us hitherto by numerical inferiority, and to pass to the offensive.'[11] This was the battle cry for what was to become the last great struggle of the war.

But back in the 'quiet' British sector, the scale of actions taking place were orders of magnitude smaller that the events embroiling the French. Despite this, in July, cracks began to appear in the German defences in front of the Australian Corps straddling the Somme River. It was during May, June and July that the Australian infantry both on the Somme and outside Hazebrouck became exceptionally proficient at what was known as 'peaceful penetration'. As the front lines re-established themselves following the German offensives in March and early April, the British and dominion divisions holding the new fronts were encouraged to conduct raids against their opposing fronts to take prisoners and gain information, keep alive the fighting spirit of the troops and inflict losses on the enemy. Unlike the old front lines, the new lines lay across ground that was relatively unscathed or which had recovered since earlier battles. Far from being desolate wasteland, spring had given no man's land in front of the Australian divisions a covering of long grass, broken occasionally by shell craters. Both the Germans and Australians pushed posts of men into forward positions along their fronts.

August arrived and with it came a flurry of activity behind the lines in the British Fourth Army sector, activity that heralded the beginning of the end of the war. It is interesting to note that the possibility of the war ending in 1918 was not seriously considered, at least by the British high command. In the Versailles Supreme War Council meeting in June, it was agreed that Woodrow Wilson should be asked to supply 100 American divisions, with the force organised by May 1919.[12] In late July, Sir Henry Wilson, Chief of the Imperial General Staff, prepared a policy which considered factors for achieving an Allied victory. The policy discussed the question of when victory could be accomplished. It proposed that it could be as early as July 1919 or as late as 1920.[13]

Following the conclusion of the German offensive against the French at the Marne River in mid-July, which ended through exhaustion rather than victory or defeat, General Foch continued to press his allies to renew the offensive against the Germans who were showing signs that they had overstretched their resources. Although still a formidable force, the Germans were now weakened and vulnerable. The stage was set for the final offensive. The Allies boasted 187 divisions on the Western Front against 206 German divisions, of which 106 were considered unfit for battle.[14]

On 28 July General Foch issued the formal order for an advance on the Amiens front. The aim was to relieve the German threat to the Paris to Amiens railway line, one of three important railway routes that provided the Allies the means to rapidly transfer troops to any part of the Western Front. The Paris–Amiens route was threatened by the salient formed by the German offensive in March which, in the French First Army sector to the south of the British Fourth Army, extended beyond Maroeuil and Montdidier on the Arve River. The proposed push was to be made by these two armies and the date for the advance was initially set for 10 August, later amended to 8 August, allowing the two armies less than 10 days to prepare.

As early as May, GHQ had drafted plans to use both its Commonwealth infantry corps, the Australian and Canadian, in a combined Anglo-French offensive extending south from the Ancre River. Both corps were still relatively 'fresh' having been spared the brunt of the German St Michael and St George offensives and both were regarded as consisting of 'shock' troops — highly skilled and battle-hardened soldiers eager to take up the fight. However plans for the British offensive were put on hold while the French struggled to stem the tide during the battles of the Aisne and Marne.

The planned advance would involve the three corps of infantry and one cavalry corps of Sir Henry Rawlinson's British Fourth Army and five infantry corps of General Eugène Debeney's French First Army. To ensure close cooperation, both armies were placed under the control of Field Marshal Sir Douglas Haig. Preparations for the advance included the transfer of the Canadian Corps from the British First Army to Amiens and the last of the Australian Divisions, the 1st, from the Hazebrouck area to join the Australian Corps. The five divisions arrived during the first week in August, bringing the number of divisions in the Fourth Army to 18, a total of 441,500 men.[15] Over 2000 artillery pieces were also transferred along with 534 tanks, including 72 of the lightweight 'whippet' tanks.

On the night of 30 July, III Corps (12th, 18th, 47th, 58th and American 33rd divisions), which held the left flank of the British Fourth Army sector, extended its front to the Somme River taking over the front previously held by the Australian 5th Division. The Australian division now occupied a support position south of the Somme River. The Australian Corps (Australian 1st, 2nd, 3rd, 4th and 5th divisions) sector therefore extended from the Somme River to the Amiens to Chaulnes railway line. From Amiens the railway passes through Villers-Bretonneux from where it angles away to the south-east, passing the villages of Marcelcave, Guillaucourt, Rosières and Chaulnes. The Canadian Corps (Canadian 1st, 2nd, 3rd, 4th and British 32nd divisions) was assigned the southern sector of the army front. Its front extended over 6800 metres from the Amiens–Chaulnes railway line on its northern boundary to the Amiens–Roye road on its south. The road formed the boundary between the British and French armies. The French XXXI Corps had pulled back part of its line allowing the Canadian Corps to take over its front north of the Amiens–Roye road. The road, like the railway, extends in a straight line from Amiens to Roye, angling slightly away from the alignment of the Amiens–Chaulnes railway line. The fronts of both the Australian and Canadian Corps thus widened as their divisions advanced east.

The Australian Corps front lay across the top of the plateau between the Somme and Arve rivers. Running down the middle of the corps front was the

Amiens–St Quentin road, a Roman road that, apart from a slight deviation here and there, runs in a straight line and crosses the Somme River at Brie. The ground was open and gently undulating with crops in the fields awaiting harvest. The plateau is populated by scattered villages and presented perfect terrain for the use of both tanks and cavalry.

In the first few days of August, as the various divisions moved towards their respective areas in readiness for the offensive, isolated withdrawals began to occur here and there along the German front line. A major Franco-American offensive had commenced in the Argonne region and the Germans were retreating from the Marne River. In the Fourth Army area, the towns of Albert and Dernancourt were relinquished by the Germans on 2 August. General Foch interpreted the withdrawals as a sign of weakness and urged the British to attack.

At 4.20 am on 8 August 1918, the eastward march of the British divisions on the Western Front commenced, a march that ultimately stopped with the end of the war. This date was famously described by Erich Ludendorff as 'the black day of the German Army in the history of this war'. The advances made by the Allied divisions on 8 August are now part of history and represented the first of many great advances that followed over the next three months. A wedge 10 kilometres deep was driven into the German *Eighteenth* and *Second armies* on the joint British Fourth and French First Army front that straddled the Somme River.

On 13 July General Birdwood paid a short-notice visit to Alphabet Company headquarters, returning on 29 August to present 13 medals to members of the unit. Victor Morse described the visit in a letter to his wife:

> It was the Coys day out. As far as regimental drill is concerned our men have not been together for a couple of years or more, the few shop hands and resting men only having an hours drill per week i.e. on Sunday mornings. This time we managed to bring in over 100 and the rehearsal early in the morning made me as pleased as punch. Well at 11 AM all was jake,[16] the salute given, the Coy formed in a hollow square, the recipients being in front and the ribbons presented, a very nice speech given by the Army Commander,[17] shop and billets inspected, men dismissed for the day and the party left at 12:30. The men did splendidly, our C.S.M. Moody being absolutely it.[18]

With the front becoming increasingly fluid in the days following 8 August, the British, Canadian and Australian tunnelling companies rapidly switched from the mundane routine of constructing support dugouts to the role of front-line scouts and explosive experts. This change in role was necessitated by the enormous and deadly problem of booby traps and delayed-action mines. Given their experience in handling and using explosives during the mining phase from late 1914 to mid-1917 when the front was bogged down in interminable trench warfare and the underground war between miners below no man's land was at its most ferocious, the tunnellers and their officers were prime candidates for dealing with the huge variety of booby traps and mines left by the retreating Germans as a means of both delaying and killing their pursuing enemy. The use of these devices was enormously varied and they were ingenious in their conception and execution. The tunnellers quickly became expert at finding and rendering safe many hundreds of tonnes of explosive with very little loss of life. It was usually the hapless infantry who suffered, although the lessons learned from their suffering were not wasted. Instead, every incident added to the knowledge base of the tunnellers and other bomb disposal squads from the Allied engineering units.

In early September, as his men followed on the heels of the advancing infantry and returned to sites hastily vacated in April during the German offensive, Victor Morse wrote of the fiendish nature of this style of war and the suspicion with which he and his men regarded any recaptured place that appeared in too ordered a state:

> Just at present I'm holding off one of my evacuated engine rooms, we've barred it up, he left it altogether too unusually clean & tidy, so we give it a few days for the hidden delay acid fuses to show up. After a few days an innocent looking house or chateau just simply disappears in smoke leaving a heap of brick and rubbish, the same with dugouts, or you'll walk in and the touching or treading on something very often one of the steps, does the trick.[19]

Due to the rapid advance of the British armies over new ground, new and updated geological maps had to be produced to assist with locating suitable sites for water supplies and dugouts. On 17 September, Lieutenant Loftus Hills was transferred to the office of the Inspector of Mines at GHQ, joining Lieutenant Colonel Edgeworth David. This brought the number of geologists at GHQ to a grand total of three. A month later, the geological contingent at GHQ was further increased with the temporary transfer of Lieutenant George Cook, MC, and Lieutenant Carl Honman of the 2nd and 3rd Australian tunnelling companies respectively.

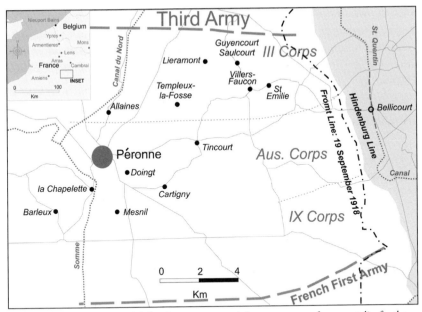

Map 28. Locations where the Alphabet Company assumed the management of water supplies for the Fourth Army from 25 September 1918, just prior to the assault on the Hindenburg Line.

At a meeting of the Geographical Society in May 1919, General Liddell explained the crucial importance of water supply at this point of the war:

> Water supply was possibly the most important … it would perhaps give you some idea of the problems which the geologists had to deal with when I instance the advance of the Third Army (to which I belong) from 21 August to November 11. We had to cross practically a desert area at the northern end about 12 miles, at the southern end about 16 miles broad in which there was practically no surface water. To take 300,000 men and 100,00 horses across an area like that is a feat, I think, which has seldom been equalled.[20]

On 25 September the Alphabet Company took over the installation and operation of water-pumping machinery for the Australian Corps, the central corps of the Fourth Army, on the southern flank of the Third Army. The company's primary task was to keep pace with the forward movement of the front lines and ensure the provision of water for men and horses. As the lines moved, which they did rapidly through August, September and October, water access points had to be quickly installed and erected at readily accessible locations. As it transpired, the access points were inevitably in heavily congested areas as men, horses and machines streamed eastward. Village hand-pumps were replaced with engine-driven pumps and numerous bottle and 'dixie' (army-issue mess tin) filling points established at each site. In rear areas deep bores were sunk and the groundwater air-lifted to waiting tanks by a truck-mounted air-compressor.

General Liddell also explained the importance of boring to locate water to the meeting of the Geographical Society in May 1919:

> Of course we depended largely on boring. During the advance, and in the face of the enemy, we made thirteen bores about 250-300 feet in depth; in some cases the boring plants were in line with the field guns, and the crews, unfortunately, in two cases were knocked out by shell fire.[21]

While Liddell was describing what occurred on his own army front, the situation was no different just south in the Fourth Army area. One of the larger bore supplies was outside the village of Driencourt, near Tincourt, which could yield water at a rate of 27,300 litres per hour. The water was diverted to an 18,000-gallon (81,000-litre) tank.

The day before the Alphabet company commenced its water supply operations with the Fourth Army east of Péronne, it began its relocation from Assinghem to Maroeuil, a satellite village on the northern outskirts of Arras. The village was located where broad and narrow gauge railways connected, and around it and its neighbouring village, Étrun, a support hub was established which included a large Royal Engineers supply depot, various camps and at least one field hospital, the Wessex Field Ambulance Hospital. A suitable location for the new workshops and headquarters was found in the buildings of an old laundry next to the Royal Engineers Depot. The first element to move from Assinghem was the machinery shop to ensure that its capacity to repair or refit its field sets suffered as little disruption as possible.

While up to his neck in managing his company's new role as water suppliers for the Australian Corps, which saw Victor Morse and his officers make daily round trips between the British sector's southern front lines and his headquarters at Assinghem, Morse also received his orders to relocate. They arrived on 29 September, as Morse later wrote:

> And what a week it has been ... we have been at it two nights running it was bed at 3 and away again at 5 and each day since has been very little different. Piper so reliable as ever, and poor old Close, it was his first real experience of us, when we got to it and I'll undertake to say he did more work in this one week than he's done for years.

Right in the middle of it came across orders to shift shop 40 miles away and I 'winced', tomorrow morning the wheels of this new shop will turn and do work in all depts. Without any one of the depts. being stopped for more than 24 hrs, during the last 4 days different depts. have been working at both places ... 'twill be a week before all our material is finally moved ... in two days early this week my car covered 340 miles.[22]

By 1 October the transfer of all the company's equipment and stores to its new home at Maroeuil was complete. Once established, the company not only supplied power and lighting to its own premises from its Maroeuil headquarters, but to those of the surrounding camps, depots and hospitals. The company also took control of pumping for the village's water supply. For the men staying at or visiting their headquarters, life was made as comfortable as possible as winter approached. Sleeping quarters were electrically lit and heated and a bath house had hot water supplied via the engine room cooling water tanks which could provide sufficient water for four showers to be run continuously.

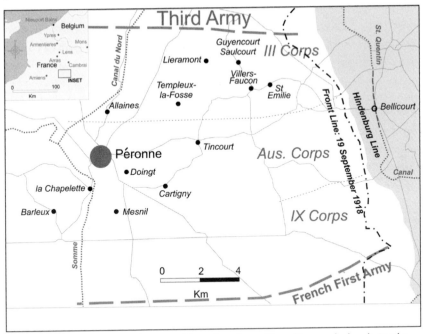

Map 29. The Alphabet Company's move to Maroeuil on the outskirts of Arras took place during the last week of September 1918. The company was compelled to move closer to the front following the collapse of the German lines after 8 August.

The start of October also saw the commencement of the German withdrawal on the British First Army front which extended from Lens in the north to Cambrai on its southern flank. The withdrawal of German forces towards the Belgian border began in earnest on 8 October 1918. By 18 October the front had been pushed back 20 kilometres east from Vimy Ridge and the town of Douai had been reclaimed. Once it had been liberated, the Alphabet Company was instructed to assist in resupplying water to the town as the Germans had destroyed the pumps at the water supply plant located in the village of Esquerchin, four kilometres to the west of Douai. However the pump station represented just a fraction of the damage wrought by the recently departed occupation force.

Plate 81. The Alphabet Company's collection of motorised transport at its Maroeuil headquarters (AWM 12778).

Plate 82. The unit's workshop at Maroeuil (AWM 12800).

On 22 October the company installed an electrically powered pump at the pump station. However, once pumping commenced, the men discovered that the 12-inch mains pipe into town had been broken in four places. The breaks were mended with a replacement pipe found at a depot in town, but this was just the start of what must have been a systematic recovery process enacted everywhere across the shattered front. The Germans had blown the bridge crossings over the Scarpe River and, in doing so, had also destroyed the water pipes which were fixed to the bridges that crossed the river. This was resolved by reconnecting the mains water pipe to the central town supply as the bridges were rebuilt. In spite of this there was still a large number of broken mains water pipes all through the town and valves had to be shut off or throttled back to secure an adequate flow of water. The Germans had also broken many of the water meters and pipes connected to house cellars which then filled with water. As the broken connections were turned off or plugged in the streets, the supply of water improved and the company could turn its attention to finding a long-term solution to the water supply problem. Civilians began returning to their homes, adding to the need for a sustainable solution.

Plate 83. Esquerchin pumping station (AWM H19513).

On the day his company established itself at Esquerchin and began resolving the water supply problem, Victor Morse described the destruction he had witnessed:

> … am very busy getting a town water supply going after the hun did his best with the big pumping station in the way of destruction before leaving a few days ago. Came through one very big town in the dark tonight absolutely deserted, the hun emptied the civilians back to his own country before leaving, destroying and looting furniture etc and as yet no other civilians allowed … finding the emergency built bridge over the river as at each stunt end one only found a chasm & broken stonework where a bridge had once been. And all over the place fires starting or burning in beautiful city mansions by his delay action incendiary bombs & our men vainly trying to get them under [control] …

> … yesterday many miles from here I came through just after the first trainload of civilians had arrived. What a pathetic sight, just what they could carry, generally a large bundle what they got away originally with, all classes … but practically no men & the few, very old, and what a cruel study in faces … the happy faces of a few who found their home more or less intact, and the sad and tearful faces of those who had arrived at their home site and found a smashed up heap of ruins.[23]

By 11 November, the day of the Armistice, the British had followed the retreating German armies back across the Belgian border on all fronts. The city of Valenciennes had fallen on 3 November on the First Army front. In the hours before the guns fell silent on the morning of the Armistice, the psychologically significant Belgian town of Mons, where the first British shot had been fired in anger four years earlier, was retaken, this time the armies simply passing through. As Morse wrote:

> The next hut is loud with a conglomeration of songs as they're turning in. I've just closed the mess evening with a toast to wives and sweethearts. The billet eased off its merry row a couple of hours ago.

> I've been very cold lately … and very few days has my car done less than 100 miles. We pulled up at our Hdq at 8 pm after a fast 3 hrs run and the first thing I was asked was for the details of the news. Well! I soon verified it & when I got to the mess, well all were off their head with the news.

It seems a pity that Germany won't feel the horrors of the war she commenced as the French here have but we must leave the past now to those above and we trust they'll make the terms 'white hot'.

I've got a fine spirited crowd and they wont like the necessary delay from now on … the day seems to have come at last …[24]

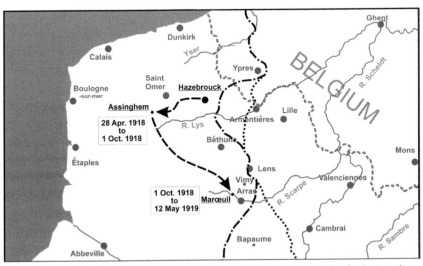

Map 30. Locations where the Alphabet Company assumed control over water supplies for the Australian Corps and later American II Corps during October 1918, following the assault on the Hindenburg Line.

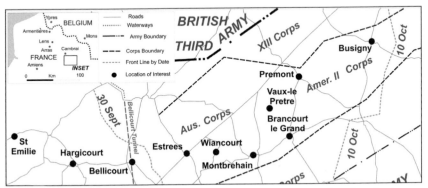

Map 31. Locations where the Alphabet Company assisted the First Army on its front from October to December 1918.

As they withdrew eastwards, the Germans systematically destroyed essential infrastructure in the towns and cities through which they passed, in an effort of slow the advance of the Allies. Once hostilities ended, the Allies occupied these places, finding almost all of them devoid of vital infrastructure. Consequently, following the Armistice, work continued unabated, particularly for those engineering units attached to the armies. This work now acquired a mounting sense of urgency, particularly the provision of essentials for human comfort in a deepening winter across the areas where hundreds of thousands of army personnel were still living, and which now saw the first trickles of returning civilians eager to see what had become of their houses and businesses in what had been a war zone. Power for warmth and lighting, and water for sanitation and cooking were the highest priorities. Re-establishing these services and opening and clearing the transport routes were key.

Plate 84. One of the three canal water supply crossings for water pipes from Neuville-sur-Escaut to the Denain reservoir constructed by the Alphabet Company during December 1918 (AWM H19508).

Prior to the Armistice, the Alphabet Company had commenced the task of providing water supplies to Esquerchin and the city of Douai. By the time of the Armistice, the need to re-establish water supplies had extended to Denain, 20 kilometres east of Douai. Here the water was sourced from a pumping station at Neuville-sur-Escaut, five kilometres from the town. Once at Denain, the water was pumped a further two kilometres to a reservoir.

Over the course of the route, three canal crossings had to be built, all the bridges having been destroyed by the Germans. These were duly completed and a bridge carried a steel pipe some 12 inches (30.5 centimetres) in diameter, which was sourced from wherever pipe could be found, including waste dumps at Valenciennes and Douai, and salvaged unused pipes from street mains in Douai.

Plate 85. The main Headquarters First Army power station in Valenciennes showing all the elements of a well-established engine room. Exhaust pipes can be seen exiting the back brick wall, fuel tanks for the generator engines are also along the back wall, water coolant pipes pass down and away from the engines and a large electric switchboard with isolation switches and gauges is evident on the left. The engine and generators appear to be Austin 24-kilowatt sets (AWM H19537).

However the electricity supply was a different matter. The Alphabet Company's role in providing power for the military and military support agencies continued to take priority. Consequently, the company was unable to supply electric power to the returning population of those townships which had been deep behind German lines for the previous four years and deprived of all creature comforts, enduring the most basic existence. Despite the onset of a harsh winter, the supply of electricity to homes and businesses would take some time to re-establish.

During the winter, in Valenciennes alone, the Alphabet Company installed 6860 metres of electric cabling from three engine rooms supplying power to 845 lights, the third largest lighting installation by the unit in the war. But, impressive though these statistics may seem, by the end of 1918 they meant nothing to the men who were working hard on such tasks. All that occupied their minds was the thought of going home.

CHAPTER 10

POST-APOCALYPSE

Celebrations at the cessation of hostilities on 11 November were fleeting as the company was forced to grapple with a host of new challenges. The first of these was the influenza epidemic — the Spanish Flu — which arrived just in time to claim the lives of many men who had survived the frenzy of killing that was the war.

Lieutenant John Royle succumbed to the epidemic on 15 November and was admitted to hospital at Wisques outside St Omer, just a few kilometres from the old company workshops and headquarters at Assinghem. His suffering was exacerbated by the tragic news that his brother, Raynes Royle, a flight lieutenant serving with the 7th Squadron, Royal Air Force, had been killed just three days before the Armistice. John Royle's influenza was so severe that he spent 16 days in hospital before being discharged, his illness perhaps prolonged by the emotional pain he must have experienced.

Plate 86. Sebourg Château, King George V's headquarters near Valenciennes, where the Alphabet Company installed electric lighting and fittings with 6 kilowatts of generating power between late November 1918 and early April 1919 (IWM Q9763).

At the same time, Victor Morse, who had a natural aversion to sick-beds, was forced to take to his own bed with illness, fearing the worst:

> I was queer for a couple of days we've had it pretty bad in the Coy and I've had some deaths inside 3 days of catching it so I sort of had the wind up for a day or so … however am O.K. now though shaky …[1]

The deaths to which he referred were those of Sappers No. 5055 John Brown and No. 3531A John Pierce who died on 6 and 17 November 1918 respectively. The epidemic went on to claim the lives of two more men from his unit, No. 1389 Sergeant Henry Piece on 2 December 1918 and finally, on 23 February 1919, No. 1167 Sapper Charles Sheriff.

In spite of the threat of the flu epidemic and the cold winter weather that added fuel to its fire, the main focus of the company's workload during the last two months of 1918 and which spilled over into early 1919 was improving the living conditions of senior staff and men from the British First Army headquarters in the city of Valenciennes. Following the headquarters' move from Auberchicourt to Valenciennes at the time of the Armistice, the company progressively extended an electricity supply via a network of five circuits to town offices, billets and town mains in the central business district of the city and another separate circuit around the château where the senior staff took up residence. So it was that, between the Armistice and when it withdrew for repatriation in April 1919, the company laid 6860 metres of cables, installed 845 lighting points and maintained six generating sets capable of supplying 101 kilowatts of power. The Valenciennes water supply pumping station had been partially destroyed by the retreating Germans and, in an effort to augment the city's water supply, the Alphabet Company and the First Army engineers decided to pump water from a pumping station at nearby Marly, which had not been damaged, to the Valenciennes reservoir. The motor which powered the water pump was replaced by a motor supplied and operated by the company from 6 December 1918 to 4 April 1919, when the motor was finally withdrawn.

This was not the first time the company had provided power to a British Army headquarters. Between July and early November, during the advance on General Sir William Birdwood's Fifth Army front, the company provided 20 kilowatts of generating power to Birdwood's army headquarters based in the château of the tiny village of Upen d'Aval outside St Omer.

Plate 87. Loading a 12-horsepower Frisco Standard motor for the Valenciennes water supply (NAA 10/32).

But the main focus of every soldier following the Armistice of 11 November was repatriation and every man wondered precisely when he would finally return home. The repatriation of millions of men, including many hundreds of thousands from dispersed and distant countries, from a devastated war zone over the winter months was a daunting logistical exercise. While the men on the ground recognised the logistical realities, after years away from home, feelings of impatience were natural and had to be quashed as far as possible.

Apart from distracting themselves with work, there were other courses open to men who wished to use their time to improve their professional civilian qualifications or learn new skills. Temporary positions in civilian businesses, generally in Britain, were opened to soldiers through the Non-Military Employment (NME) program. Educational courses were also offered covering a wide range of subjects. During December, two of the company's key junior officers, Lieutenant John Close and Lieutenant William Anderson, MC, took leave in England and also completed a period of NME. William Anderson joined John Lysaught & Sons at Lincoln and the Dalzell Steel Works at Motherwell in Scotland. John Close gained experience with British Thomson Houston Coy Ltd in London. William Anderson's NME leave was extended to the point where he did not return to the Alphabet Company but was repatriated directly to Australia, paying his own fare. John Close rejoined his unit in mid-February 1919.

On 4 December 1918, the Alphabet Company was mentioned in Sir Douglas Haig's Special Order of the Day and General Sir William Birdwood, who had formed a close association with Morse during the war, sent his own letter of congratulations.[2] Morse drafted a letter in response:

Dear General

I am very grateful to you for your letter of congratulation to us in connection with our mention in the c. – in – c's order for the day (Dec. 4). It indeed came as a surprise, and we feel it a grand finale to our efforts in this war. Our success has been due to the loyal and untiring support given me by all ranks at times when they seemed to be attempting the impossible. The Coy's work was little known outside, as during siege warfare and operations, the nature of the work; in mining, with our coy covering practically all systems along the front necessitating strict company secrecy as was also the case during pending big operations which became obvious to the men working for them in the weeks or months previously.

I have just returned from an inspection of our water boring work at the Independent Air Force aerodrome south of Nancy, so you see our scope of work at the one time has stretched from Nieuport at the coast to very nearly the Swiss border. At present we are keeping busy on general power, lighting, water and sewerage work and I am giving a refresher course and training to over 100 O.R's [soldiers] per month from the A.I.F. in practical internal combustion engines, electrical work, general plumbing and pipe laying. Though naturally all anxious to get back quickly I do not anticipate trouble, will keep too busy for that.

Your letter to me is one I'm extremely proud to have and will be a valuable 'war souvenir' to my family. The Coy's very best wishes to you Sir for Christmas and New Year.

Yours sincerely.

Christmas Day 1918 arrived with the knowledge that the war was over, but was marked by muted celebrations. The unit was still hard at work in the depths of another French winter and, as was the norm, its men were spread over a wide area: Maroeuil, Douai, Denain, Montigny, Lille, Roubaix and Valenciennes. The unit was also beginning to scatter further afield, with some men on leave or filling positions under the NME. Of those, several would not return to the unit. As Morse wrote to his wife:

> Our Xmas will be tame only Norfolk & myself of us, we got Hills down to join us and a couple of strangers passing through the empty (except for Vin blanc) hole we've invited in. I've been pushing work hard to get as many of the mens Xmas messes lit for Xmas around the country. It means such a lot to them. The infantry Divs, with their homes so near and them just camped waiting. We've had a good day, a splendid dinner, a goose. I've not been in the Xmas mood today. I just feel so homesick all day the feeling just won't leave me.[3]

On 8 January 1919, Victor Morse took leave in Britain, handing temporary command of the unit to Captain Percy Piper. Morse's thoughts were focused on arranging movement orders for his unit and, if possible, finding NME positions for men who wished to take the opportunity to gain valuable work experience in British or French industries. He spent several fruitless days at AIF Headquarters in London being passed from one section to another as he sought to gain some indication of when he might expect to get his men away. He returned to France none the wiser, although he had managed to arrange positions for some of his men in British firms while they waited.

On his return to the company on 11 February, having been away for a month, he discovered that his unit was on the brink of mutiny. Percy Piper related what had occurred while Morse had been away. Just a week after his departure, a game of football had been arranged with the 3rd Australian Tunnelling Company, then based in the city of Courtrai repairing destroyed and damaged bridges. At the time, the tunnelling company was embarking on a 'tools down' and 'go slow' program with its officers, born of the frustration of continuing to work while other units appeared to be relaxing and in the process of being demobilised. The discontent spread to the Alphabet Company and several men persuaded others in the unit to abandon their military routines. The few remaining men attempting to enforce order and discipline were left high and dry. It was only when Victor Morse returned that, out of respect for his authority, the men responded to his insistence on a return to the standards of behaviour he had always demanded of his unit. Even then, it took some effort to regain control. As Morse wrote later:

> I found the men had decided a few weeks ago not to have parades etc we considered necessary, though heaven knows they are few enough, roll

call each day, and one rifle inspection each week. They even told Piper that they could hand their rifles in so they wouldn't have to clean them … you can imagine my feelings and the job I had to pick things up when this lasted three weeks, especially as most of my holiday was spent in arranging better things for the crowd. I can tell you I felt particularly fed up … The CSM has just come along with a grin all over his face (wasn't there before the parade), 'All correct, Sir.' Old Moody the CSM is wonderfully conscientious, but was fearfully down, don't think he slept much last night.[4]

While the discontent was quelled, it would simmer as the men continued to wait and flared again on one final occasion in early April, resulting in the fire in the mess that destroyed much of the unit history and a number of Victor Morse's belongings. A few days after re-establishing control over his unit at Maroeuil, Morse received the long-awaited instruction to travel to Rouen for discussions on demobilisation arrangements. From that point, the process of repatriation began.

The first men selected for return to Australia were those over 45 years of age. This was followed by drafts of men separated by year of enlistment, with the 1914–15 men the next draft to go. The last draft comprised the 1917–18 men. The bulk of men in the unit had enlisted in 1916, and were scheduled to leave in April.

With the general demobilisation and repatriation across the armies, Victor Morse received the first of a number of letters from senior military commanders offering their best wishes. The Engineer-in-Chief of the BEF in France, Major General Gerard Heath, penned a letter dated 26 February 1919:[5]

My dear Morse,

I am sorry to hear you are leaving us so soon – but no doubt you will be glad to get back to your own country. I cannot let you leave without writing to thank you for the very large amount of helpful work you have put in for the British Armies in France. Your specialist knowledge of electrical and mechanical engineering was of great value more especially with regard to our Mining operations and electric light work, and boring operations at the front, and more recently in connection with the supply of water to the troops and reconstruction of water and electric light installations of the devastated towns.

Also I should very much like to thank the officers, N.C.O's and men of your company who have worked so zealously in the common cause. They laid themselves out to help all comers in every difficulty. In fact it almost became a habit to ask for the help of the Australian E. & M. M. & B. Company when results were wanted quickly.

Very best of luck to you for the future years.

Yrs. Sincerely.

G.M. Heath.
Major. General.
Eng. in Chief.

Prior to his appointment as senior engineer for all the British armies, General Heath had been Engineer-in-Chief, First Army, and was therefore the officer responsible for engineering work associated with such actions as the taking of Vimy Ridge in April 1917. The significant involvement of the Alphabet Company at Vimy Ridge thus raised the profile of both the company and its CO with the man who would oversee all the Commonwealth engineering units in France. His letter expressed gratitude for the two characteristics that Victor Morse strove to instil in his company, reliability and dependability. To have these confirmed by both the supreme commander in the Special Order of the Day on 4 December, and the general leading the specific branch of the service, was no doubt a source of considerable pride.

By the first week of March, some 200 men were awaiting demobilisation; four weeks later, the number had fallen to 100. As the date for his own departure from the front approached, Victor Morse took time to muse on the military authority's pragmatic approach to accounting for its equipment, which after years of use in the field was clearly well worn. He wrote:

The A.I.F. considering the sentiments of her fighting troops so much decide that an officer can retain his equipment belt, sword, strap, whistle, etc by paying 2/3^{rds} of their original value. In fact if they are not handed in the amount is deducted in your pay book. i.e. my belt 3½ years old and only fit for another 6 months can be retained by me paying ⅔ i.e. £1-2-0. My whistle same age 4 s, my revolver cleaning rod 3½ years old and lost 2½ years ago will be debited 10 s … isn't Australia commencing to look after the interests of her dear!!!! soldier officers.

As March turned to April and the work of the company across the cities and towns of north-eastern France began to wind down, the unit's hardware was disconnected and returned to the workshops in Maroeuil. The last 100 men awaiting their turn to leave were firmly focused on their return home and it was an impatient wait for many. The disastrous fire in the early hours of 6 April was a product of this impatience, as Victor Morse explained:

> ... during the night one or more of them under the influence of drink bringing the worst out got to the old game fire. They set fire to the mess just after midnight with the aid of petrol, the mess staff just got out in time, they weren't even able to save their own belongings and my luck, I've been using the place for getting our history records together, our cook who knew they were there managed to grab the Coy letters, the only thing saved, all my photo films from the beginning of the Coy burnt, only took them there a few days ago to sort out in connection with our history ...

Also lost were cash and valuables amounting to over £170. Given the trials of the previous three years, the fire almost broke Victor Morse's spirit as his anguished memories of the attempted robbery and fire at the Hazebrouck headquarters in November 1917 returned to haunt him. Perhaps that experience had strengthened him as he quickly recovered his resolve and, by the following day, three men had been placed under arrest.

However the loss of money and personal photographs represented the least of the consequences of the fire. Only Victor Morse, as the unit's CO, was equipped with the complete knowledge of the unit's working history, its achievements and the reasons it had served in its various locations. The prospect of having to rewrite the unit's history from memory with the aid of just a few remaining pages — although, by sheer good fortune, most of the maps and plans had not been burnt — was so daunting that Morse could not face this massive task until he had psychologically braced himself. It took several weeks for this psychological journey to reach its conclusion. By the end of April he had embarked on his monumental task, writing initially by hand and later transcribing these notes by typewriter, establishing a collection of reminiscences of all the major works in which the company had been engaged from the time of its arrival in France.

On 24 April, the longest serving officer in the unit after Victor Morse, the stalwart Lieutenant George Norfolk, MC, finally left with a contingent of 60 men and the remaining officers. Six more men followed three days later, leaving just 25 men under the command of Victor Morse. His impending departure from Maroeuil and France sparked a period of reflection, and Morse confided to his wife:

> I can surely say that during the war not more than a dozen people in the Army knew of its [the Alphabet Company's] existence as a whole, even our own men in the different sectors did not know of its range. At the Wings Way sector Clive [Morse's brother-in-law, Sergeant Clive Neill] was for some time. He'll have many a time wandered quietly as possible through that mining lateral which was crumped & cable smashed and wondered whether both sides of him would get blown in before return, and how many huns are listening to him. That gallery was mostly 4' 6' x 2' 3' I can tell you I was a tired individual after I'd finished that round, meeting my N.C.O.s at each sector along. The engine room at the left is at its 6th position all the others became destroyed as he located them. We lost a lot of men there during these last three years. You'll note the length of overland cable which has to be maintained, my it used to get shot up badly. The engine rooms were all secret. Rank was nothing re-entering them, many a high and mighty personage has come down to earth in his importance after daring to enter a Mining Engine Room or lateral. Very few folk did know us outside the mining world and higher authorities as our existence depended on our secrecy, it didn't take long for an engine room to disappear after he got its location. At The Bluff near Hill 60 he searched [for] us with the amour piercing shells until he got one inside, and that was caused by a chance shell cutting our exhaust engine pipe between Eng. & silencer and we not noticing it for some minutes. Other stations went the same way, at times with the staff.[6]

On Friday 9 May, the company's remaining work was handed over to the British 350th Electrical and Mechanical Company, Royal Engineers. On 13 May 1919 the cadre arrived at Le Havre with five lorries loaded with the last of the unit's machinery, the kits belonging to the remaining men and the contents of the unit's office. It was a far cry from three years earlier when they had arrived with over 10 times that amount. The small collection of men who remained with their CO comprised:

Company Sergeant Major: No. 388 Arnott Moody, DCM

Company Quartermaster Sergeant: No. 265 Hartley Sandow, MSM

Staff Sergeants: No. 4154 Charles Scorgie, MSM, No. 2348 Alan

Denton, DCM, and No. 831 Reginald Whitwell, MSM

Sergeants: No. 18715 Clive Neill, No. 705 Henry Somerset, MSM, and No. 379 Alfred Davies, MSM

Corporal: No. 1268 Raymond Ranger Stanley

Lance Corporals: No. 17 William Roberts, No. 3946 John Buckie and No. 739 Ian Wilson

Sappers: No. 3892 Arthur McPherson, No. 6100 Albert Dinger, No. 16947 Henry Ayres, No. 3349 Arthur Pearson, No. 7272 Harold Tapner, No. 1396 William Wake, No. 7833 Charles Fooks, No. 7541 Maurice Roseburg and No. 2821 James Thornton

Motor Drivers: No. 2346 Corporal Robert Cobcroft, No. 2493 Thomas McKell and No. 4044 Alfred Jinks.

Five days later, on 18 May 1919, these last remaining men of the Alphabet Company boarded a ship with the small amount of equipment they retained, and left France.

Once on English soil, Victor Morse resumed his chore of rewriting the unit history. It was to be a solitary task that would take him another month to complete. During that time he stayed with family friends at Forest Hill on the southern outskirts of London. After a supreme effort, the hand-typed version of the unit history was completed and, in mid-July, submitted to the former Inspector of Mines, Brigadier General Robert Harvey, at the War Office in Whitehall. In a note of thanks, General Harvey wrote that he felt sure no other electrical and mechanical company could have submitted such a record of works.

While Morse was musing over the contribution of his men to the war, others at a much higher level were likewise considering the aftermath of the war, albeit on a more globally significant scale. Following months of negotiation, the Treaty of Versailles was finally signed by the Allied powers and Germany on 28 June 1919. It was only then that the 'war to end all wars' officially ended. A celebration was in order and a Peace Day was planned for 19 July 1919. This day marked a massive celebration in all the Allied countries which had paid so dearly in their quest for peace. Of the almost nine million men and women mobilised from the countries that comprised the British Empire, just over two million had been wounded, over 900,000 had been killed or died of wounds and 191,000 had been reported missing or taken prisoner.

Plate 88. Peace Day parade crowd outside Buckingham Palace, 19 July 1919 (IWM Q28765).

Parades and celebrations were organised in affected countries across the globe. One of the biggest was in London. To the sound of tolling bells and cheers from a huge crowd which lined the streets from Battersea to Kensington Gardens, a parade of soldiers, sailors, airmen and servicewomen was led by Admiral Sir David Beatty, Sir Douglas Haig, Marshal Foch and General Pershing. Among the crowd was Victor Morse who had travelled from Forest Hill to experience the event. By that time most members of his unit had departed English shores, so he watched the parade alone. He related his impression of the event to his wife:

> Watching that long wonderful procession with all its representations and colours and flags went in very deep and I think as I stood there many of the past 'war sights' came vividly to my mind for the first time … the procession seemed to appear to me in a very serious mood and I realised for the first time that it was really over and a thing of the past.[7]

One of the most sombre scenes that must have struck a chord with him through all the colour of what should have been a joyous day, occurred after the passing of the troops. Then came a long procession of ordinary people, slowly filing past a temporary cenotaph outside Whitehall, leaving a pile of wreaths around its base. Made of wood and plaster, the cenotaph was designed by Sir Edwin Lutyens, who also designed the Memorial to the Missing at Thiepval and the Stone of Remembrance which features in large British military cemeteries across Flanders and northern France. Such was the impact and depth of feeling for the cenotaph as a public memorial to the dead that, within two weeks, the decision had been made to replace the structure with an identical, permanent memorial, which was unveiled by King George V on 11 November 1920. It still stands at Whitehall today.

Plate 89. Group of officers and a nurse during the return voyage to Australia in late1919, many displaying decoration ribbons on their tunic breast. The mustachioed Victor Morse is seated in the centre, middle row. The chevrons on the sleeves of several men are service chevrons, one for overseas active service and an additional one for each year served abroad (Victor Morse collection).

Following the festivities, plans were made for the remnants of the Alphabet Company to return home. In early August, Victor Morse was advised that he had been placed in charge of the hospital ship *Kanowna*, due to leave Southampton on 17 August, although its departure was eventually delayed for a week. During that time, Morse chanced on one of his former senior NCOs, Sergeant Hugh Thurlow, in the street. He successfully sought permission for Thurlow to join him on the voyage as a staff member. Thus the last of the

Alphabet Company to return to Australia were its CO and one of his most trusted, long-time senior NCOs.

The hospital ship finally left Southampton on 28 August 1919. Victor Morse was in charge of a contingent of 77 officers from a range of units, several of them majors like himself and one colonel, a chaplain. Of the almost 700 patients, over half were bedridden and many were amputees. During the voyage, Morse strove to lighten their suffering (or perhaps add to it, depending on one's perspective), giving a lecture on a subject close to his heart and vivid in his memory, entitled 'War Mining on the Western Front'.

The voyage proceeded smoothly across the hemispheres and Fremantle came into view on 15 October followed by Sydney nine days later, the ship pausing along the way to disembark men and patients in both Adelaide and Melbourne. The Alphabet Company, at least in the form of its stalwart CO, was finally home after a round trip of three years and 249 days.

All home? Not quite. One 'Alphabetical' stayed on as possibly one of the last Australians in France. Perhaps in response to the horror he had witnessed and his grief at the loss of so much life or for other reasons stemming from his experiences there, former No. 17 Lance Corporal William Roberts remained. Roberts had acted as Victor Morse's batman for a period and, at the time of his enlistment, had stated that he was married with a son. Whatever his reasons, in late 1919 he had discharged from the AIF in England and immediately applied to the Imperial War Graves Commission for a position as a gardener, tending newly established War Graves Commission cemeteries in France.[8] Once his application was approved he immediately commenced his new career, cutting all ties with his former life in Australia, although he remained in touch with the family of his former CO. In August 1937, a letter to the editor appeared in the *Sydney Morning Herald* from Morse's widow, Aileen, which revealed that William Roberts was still living in France, had married a French girl and was father to a 15-year-old daughter.

Between May 1916 and April 1918, the Alphabet Company, that little band of men led by an even smaller band of grossly overworked officers, was responsible for 590 installations involving power-generating sets, shallow-water-pumping sets, air-ventilation sets, soil-haulage sets and deep-water-bore pumping sets. The men also laid around 377,000 metres of heavy and light gauge electrical cabling combined, installed some 11,500 lighting points and provided a cumulative power supply across all the unit's power plants of 2070 kilowatts of electricity. Most of these installations occurred well within range of high explosive artillery and small arms fire. The men effectively powered the equivalent of a small town continuously through the war, alleviating the appalling living conditions of countless individuals while also enhancing the success of the pivotal Messines mines in June 1917. Added to this was the unit's role, directly or indirectly, in the obtaining and analysis of data from in excess of 1000 hand-drilled dugout exploration boreholes, totalling around 10,670 linear metres, which peppered the front and led to the construction of many of the dugouts that protected thousands of men from shot and shell on a daily basis.[9] The boring section of the unit, which was one of six water-boring sections working for the British armies, contributed proportionately to the approximately 500 deep water boreholes drilled by the boring sections to an average depth of 90 to 120 metres.[10] This output is staggering for a unit that started without even a name, let alone a defined role in the war.

With the end of the war, the passing of those who experienced that war, and the lapse of a century, it is time to reflect on the magnificent contribution of the little company of men who achieved so much. The honours awarded to the men of the Australian Electrical and Mechanical Mining and Boring Company — the Alphabet Company — is one yardstick for measuring the mettle of its members during the First World War.

Honour	Number Awarded
Member of the Order of the British Empire (MBE)	1
Distinguished Service Order (DSO)	1
Distinguished Conduct Medal (DCM)[+]	5
Military Cross (MC)	2
Military Medal (MM)	3
Meritorious Service Medal (MSM)[++]	15
Italian Bronze Medal for Military Valour	1
Mention in Despatches[+++]	7

+ Includes one bar
++ Includes one medal rejected by recipient
+++ Includes one man mentioned twice

Particular mention must be made of those individuals from the Alphabet Company who distinguished themselves in the war, rising through the ranks to gain a commission and who were also decorated for acts of gallantry or outstanding devotion to duty. Foremost among these men is Captain

Percival Charles Piper, DCM, who enlisted as a sapper with the original Australian Mining Corps. He won his DCM as a staff sergeant for sustained exceptional work leading up to the battles of Messines and Vimy Ridge in early 1917.

Of the men who left Australian shores with the Australian Mining Corps or reinforcing units and who went on to serve with the Alphabet Company or its predecessor, 15 are now listed on the Roll of Honour. Of these, 14 are interred in French and Belgian soil and one is buried in England.

However, accurate figures for the casualties incurred by the company on active service are not readily available as, ironically, that information was itself a casualty of the fire that destroyed much of the unit's war diary. The figures for a period of five months from January to June 1918 (April's data is missing) reveal that casualties were being incurred at a steady rate each month, ranging from five during January to 25 in March, the other months recording between 15 and 19. At full strength, when the unit totalled around 245 with a variable number of up to 90 men attached from British units, monthly casualties averaged 15 men, representing a monthly casualty rate of around 5%. Most will have been minor afflictions, including sickness, and these men would have quickly returned to the unit. Other casualties, however, were far more serious, resulting in their repatriation, as was the case with No. 5 Lance Sergeant Penleigh Boyd, who was gassed during the Third Battle of Ypres, and No. 1276 Sapper Albert Booth whose left knee was smashed by a bullet in September 1916. Booth's case was mentioned in one of Victor Morse's letters home. Others suffered serious wounds but managed to return to the unit after several months' convalescence, such as No. 229 Sapper John Parker, MSM, who was badly wounded in the right leg during the German offensive at Givenchy in early April 1918, rejoining his unit three months later. Clearly, like any other unit at the front, the Alphabet Company suffered its fair share of casualties. However it is remarkable that, given the many front-line locations at which the company served, and the length of time it served at those perilous places, only nine men were killed in action or died of wounds.

While most of the old soldiers returned to Australia and attempted to rebuild their lives, slowly adapting to the monotony of their civilian existence, others went on to became recognised leaders in their professions.

The first Tunnellers and Alphabeticals' Reunion Dinner was held on the second anniversary of the opening of the Battle of Messines on 7 June 1919.

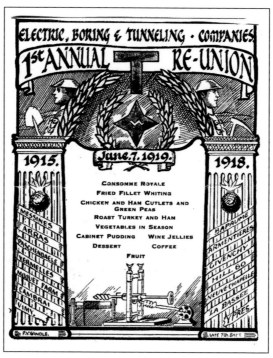

Plate 90 (left). The menu card from the first dinner bears a simplified depiction of the Wombat borer.

Plate 91 (right). An invitation to the 1941 Tunnellers and Alphabeticals' Reunion Dinner in Melbourne. A.K. Girling was No. 569 Sergeant Alexander Girling, formerly of the 2nd Australian Tunnelling Company and a Belgian Croix de Guerre winner. H.D. Hopkins was No. 6115 Sapper Harry Hopkins, formerly of the Alphabet Company (photos courtesy of Mr Ray Jacobs).

Edgeworth David returned to Australia in March 1919 with the rank of lieutenant colonel and resumed his academic career. As in so many other facets of his life, he had distinguished himself, having been awarded a DSO and been Mentioned in Despatches on two occasions. The following year he was created a Knight Commander of the Order of the British Empire (KBE). On 28 August 1934, at the age of 76, Sir Tannatt William Edgeworth David, KBE, DSO, FRS, MA, DSc, LLD, died in Sydney and was honoured with a state funeral.

While the war affected its participants in uniquely personal ways, it also bound them together in a way that has rarely been seen in Australia since. The war experience was such a wrench from their former existence that many men struggled to come to terms with the reality of life back in a civilian world, a world that was war fatigued and in which any remaining energy was spent in mourning the lost.

The special bond that formed between the men could not be translated into the wider Australian community. These were now men set apart from their non-combatant compatriots, whether they liked it or not. As was the case with many units that fought, an association of returned tunnellers was formed almost as soon as the men began arriving in Australia. As early as July 1919, even before many of the men had returned to Australian shores, the first of the Australian tunnellers' reunion dinners was organised.

A worldwide Tunneller's Old Comrades Association (TOCA) was established as a means for the tunnellers to maintain contact with one another across the globe. An Old Comrades Association was also formed in 1925 for the 985 tunnelling company officers who served in the war. Its formation was coordinated by Robert Stokes, DSO, OBE, MC, former Controller of Mines for the First Army, from his base in Kimberley, South Africa, where he was working for the diamond company De Beers. Bulletins were published regularly and mailed to the ex-officers spread across the globe.

In Australia, the TOCA held annual dinners on the Saturday evening closest to 7 June, the anniversary of the Battle of Messines. Meetings were held at the Imperial Services Club in Sydney. During the early days, arrangements for the Australian officers' association were made by Edgeworth David and John Royle, both with a close connection to the Alphabet Company.

A 'Tunnellers and Alphabeticals Association' was also formed for the non-commissioned ex-servicemen. Annual reunion meetings were organised, usually within each state. Most reunion dinners were held on the eve of the Anzac Day march when the men would congregate in their respective state capital cities. It was difficult for the Alphabet Company, which had consisted of such a small band of men from across Australia, to meet again in any great numbers. Regular reunions were held in the capital cities where there were sufficient numbers of men, chiefly Sydney and Melbourne. In Sydney in particular, Alphabet Company picnic reunions were held in February every year until the Second World War, on the Saturday closest to the anniversary of the Mining Corps' departure from Sydney in 1916. Likewise, those men from the tunnelling companies and the Alphabet Company resident in Sydney marched together in Anzac Day parades under the same banner and gathered afterwards for a reunion at Sargent's Café at 55 Market Street.

Plate 92. Men from the tunnelling and Alphabet companies marching together in the 1955 Anzac Day parade in Sydney (photo courtesy of Mr Tom Murphy).

The adjustment to a 'normal' way of life was as difficult for these men as it was for the remainder of the returned servicemen and women from the AIF. The silent, invasive condition that is today recognised as post-traumatic stress disorder was, in those days, neither understood nor acknowledged. The men arrived home, rejoiced in the reunion with their loved ones, and picked up their lives as best they could. But the years of extreme physical and mental stress and surges of adrenaline produced by the raw terror of war affected a very high proportion of men. Added to this were the countless memories of indescribable sights, smells and sounds, a sensory overload of a hellish experience that left its imprint as scars on their souls.

The wartime experience bound the men together and, in many ways, this bond was one of the few avenues of healing and coping with their memories that was available to them. For some, there would be no healing and, on their return home, they began a slow decline into a place of loneliness and separation that led ultimately to death at their own hand.

Soldier: 'Struth Bill! Tom didn't half cop it, did he?'

Plate 93. A cartoon by Hugh Thurlow attempting to make light of the reality of the situation in which men on the front found themselves — the possibility of having to scrape the remains of friends into bags for burial. Humour was a universal strategy for dealing with those brutal facts of life and experiences that survivors carried with them for the rest of their lives (AWM 3DRL/4059).

But their experiences on the Western Front made them part of a brotherhood that was indestructible, lasting the rest of their lives, whether they sought the company of their mates or not. The inevitable decline in the noble band of survivors began almost as soon as the wake of the last transport ships washed ashore in the ports around Australia and their ranks grew thinner with each passing year. The vicissitudes of civilian life, assisted no doubt in many cases by the ravages of their military service, gradually whittled away the numbers of the brotherhood. The ranks of the men had already thinned by the time the first of the official TOCA reunion dinners was being organised in Sydney in 1925.

Victor Morse was one of those who died prematurely. When he returned to his wife and three children in late 1919, his vitality had been eroded, the combined effect of his health breakdown at the end of 1916 through overwork and his gassing on active service. He took up a position working for the Tasmanian Hydro-electric Department before becoming Chief Assistant Electrical Engineer with the NSW Department of Public Works. Constitutionally weakened, he fell ill while on an inspection tour of the Murrumbidgee Irrigation Area and did not recover, dying on 26 January 1925. He was just 39. The death of one of his most trusted and long-serving officers, former Lieutenant George Norfolk, MC, followed just a few years later, on 28 October 1931, at the age of 59.

Perhaps one of the most tragic yet ironic post-war deaths was that of Arnott Moody, the former Company Sergeant Major and a DCM winner. Within months of his return to Australia, Arnott married. He went on to have two children, established Moody and Company, a successful electrical engineering business, became a leading member of the local community and was an active member of the Alphabeticals reunion committee in Sydney. One weekend in late November 1937, he travelled to his mother's house to work on a porch light. Perhaps as a result of complacency and the familiarity of his surroundings, he broke the golden rule of the electrical profession and did not check that the power was turned off before working on the wiring through the manhole. He was electrocuted and died, aged just 50.

War Memorial War Equipment

Victor Morse was immensely proud of the work of his unit during its time in France and he was passionate about conveying to his fellow Australians what his men had done. One of the best ways to do this was to display items of equipment they had used and describe how and where these were employed.

When Morse returned to England on leave in January 1919, one of the tasks he set himself was organising and gaining approval for the transportation of a selection of unit's salvaged equipment back to Australia, with the intention of displaying these as items of historical interest to the nation. He managed to elicit the support one of the most senior officers in the AIF, Lieutenant General Sir Cyril Brudenell White who, in a letter to the War Office, argued that the Australian government was entitled to that portion of the Alphabet Company's equipment brought out by the unit and not requisitioned from England. He also sought the donation of items deemed of historical interest or which might be useful for training purposes in Australia.

There followed a period of sorting through the unit's mass of stores held at its former workshops at Maroeuil, including a selection of captured German generators, pumps and fans. A number of items were selected as representative of the equipment the unit had used, then collated and packed into cases. The bulk of the unit's remaining stores and equipment were then to be handed back to the British military authorities. Victor Morse spent considerable time and effort justifying his selection of items to the Repatriation and Demobilisation Department at AIF Headquarters in London, where the Deputy Director was the Chief Engineer of the Australian Corps, Brigadier General Cecil Foott, who ultimately authorised the return of all the selected stores to Australia.

Over 20 cases of equipment returned aboard the transport ship HMT *Boorara* in July 1919 and were placed in storage at the Army Ordnance Stores in Sydney where they languished pending possible selection of items for a proposed War Memorial Museum. The Australian War Memorial Museum, established as a venue for the display of war relics of national significance, was first opened on 25 April 1922 in an annexe (now removed) of the Exhibition Building in Melbourne where it remained until 1925. It was then moved to the Exhibition Building in Prince Albert Park in Sydney. It was not until 1941 that the current, purpose-built Australian War Memorial was officially opened in Canberra and most of the artefacts transferred to the new space where they were subsequently supplemented by relics and items from other wars and conflicts in which Australians have been involved since that time.

However, by early 1921 the Australian military authorities had decided that there was no place or use for the equipment shipped back to Australia by the Alphabet Company and it was listed for sale. With outstanding prescience Victor Morse protested the proposed sale. Included were items unique in Australian and indeed British military history, such as the Wombat borer, which is mentioned in several official histories of the war, and in many front-line unit diaries. Likewise the portable Acme drilling units, used to determine the siting of many of the dugouts across the Western Front, particularly in the Ypres salient, were unique pieces of machinery. There was also equipment used at Givenchy, Messines Ridge and under Vimy Ridge. In the end, Victor Morse's protestations proved to no avail and, by the time the first iteration of the Australian War Memorial opened its doors to the Melbourne public, the Alphabet Company's Great War relics were not among those arranged in the glass cases. By then the opportunity for any of them to be seen or appreciated by the general public had been lost.

Adieu

The Alphabeticals who played their part in that nation-shaping war 100 years ago have now passed away. It has taken a century for the achievements of the men who served in the Alphabet Company to be documented in some way. It should be a source of enormous regret to this country that they died without being publicly afforded the same level of recognition as the better known Australian infantry units of that war. Theirs was a unique and extraordinary story and richly deserves to be told.

APPENDIX

THE ROLL OF THE AE&MM&B COMPANY

Died	Regimental No.	Rank	First	Second	Surname	RTA	Award
	371	Spr	Tom		Alderton	16-Jun-19	
		Lt	William	Thomas	Anderson	1-Nov-19	MC
	3553	L/Cpl	Frederick	William	Atkinson	11-May-19	
	3554	Spr	Richard	Ralph	Atkinson	16-Jun-19	
	16947	Spr	Henry	James	Ayres	6-Jul-19	
	1404	Spr	Francis		Bailey	5-Apr-19	
†	804	Spr	Percy	Clarence	Baker	DOW (2-Jun-17)	
	3567	Spr	George	Henry	Baldock	27-Aug-17	
	41	Spr	Richard	Patrick	Baillie	31-Mar-19	
	2339	Spr	John	Irwin	Balls	15 Aug 1918*	
	541	Spr	Arthur		Barnes	8-Jan-19	
	5344	Spr	Precival	Gregory	Barry	16-Jun-19	
	345	Sgt	Richard		Bartlett	27-Apr-19	
	16953	Spr	Thomas	Henry	Beardsell	9-Aug-19	
	3961	Spr	Walter		Benson	20-May-19	
†	2317	Spr	Frank		Bidulph	DOD (17-Jul-17)	
	1217	St. Sgt.	James	Washington	Binney	11-May-19	MiD
	2457	Pte	Charles	Gordon	Binney	21-Mar-19	
	6101	Spr	Clarence	Herbert	Bird	19-Oct-17	
	4206	Sgt	Leslie		Blair	31-Mar-19	
	3944	Spr	William	James	Bloxom	11-May-19	
	5051	Spr	Cyril	Edward	Bomford	11-May-19	
	3526	L/Cpl	Charles	Edward	Booth	11-May-19	
	1342	L/Cpl	John	Patrick	Bourke	11-May-19	
	5	L/Sgt	Theodore	Penleigh	Boyd	21-Mar-18	
	16782	Spr	Neil		Boyle	1-Aug-19	
	7825	L/Cpl	Clifford	Ernest	Braybon	22-Sep-19	
	1410	L/Cpl	Edward		Breadman	4-Jul-19	
	5077	Spr	Edward		Brennan	11-May-19	
	3812	2 Cpl	Sydney	Hall	Brown	11-May-19	
	4284	L Cpl	Donald		Brown	25 Aug 1919*	
	3304	Cpl	Hugh	Phillip	Brown	8-Oct-19	MiD

Died	Regimental No.	Rank	First	Second	Surname	RTA	Award
†	5055	Spr	Walter	John	Browne	DOD (6-Nov-18)	
	1343	Spr	George	Stuart	Bruce	11-May-19	
	3946	L Cpl	John	Francis	Buckie	4-Jul-19	
	368	Spr	Harold		Buckingham	15-May-19	
	56	Spr	Harry	William	Bugg	12-Jul-19	
	806	Spr	Edward		Burns	12-Jul-19	
	4291	L/Cpl	Ethelbert	Stephen	Bushell	1-Jun-19	
	5500	Spr	William	George	Byrne	16-Jun-19	
	375	Spr	William	John	Cairns	16-Jun-19	MSM
	374	Spr	Charles	Arthur	Calf	5-Apr-19	
	966	Spr	Alexander		Carlton	1-Jun-19	
	2413	Spr	Henry	Herbert	Carpenter	16-Jun-19	
	3576	Spr	James	Gregory	Chessell	24-Jan-19	
	5123	Spr	Pierre	Eric	Chrissen	11-May-19	
	7250	Spr	Henry	Ferdinand	Clarke	3-Jul-19	
†	3943	Spr	William	Edward	Clarke	KIA (14-Aug-16)	
		Lt	John	Campbell	Close	1-Jul-19	
	2346	Dvr	Robert	Cecil	Cobcroft	6-Jul-19	
	810	Spr	Alexander	John	Collins	10-Dec-18	
	7531	Spr	Eric	Edward	Collins	16-Jun-19	
	4301	L/Cpl	Rupert	Napier	Coombes	21-Mar-19	
	1447	Spr	Walter	James	Court	1-Jun-19	
	1347	Spr	Frederick	James	Cram	20-Jul-19	
	3596A	Spr	George	Newton	Crock	16-Jun-19	
	376	Spr	John		Crosby	16-Jun-19	
	1348	Spr	Walter	Charles	Cullen	17-May-19	
	7163	Spr	John		Currie	25-Sep-19	
	1291	CSM	William	Henry	Curtis	16-Jun-19	
	5316	Spr	James		Daly	10-Dec-18	
	379	Sgt	Alfred	Douglas	Davies	22-Nov-19	MSM
	413	Spr	William	John	Davies	16-Jun-19	
	5721	Pte	Henry		Davis	20-May-19	
	2348	St. Sgt.	Alan	Ede	Denton	6-Jul-19	DCM
	4753	Cpl	Gordon	Thomas	Dewhurst	20-Jul-19	
	6100	Spr	Albert	Vincent	Dinger	4-Jul-19	
	4209	Sgt	Edward	Gilmore	Dodd	6-Oct-19	
	7252	Spr	Alexander	Wilkie	Donaldson	19-Aug-19	
	7102	Cpl	Harold		Dowling	16-Jun-19	
	4035	Spr	Thomas		Dowling	4-Dec-18	
	1352	Spr	Hubert	Sheppard	Down	16-Jun-19	
	4754	Sgt	Vere		Downie	4-Jan-20	

Died	Regimental No.	Rank	First	Second	Surname	RTA	Award
	10	Cpl	Thomas	Francis	Doyle	8-Aug-18	
	4034	Spr	Robert	Seth	Duvall	22-Sep-19	
	4897	Spr	W illiam	George	Etherington	16-Jun-19	
	15310	Spr	Henry		Fairweather	16-Jun-19	
	1354	Spr	George	William	Fawkner	2-Mar-19	
	2768	Spr	Alexander	William	Ferguson	14-May-20	
	2477	Spr	William	Joshua	Ferguson	29-Sep-19	
	756	Spr	Thomas		Fewtrell	21-Apr-18	
	7106	Spr	Sydney	Charles	Fisher	28-Feb-19	
†	2350	Spr	William	Hanlon	Fisher	DAI (18-May-17)	
	2476	Spr	Leslie	Frederick	Fitterer	26-Dec-19	
	3599	Pte	William	Arthur	Fletcher	12-Jun-19	
	7833	Spr	Charles	Philip	Fooks	1-Jan-19	
	11	Cpl	George		Forbes	23-Mar-19	
	2825	Spr	John	Edward	Ford	12-May-18	
	7834	Spr	Arthur		Forest	3 Jul 1919*	
	2351	Spr	James	Joseph	Forrester	21-Mar-19	
	7402	Spr	Roy	Alton	Forsyth	5-Apr-19	
	108	Spr	Harry		Foulkes	17-Mar-19	
	1356	Spr	James		Franklin	8-Apr-18	
	1357	Spr	Walter	Andrew	Fraser	18-Jul-19	
	380	Spr	Ernest	Barrett	Fry	16-Jun-19	
	3399	Spr	Robin	Gordon	Gale	16-Jun-19	
	4757	Spr	William		Gannon	16-Jun-19	
	7253	Spr	David		Gardner	19-Aug-19	
	6112	Spr	Fred		Gaydon	1-Apr-19	
	1358	Spr	Charles	Edward	Gilbert	1-Jul-19	
	567	Pte	John	Francis	Gilbert	13-Feb-17	
	199	Pte	Arthur	Sydney	Giles	17 Oct 1919*	
	2324	Cpl	Frank	Taylor	Gooden	11-May-19	
	7255	Spr	John		Graham	29-Aug-18	
	382	L Cpl	Richard		Grieve	10-Feb-20	MM
	6085	Spr	Charles	Culbert	Grieves	26-Dec-18	
	383	Spr	Charles		Groves	21-Jun-19	
†	1023	Pte	Abraham		Haley	DOD (19-Nov-16)	
	2357	Spr	Frederick	Charles	Halkyard	8-Jul-19	
	15869	Spr	Henry	Norman	Hall	21-Mar-19	
†	2664	Cpl	John	Bertie	Hambidge	KIA (14-Aug-16)	
	784	Spr	William		Hanlon	31-Oct-17	
	1361	Spr	James	Henry	Harvey	21-Dec-17	
†	1026	Cpl	Frank		Hawtin	DOW (1-Jun-17)	IMB
	1245	Pte	Herbert	Leslie	Henery	16-Jun-19	

Died	Regimental No.	Rank	First	Second	Surname	RTA	Award
	16662	Spr	Robert	Patrick	Hennessy	16-Jun-19	
	7669	Spr	William		Herd	1 Oct 1917*	
	1260	Spr	Thomas	Henry	Hillman	11-May-19	
		Lt	Loftus		Hills	3-Mar-19	MBE
	8150	Spr	Andrew		Hobbs	15 Apr 1919*	
†	5144	Cpl	Cyril	Freeman	Hobbs	KIA (9-May-18)	MSM
†	4356	Spr	James	John	Hood	KIA (21-Aug-17)	MM
	6115	Spr	Harry	David	Hopkins	22-Sep-19	
	4255	Spr	George	Henry	Hopkins	5-Nov-17	
	4357	Spr	Frederick	Sydney	Hopkins	16-Jul-19	
	383	Spr	John	McGeachie	Hotchkis	21-Jul-17	
	2818	Spr	Leslie	James	Hughes	25 Oct 1919*	
	5070	Spr	William	Kight	Hunt	11-May-19	
		Capt	Stanley	Burrell	Hunter	10-Mar-18	MiD
	3308	Pte	Walter	Edward	Hurst	21-Dec-17	
	564	Spr	Sydney	Arthus	Hyde	4-Jul-19	
	8037	Spr	Cyril	Gavan	Hylton	5-Mar-19	
	4362	Spr	Harry		Ibberson	5-Nov-17	
	1040	Spr	Vivian	Harold	James	16-Jun-19	MSM
	5112	Spr	Percival	Marcus	James	1-Jun-19	
	2353	Spr	George	Henry	James	11-May-19	
	7839	Spr	Gordon	William	James	5-May-19	
	4044	Spr	Alfred	Clarence	Jinks	23-Jul-19	
	2327	Pte	James		John	31-Mar-19	
	8122	2/Cpl	Francis	Joseph	Jones	6-Sep-19	
	1277	Spr	Patrick	Joseph	Kiely	2-Feb-18	
	1365	Spr	Douglas	Barry	Kilburn	11-May-19	
	821	Spr	Arthur	Edward	King	16-Jun-19	
	8203	Spr	Henry		Knight	16-Jun-19	
	1366	Spr	James		Knox	5-Mar-19	
	385	Spr	Lawford	Howard	Leach	22-Jul-19	
	623	Spr	Robert	William	Lee	31-Jan-19	
	1367	Spr	Reginald		Leslie	22-Sep-19	
	2388	Spr	Thomas	Louis	Leverman	3-May-19	
	3635	Spr	William	John	Lithgow	16-Jun-19	
	16796	Spr	James	Lewis	Little	25-Mar-19	
	848	Spr	James	Alfred	Lockrey	9-Dec-18	
		Lt	William	Hull	Logie	26-Sep-17	
	1436	Pte	Frank	Albert	Long	8 May 1919*	
	1422	2/Cpl	Joseph	George	Lord	7-Feb-19	
	1371	Spr	John	Alexander	MacGregor	31-Mar-19	
	1423	Spr	William	Edwin	Maddison	16-Jun-19	

Died	Regimental No.	Rank	First	Second	Surname	RTA	Award
	6715	Spr	Fred		Marriott	11-May-19	
	4212	Sgt	Hubert	Henry	Marsh	30-Apr-19	MM
†	840	Spr	Alfred	Henry	Marshall	DOD (27-Aug-16)	
	176	Spr	Harry		Maxfield	23-Jun-19	MSM
	5779	Spr	Henry		Maxwell	6-Sep-19	
	3529A	Spr	Arthur		McCullum	15-Jan-19	
	3532	Spr	James		McLean	25-Sep-19	
	2394	Spr	Alexander		McDonald	16-Jan-19	
	641	Spr	Duncan		McDougall	21-Jul-17	
	5586	Spr	George	Aitcheson	McFadyen	9-Feb-19	
	7263	Spr	Albury	George	McFarlane	22-Nov-19	
	2493	Dvr	Thomas	Edward	McKell	6-Jul-19	
	2424	Spr	Bernard		McManus	16-Jun-19	
	1427	Spr	William		McMurray	11-May-19	
	1097	Spr	Charles	Arthur	McParlin	8-Aug-18	
	3892	Spr	Arthur		McPherson	6-Jul-19	
	2393	Spr	John	McClure	McPherson	1-Jun-19	
	343	Spr	Phillip	John	McShane	20-Dec-17	
	1087	L/Cpl	William	Woodger	Meldrum	1-Jul-19	
	4172	Spr	Milfred	Leslie	Merchant	8-Oct-19	
	850	Spr	William	John	Merriel	16-Mar-18	
	370	Sgt	William	Harrison	Millar	22-Aug-19	MSM
	16789	Spr	Robert	McMurtrie	Mitchell	1-Aug-19	
	18178	Dvr	Kenneth	Dudley	Moffat	7-Jul-19	
	3603A	Spr	Joseph		Monkhouse	1-Feb-18	
	3602A	Spr	Robert		Monkhouse	6-Sep-19	
	1374	Spr	Hector	Joseph	Mood	6-May-19	
	388	CSM	Arnott	Victor	Moody	6-Jul-19	DCM
	24	Spr	Benjamin		Moore	6-Sep-19	
	2425	L/Cpl	Albert	Edward	Moorhouse	16-Jun-19	
	3890	S/Sgt	David		Morgan	30-Apr-19	
	1376	L/Cpl	Charles		Morris	8-Sep-19	
		Major	Richard	Victor	Morse	28-Oct-19	DSO, MiD
	5580	Spr	Patrick	Joseph	Murphy	1-May-19	
	8125	Spr	William	Henry	Murphy	16-Jun-19	
	843	Spr	Charles	Arnauld	Murray	11-Jan-18	
	135	Spr	Alexander		Myhill	27-Jul-17	
	1306	Cpl	Jack		Nancarrow	5-Mar-19	DCM & bar, MiD
	2817	L/Cpl	William		Napier	11-May-19	
	6859	Spr	George	William	Napier	16-Jun-19	

Died	Regimental No.	Rank	First	Second	Surname	RTA	Award
	4425	Spr	William	Percival	Nasmith	16-Jun-19	MiD
	1302	Spr	Reginald		Naughton	21-Jun-19	
	4257	Spr	Thomas	William	Northcote	11-May-19	
	2488	Spr	Walter	John	Northcote	23-Mar-19	
	18715	Sgt	Clive	Lander	Neill	6-Jul-19	
	3410	Cpl	Edward		Newton	5-Apr-19	
	4430	Spr	Alfred		Nicholson	8-Aug-18	
	823	Spr	Roy	Charles	Nilsson	7-Jun-18	
		Lt	George	William	Norfolk	16-Jun-19	MC
	4257	Spr	Thomas	William	Northcote	11-May-19	
	2468	Spr	Walter	John	Northcote	25-Mar-19	
	824	Spr	Claude	Cecil	Nunn	21-Jun-19	
	5012	Cpl	Josiah	Charles	Oates	1-Jun-19	
	395	Spr	Arthur		Olsen	23-Sep-19	
	17005	Spr	Alexander	Charles	Olsen	16-Jun-19	
	4908	Spr	William	Herbert	Osborn	11-Jan-18	
	1378	Spr	Frank		Owen	25-Mar-19	
	1257	2 Cpl	Frederick	Lindsay	Page	6-Sep-19	MSM
	3666	Spr	James	Gordon	Page	28-Mar-19	
	229	Spr	John	Gillon	Parker	2-Feb-20	MSM
	4781	Spr	William		Parsons	21-Jan-19	
	7244	Spr	William		Patrick	26-Jun-19	
	3349	Spr	Arthur	Godfrey	Pearson	21-Jun-19	
	5803	Spr	Henry	William	Pearson	11-May-19	
	4782	Spr	Cecil	James	Peart	16-Jun-19	
	2359	Spr	Frank		Peet	11-May-19	
	6770	Spr	Frederick	Norman	Pengelly	23-Mar-19	
	48	Spr	Harold	William	Perkins	23 Jul 1919*	
	7064	Spr	Alfred	William	Petherick	10-Apr-19	
	5600	Spr	Rubble	Whitford	Phillipps	16-Jun-19	
†	3531A	Spr	John	Patrick	Pierce	DOD (17-Nov-18)	
		Capt	Percival	Charles	Piper	23-Jun-19	DCM
	2513	Spr	William	Henry	Pitt	27-May-19	
	1379	Spr	George		Porteous	3-Mar-19	
	1385	Spr	Moorcroft	Rickards	Pugh	11-May-19	
	1383	Cpl	Albert		Pumfrey	25-Oct-19	
†	1386	Sgt	Harrie	Osborne	Quince	DOD (2-Dec-18)	
	4453	L/Cpl	Arthur	George	Quinn	15-Feb-18	
†	3807	Spr	Henry		Ralph	DOW (29-Nov-17)	
	1268	2 Cpl	Raymond	Edward	Ranger	6-Jul-19	
	54496	Pte	Robert	Herbert	Rankine	6-Sep-19	
	17007	Spr	Henry	Alfred	Read	12-Mar-20	

Died	Regimental No.	Rank	First	Second	Surname	RTA	Award
	3669	Spr	Alfred		Rees	28-Mar-19	
	248	2/Cpl	Lewis	Beaton	Reid	8-Nov-18	
	7851	Pte	Arthur	Victor	Riches	22-Sep-19	
	1140	Spr	Henry		Ricketts	1-Jun-19	
	7130	Spr	John	Philip	Ridgway	16-Jun-19	
†	2462	Spr	Earl		Riley	KIA (16-Jul-16)	
	17	L/Cpl	William	Clement	Roberts	Remained in France	
	793	Spr	Allan		Robertson	25-Nov-17	
	1256	Spr	Ernest	Raymond	Robinson	8-Aug-16	
	5736	Spr	Harry		Robinson	23-Sep-19	
	7270	Spr	Harry		Robinson	16-Jun-19	
	1439	Spr	Arthur	Percival	Roe	6-Oct-19	
	7158	Spr	Richard	James	Rogers	18-Jul-19	
	7541	Spr	Maurice		Roseberg	25-Sep-19	
	16792	Spr	John	Lawson	Rossini	1-Aug-19	
	1440	Spr	Maurice	Kenny	Royal	7-Feb-19	
		Lt	John	Mcdiarmid	Royle	25-Mar-19	MiD
	20391	Spr	George		Russell	6-Jul-19	
	265	Spr	Hartley	Reynolds	Sandow	6-Jul-19	MSM
	3684	Spr	James	Francis	Savage	28-Mar-19	
	4154	S/Sgt	Charles	Christie	Scorgie	8-Jul-19	MSM
	469	Spr	Roy		Shaw	16-Jun-19	
†	1167	Spr	Charles	MacKern	Sheriff	DOD (23-Feb-19)	
	3806	Spr	Thomas	Dales	Simpson	16-Jun-19	
	1261	S/Sgt	Alexander		Sinclair	1 Sept 1919*	MSM
	3678	Pte	Cyril	William	Smith	16-Jun-19	
	1389	Spr	John		Smith	11-May-19	
	281	L/Cpl	John	Patrick	Smith	16-Jun-19	
	3864	Spr	Richard	Percival	Smith	16-Jun-19	
	392 (6)	Spr	William	Lewis	Smyth	4-May-17	
	705	Sgt	Henry	Charles	Somerset	18-Jul-19	MSM
	290	Spr	Walter		Steadman	31-Mar-19	
	7013	Spr	Walter	John	Stevens	16-Jun-19	
	1390	Spr	Robert		Stirrat	9-Aug-19	
	3380	Spr	James		Strubie	31-Jan-18	
†	3682	Spr	John	Francis	Summers	KIA (23-Sept-17)	
	1382	Spr	Joseph	Renshaw	Swindon	11-May-19	
	295	Spr	James	St Lawrence	Tacey	8-Nov-18	
	7272	Spr	Harold	James	Tapner	3-Jul-19	
	7712	Spr	Clyde	William	Taylor	16-Jun-19	
	7862	Spr	Jack	Raymond	Taylor	13-Jul-19	
	4483	Spr	James	Murell	Taylor	17-Jun-18	

Died	Regimental No.	Rank	First	Second	Surname	RTA	Award
	2762	Pte	William		Taylor	16-Jun-19	
	4792	Spr	William	Henry	Taylor	21-Mar-19	
	4492	Spr	Frederick	John	Teale	7 Sept 1919*	
	7542	Spr	Phillip		Tempest	16-Jun-19	
†	3961	Spr	Victor	John	Thompson	KIA (18-Dec-17)	
	2821	Spr	James	Edmund	Thornton	21-May-19	
	1431	Sgt	Hugh	Clopton	Thurlow	28-Aug-19	MSM+
	7138	Spr	Frank	Charles	Towill	16-Jun-19	
	401	Spr	William	Charles	Turk	11-May-19	
	861	Cpl	Ernest		Turner	9-Feb-19	
	5090	Spr	Charles		Valentine	11-May-19	
	1264	Spr	George	Oliver	Venteman	6-Jul-19	
	2646	Spr	David		Vickery	11-May-19	
	1287	Spr	Harlod	Sidney	Violetta	1-Apr-19	
	1396	Spr	William	Henry	Wake	6-Jul-19	
	2367	St. Sgt.	Charles	Clemson	Walker	24 Aug 1919*	MSM
	3537	Sgt	Wallace	Allan	Warburton	18-Nov-19	
	3610	Spr	Henry	John	Ware	9-Aug-19	
	3539	Spr	Norman	Douglas	Watt	3-Mar-19	
	319	S/Sgt	Frederick	Arthur	Weeks	20-Feb-20	
	3699	Pte	William	Henry	Wehlan	23-Sep-19	
	1298	2/Cpl	Douglas		Wellwood	3-Sep-19	
	4504	Spr	Frederick	William	Whitbourn	1-Jun-19	
	831	St. Sgt.	Fred	Ewen	Whitwell	6-Jul-19	MSM
	832	L/Cpl	Reginald		Whitworth	3-Sep-19	
†	4509	L Cpl	Arthur	Thomas	Wigzell	DOW (8-Mar-18)	
	3700	Spr	Frederick	James	Williams	11-May-19	
	862	Spr	John	Charles	Williams	16-Jun-19	
	8134	Spr	Eric	Walter	Williams	3-Sep-19	
	1307	Spr	Arthur		Williamson	23-Jan-19	
	1259	Spr	Henry	McDonald	Wilson	27-Apr-19	
	739	L/Cpl	Ian	McAlister	Wilson	17-Apr-20	
	15443	Spr	John		Wood	15-Nov-19	
	833	Spr	Francis	Henry	Woodriff	2-Dec-19	
	1262	Spr	Lionel	Geoffrey	Woolf	15-Nov-19	
	7261	Spr	John	Leslie	Woolnough	16-Jun-19	
	1400	2/Cpl	John		Yarroll	18 Mar 1919*	

Possible and/or Transient Connection

Died	Regimental No.	Rank	First	Second	Surname	RTA	Award
	4454	Pte	Herbert	Sydney	Clabburn	11-May-19	
		Capt.	Harry	Wheeler	Brown	8-Aug-19	
	3494A	Spr	Sydney	Harold	Clerke	22-Jul-17	

Died	Regimental No.	Rank	First	Second	Surname	RTA	Award
		Lt. Col.	Tannatt	William	David	8-Mar-19	DSO, MiD
	97	Spr	Lawrence	Joseph	Doyle	18-Dec-18	
†	560	Spr	Edward	John	Flowers	KIA (29-Jun-16)	
†	118	Spr	Harold		Grabham	KIA (20 Jun-16)	
	1435	Spr	Norman	Henry	Graff	27-Sep-17	
	1723	Pte	Thomas		Hook	11-May-19	
	4044	Drv	Alfred	Clarence	Jinks	23-Jul-19	
†	427	Spr	Archie		Kennedy	KIA (20 Jun-16)	
	4386	Dvr	John		Leroy	22 Jul 1920*	
	16996	Spr	William	John	Minnis	16-Apr-20	
	4409	Spr	James	William	Murphy	25-Aug-17	
		Major	James	Barclay	Shand	10-Sep-17	
	7001	Spr	Henry		Somerville	5-Sep-19	
	2365	Dvr	John	Thomas	Stanley	6-Jul-19	
	348	Sgt	William	Charles	Gilbert	22-May-19	MC

Abbreviations

DAI   Died of Accidental Injuries
DCM   Distinguished Conduct Medal
DOD   Died of disease
DOW   Died of wounds
DSO   Distinguished Service Order
IBM   Italian Medal for Bravery
KIA   Killed in action
MBE   Member of the Most Excellent Order of the British Empire
MC   Military Cross
MiD   Mentioned in Dispatches
MM   Military Medal
MSM   Meritorious Service Medal
RTA   Returned to Australia

Symbols

†   - Died on active service
*   - Discharge date
+   - Not accepted by recipient

Note - this roll may omit some names. The author has sought, from a range of archival sources, to identify as many men as possible who served with the unit.

ENDNOTES

Chapter 1

1. Ernest Scott, *Official History of Australia in the War of 1914-1919*, Vol. XI, *Australia during the War*, Angus & Robertson Ltd, Sydney, 1940, p. 335.

2. Edgeworth David later attributed the idea of a mining corps to a mining engineer from Western Australia, Lieutenant John Thomson, who was to serve briefly with the 3rd Australian Tunnelling Company.

3. R.R. McNicoll, *The Royal Australian Engineers 1902 to 1919*, Royal Australian Engineers Corps Committee, 1979, p. 56.

4. The organisation of the Mining Corps was drafted officially by 'the Australian Department of Defence Head-Quarters' on 14 October 1915 under Circular 495, A.I.F. 143/2/8 – Formation of a Mining Corps – A.I.F.

5. AWM 224, MSS 80, Australian Mining Corps, Brief Record.

6. Oliver Holmes Woodward, *The War Story of Oliver Holmes Woodward, Captain, First Australian Tunnelling Company AIF*, MacDougalls Limited, Private Circulation, 1932, p. 10.

7. Ibid.

8. Based on the proportion of Australian tunnelling officers to other ranks who did not return from the war, the total number of Allied tunnellers lost during the war is estimated to be in the order of 5500.

9. Captain J.C. Dunn, *The War the Infantry Knew*, Abacus, London, 1994 (1938), p. 145.

10. Ibid.

11. H.D. Trounce, 'Mine Rescue Work', Professional Memoir 10, US Army Corps of Engineers, 1918, pp. 559–60.

12. Alexander Barrie, *War Underground*, Spellmount, Staplehurst, UK, 1962, p. 93.

13. Infantry subways were tunnels dug specifically to allow the safe movement of infantry from reserve trenches to the front lines.

14. Oliver Holmes Woodward, 'Notes on the Working of an Australian Tunnelling Company in France', Australian Institute of Mining & Metallurgy Proc, new series, No. 37, 1920, p. 16.

15. AMW4, Series 16/2, War Diary of the 1st Australian Tunnelling Company.

16. Woodward, 'Notes on the Working of an Australian Tunnelling Company', p. 43.

17. AMW4, Series 16/4, War Diary of the 3rd Australian Tunnelling Company, Appendix 14, April 1917.

Chapter 2

1. Private letter, Victor Morse to his wife Aileen, dated 1 March 1916.

2. Ibid., dated 10 March 1916.

3. Ibid.

4. Ibid., dated 14 March 1916.

5. *Sunday Times*, Perth, 26 March 1916.

6. Or, in 2016 currency, around $5 per day (source: Reserve Bank of Australia Pre-Decimal Inflation Calculator).

7. C.E.W. Bean, *Official History of Australia in the War of 1914–1918*, Vol. III, *The AIF in France 1916*, Angus & Robertson Ltd, Sydney, 1940, p. 65.

8. Barrie, *War Underground*, p. 191.

9. Bert Cleary, The Private War Diary of Sapper Bertie Cleary, unpublished private diary of No. 510 Sapper Bert Cleary.

10. The other sisters were Gertrude Jessie Andrews, (awarded the Royal Red Cross 2nd Class), Sarah Bell, Johanna Fleming and Julia Mary Hart (awarded the Royal Red Cross 1st Class and Mentioned in Despatches).

11. Constance Keys served in France as a senior sister with the Australian Army Nursing Service and returned to Australia in early 1920 having been twice Mentioned in Despatches, awarded the Royal Red Cross (1st and 2nd Class) and the French *Médaille des Epidémies*.

12. Cleary, The Private War Diary of Sapper Bertie Cleary.

13. This story was related by Major Victor Morse in a letter to his wife in which he named the sergeant for convenience only, as there is no record of a Sergeant Birnie (or spelling variant) aboard the HMAT *Ulysses* on that voyage.

14. D. Branagan, *T.W. Edgeworth David: A Life*, National Library of Australia, Canberra, 2005, pp. 268–69.

15. Cleary, The Private War Diary of Sapper Bertie Cleary.

16. HMS *Ausonia* was later torpedoed twice, the first time off the southern coast of Ireland in June 1917. A second and fatal attack took place on 30 May 1918, some 1000 kilometres west of Ireland. Forty-four crew members were lost and the remainder were adrift for eight days before being rescued. The ship's captain, Captain Robert Capper, was awarded the Distinguished Service Cross for his leadership during and following the sinking.

17. There were two ships named *Ausonia* at the time. Formerly named SS *Tortona* and built in 1909, the Cunard Line ship was torpedoed in May 1918 by the German submarine *U-62* with the loss of 44 lives. The second was an Italian-owned cargo steamer, built in 1883. It too was sunk by a German submarine, the *U-64*, in September 1917.

18. AWM PR84/272, letters of Sergeant Theodore (Penleigh) Boyd.

19. During the Boer War, Lord Methuen had commanded the British 1st Division, which suffered the ignominious fate of several defeats at the hands of the Boers. He had been Governor of Malta since 1915.

20. Private letter, Victor Morse to his wife Aileen, dated 9 May 1916.

21. One other tunnelling company, the Portuguese Mining Company, later served on the Western Front, arriving in France in 1918.

22. W. Grieve and B. Newman, *Tunnellers – The Story of the Tunnelling Companies, Royal Engineers, During the World War*, Herbert Jenkins Ltd, UK, 1936, p. 111.

23. Captain Hill was assistant to Colonel Stevenson.

24. Woodward, *The War Story of Oliver Holmes Woodward – 1st Australian Tunnelling Company Australian Imperial Force*, p. 83.

25. In December 1916 he assumed command of the I Anzac Light Railways where he won a Distinguished Service Order and was Mentioned in Despatches on three occasions. However, illness forced his early return to Australia in January 1918. He later served in the Second World War as a major general commanding the 1st Australian Division in 1940 and 1941. He died in October 1950.

26. Norman Macrae was killed in action on 2 October 1917 during the Third Battle of Ypres. Another who transferred from Australian Mining Corps headquarters to the 4th Pioneer Battalion was Regimental Sergeant Major Bertram Edgar.

27. Interview with Albert Fewtrell, 'Colonel Fewtrell's Return – Mining and Railway Work', *Sydney Morning Herald*, 30 March 1918, p. 12.

Chapter 3

1. McNicoll, *The Royal Australian Engineers 1902 to 1919*, p. 180.
2. Private letter, Victor Morse to his wife, Aileen, dated 16 July 1916.
3. These were the British 350th, 351st, 352nd, 353rd and 354th Electrical and Mechanical companies, Royal Engineers, attached to the 1st, 2nd, 3rd, 4th and 5th armies respectively.
4. Private letter, Victor Morse to his wife, Aileen, dated 9 July 1916.
5. Ibid., dated 21 November 1916.
6. The wording of the original military order actually specified the unit as a 'Section'. This was later amended to 'Company' under Military Order 353/1917.
7. AIF Order 143/2/372.
8. Morse's appointment as CO, along with the posting of Captain Stanley Hunter, was formalised under Military Order 40/1917.
9. Private letter, Victor Morse to his wife, Aileen, dated 13 October 1916.
10. Ibid., dated 21 November 1916.
11. Ibid., dated 12 May 1918.
12. George Norfolk died in 1931.
13. William Anderson died in 1968.
14. Private letter, Victor Morse to his wife, Aileen, dated 7 August 1916.
15. Morse is referring to captured German equipment which was reused by the company.
16. Private letter, Victor Morse to his wife, Aileen, dated 6 October 1916.
17. Ibid., dated 22 October 1916.
18. Ibid., dated 7 January 1917.
19. Morse was hit by a shell fragment.
20. Private letter, Victor Morse to his wife, Aileen, dated 4 February 1917.
21. Ibid., dated 1 March 1917.
22. Ibid., dated 27 August 1916.
23. Private letter, Victor Morse to Richard Morse dated 23 June 1917.
24. Private letter, Victor Morse to his wife, Aileen, dated 14 June 1917.
25. Ibid., dated 15 October 1917.
26. Usually No. 2346 Driver Robert ('Cobby') Cobcroft, ex-Alphabet Company, who was transferred to the 6th Australian Motor Transport Company in July 1917 but remained with the Alphabet Company as a driver.

27. The German *Minenwerfer*, referred to by the British as a 'minnie', was a German trench mortar, one of the most feared weapons on the front. These weapons were terrifying because they could be heard when fired and the projectile could be seen descending vertically, delivering a massive, destructive explosion to front-line trenches.

28. Private letter, Victor Morse to his wife, Aileen, dated 21 October 1917.

29. Private letter, Victor Morse to Richard Morse dated 23 June 1917.

30. Private letter, Victor Morse to his wife, Aileen, dated 7 June 1917.

31. The shop storeman was Sergeant Penleigh Boyd, who then remained in the Ypres salient during August and September until he was gassed and his time with the Alphabet Company drew to a close. He then returned to Australia.

32. Private letter, Victor Morse to his wife, Aileen, dated 30 July 1917.

33. Source: Reserve Bank of Australia, online pre-decimal inflation calculator.

34. Victor Morse's wife was a member of the 'Cheeros', a performing troupe of women who raised funds by whistling popular songs and tunes.

35. The Tasmanian-based Australian Mining Corps Comforts Fund is reported to have raised a total of £559 or, in today's currency, around AU$200,000 (based on equivalent average earnings).

36. Private letter, Victor Morse to his wife, Aileen, dated 12 November 1916.

37. No. 1393 Sapper Albert Torzillo who transferred to the 2nd Australian Tunnelling Company in October 1916 before moving to 4th Division headquarters.

38. AWM PR 84/272, private letters, Sergeant Penleigh Boyd, May 1916.

39. Q.M.S. — quartermaster sergeant, the person responsible for the requisition and issue of stores and equipment to men of a military unit.

40. AWM PR 84/272, private letters, Sergeant Penleigh Boyd, October 1916.

41. These men are No. 2348 Sergeant Alan Denton (DCM), No. 382 Lance Corporal Richard Grieve (Military Medal) and No. 4212 Sergeant Hubert Marsh (Military Medal), all awarded medals for gallantry during the Battle of Messines in June 1917.

42. Private letter, Victor Morse to his wife, Aileen, dated 15 July 1917.

43. AWM PR 84/272, private letters, Sergeant Penleigh Boyd, May 1916.

44. Ibid., October 1916.

45. Private letter, Victor Morse to his wife, Aileen, dated 15 July 1917.

46. With the end of the conflict later that year, William Curtis was authorised for release from prison on 12 December 1918. He joined the Australian General Base Depot at Le Havre and was repatriated to Australia in June 1919.

47. Private letter, Victor Morse to his wife, Aileen, dated 2 December 1917.

48. No. 623 Sapper Robert William Lee.

Chapter 4

1. Barrie, *War Underground,* p. 37.

2. As early as 8 February 1915, within months of the front lines along the Western Front assuming a permanent aspect, Lieutenant General Sir William Robertson, the Chief of the General Staff, had stated that 'capture of the Messines Ridge would straighten out the salient and remove anxiety in that quarter.'

3.   AWM 224 - Australian Electrical and Mechanical Mining and Boring Company Diary May 1916 – Apr. 1919, May 1916 S.P. 11 Peckham, near Kemmel.

4.   Woodward, *The War Story of Oliver Holmes Woodward,* p. 74.

5.   Ibid., p. 17.

6.   J.E. Lewis, *True World War 1 Stories,* The Lyon Press, London, 2001, p. 114.

7.   Later Major General Lambert, GOC 32nd Division.

8.   Lewis, *True World War 1 Stories,* p. 71.

9.   In addition to supplying and powering two water pumps and five ventilation fans in the mine galleries, power was also supplied to 445 lights in the mine and nearby dugouts.

10. Private letter, Victor Morse to his wife, Aileen, dated 27 August 1917.

11. Private letter, Victor Morse to Dangar, Gedye & Co, dated 30 August 1920.

12. Barrie, *War Underground,* p. 116.

13. Ibid., p. 118.

14. Hugh Thurlow was awarded the MSM, but refused to accept the award as he felt its value had been undermined due to the number awarded and the quality of those recipients he knew personally. His medal was returned unopened to the War Office. However, he eventually accepted it when it was sent to him in Australia after the war.

15. The men provided power for 400 lights and three ventilation fans in the mine galleries and associated dugouts.

16. P. Barton, P. Dolye and J. Vandewalle, *Beneath Flanders Fields,* Spellmount Limited, 2004, p. 180.

17. Ibid.

18. E.R.M. Fryer, *Reminiscences of a Grenadier, 1914-1919,* Digby, Long & Co., London, 1921, pp. 36–37.

19. J.E. Edmonds, *Military Operations: France & Belgium 1917,* Vol. I, Macmillan, 1932, reprint IWM/Battery Press, 1994, p.192.

20. Ibid., pp. 186–87.

21. Frank Hawtin died of wounds on 1 June 1917. His Italian Bronze Medal of Valour had appeared in the London *Gazette* just one week earlier, awarded for an act of gallantry on 10 March 1917. Percy Baker died of wounds on 2 June 1917.

Chapter 5

1.   Dunn, *The War The Infantry Knew,* p. 217.

2.   Grieve and Newman, *Tunnellers,* p. 277.

3.   AWM4, Series 16/1, War Diary of the Australian Electrical and Mechanical Mining and Boring Company, May 1918.

4.   Private letter, Victor Morse to his wife, Aileen, dated 5 May 1918.

5.   J.E. Hills, *The Fifth Leicestershires,* Echo Press, 1919, pp. 216–18.

6.   See Map 33 for detail of the series of British tunnels extending the length of the Hohenzollern Redoubt.

7.   E. Dodd, Private Diary of Sergeant 4209 Edward 'Hughie' Dodd, Australian Electrical and Mechanical Mining and Boring Company, unpublished private diary.

8.   The fighting strength of a battalion at that time was in the order of 700 men. Thus the

losses suffered by the four Scottish battalions amounted to around 80% of the fighting strength of the 44th Brigade.

9.   This is possibly a reference to the detonation of a German camouflet in the deep Black Watch mine workings in the early hours of 27 November 1916 where a team of men from the 3rd Australian Tunnelling Company was charging its own camouflet. The blow killed 20 miners outright and wounded another nine. This tragic event was the worst single loss of life to Australian tunnellers in the First World War.

10.   Private letter, Major Leslie Coulter to Major Victor Morse, dated 6 May 1917.

11.   Crassier dimensions as cited in Grieve and Newman, *Tunnellers*.

12.   The two large waste rock piles that are known today as the Double Crassier at Lens are not the same as those of the First World War, although they lie partially over the footprint of the earlier crassiers.

Chapter 6

1.   Louis Barthas, *Poilu, The World War I Notebooks of Corporal Louis Barthas, Barrelmaker 1914-1918* (trans. Robert Cowley), Yale University Press, 2015. Originally published as *Les carners de guerre de Louis Barthas, tonnelier, 1914-1918*, Editions La Découverte, Paris.

2.   He was Captain Plummer, MC, of the 185th Tunnelling Company. P. Robinson and N. Cave, *The Underground War, Vimy Ridge to Arras*, Pen & Sword, 2011, pp. 130–31.

3.   G.W.L. Nicholson, *Canadian Expeditionary Force 1914-1919: Official History of the Canadian Army in the First World War*, R. Duhamel, Queen's Printer and Controller of Stationary, Ottawa, 1962, p. 250.

4.   Robinson and Cave, *The Underground War, Vimy Ridge to Arras*, pp. 85–86.

5.   The Durand Group is an association of military experts whose special interest is military mining. There were a number of mines and camouflets placed by the British in readiness for the attack on Vimy Ridge on 9 April 1917 but which were not used and, as far as can be ascertained, remain in the ground where they were placed in 1917. Several were in the area now covered by the Canadian Memorial site and posed a potential threat to the site. The Durand Group was established to investigate the threat posed by these mines, namely those placed near the Broadmarsh, Duffield and Durand craters and, if necessary, render them harmless. The story of the investigation of the Durand and Broadmarsh mines is told in a documentary entitled *One of Our Mines is Missing* (Fougasse Films Ltd).

6.   Robinson and Cave, *The Underground War, Vimy Ridge to Arras*, p. 47.

7.   The preparatory Canadian artillery bombardment had commenced on 20 March and intensified on 2 April.

8.   Edmonds, *Military Operations: France & Belgium 1917*, Vol. I, p. x.

9.   Within the larger context of the battle, fierce actions took place that are now as associated with the Battle of Arras as Passchendaele is with the Third Battle of Ypres. The ferocious battles for control of Vimy Ridge and Bullecourt are just two of a host of battles intimately linked within the fabric of the larger offensive.

10.   Edmonds, *Military Operations: France & Belgium 1917*, Vol. I, p. 192.

11.   Ibid., p. 499.

12.   AWM 224 – Australian Electrical & Mechanical Mining & Boring Company Diary May 1916 – Apr. 1919.

Chapter 7

1. The common term for a 5.9-inch German shell.

2. *Wipers Times*, Vol. 2, No. 4, Monday 20 March 1916.

3. Unfortunately, the name and number of the Sergeant Wilson mentioned is not specified in the unit diary and a search of publically available databases did not identify a Sergeant Wilson serving with the A.E.&M.M.&B. Company. It is possible that this man was serving with another unit when he returned to Australia at war's end and his name therefore appears on the Australian World War I nominal roll as belonging to that unit.

4. Lieutenant Alexis Helmer was killed in action and buried in a plot in the vicinity of Essex Farm on 3 May 1915. John McCrea wrote the famous poem after the burial. Helmer's grave was subsequently lost.

5. The offensive, which General Robert Nivelle sold as a means of breaking through the German defences along the Aisne front, lasting no more than 48 hours, with few casualties, proved to be a month-long affair costing the French over 100,000 casualties with limited gains in territory. This led to a dramatic loss of morale in the French forces and the desertion of thousands of men, while entire divisions mutinied. Nivelle was removed from command and replaced by Pétain. It took months for the French to recover as a cohesive fighting unit and during this time the French sector was vulnerable to attack.

6. M. Farndale, *History of the Royal Regiment of Artillery, Western Front 1914-18,* Royal Artillery Institution, Dorset Press, UK, 1986, p. 208.

7. The gains of those brief days did not come without cost. The 11 Allied divisions involved in the fighting during the Battle of Menin Road suffered over 20,200 casualties, almost 12,300 from the Second Army divisions on the Gheluvelt Plateau.

8. Farndale, *History of the Royal Regiment of Artillery, Western Front 1914-18*, p. 844.

9. Eight Victoria Crosses were awarded on that day, six British and two Australian, most awarded for actions in taking German pillboxes.

10. J.E. Edmonds, *Military Operations: France & Belgium 1917,* Vol. II, HMSO, 1948, reprint IWM/Battery Press, 1991, p. 316.

11. This figure excludes lightly wounded, the numbers of whom were not recorded. The 12 Allied divisions that took part in the battle suffered over 20,000 casualties, of which the two Australian corps suffered just over 8000.

12. Edmonds, *Military Operations: France & Belgium 1917*, Vol. II, p. 347, n. 1.

13. Bean, *Official History of Australia in the War of 1914–18*, vol. IV, *The AIF in France 1917*, Angus & Robertson, Sydney, 1941, p. 931.

14. A sizeable advance had also been achieved by the 29th Division. Three Victoria Crosses had been won by the division that day and another by the 11th (Northern) Division. Elsewhere, advances were made to only half the distance laid down for the day's objective while, in the village of Poelcappelle, virtually no gains had been made at all.

15. Captain Clarence Jeffries of the 34th Battalion (3rd Australian Division) captured two machine-gun emplacements, six guns and over 60 prisoners. He was killed leading an attack on a third emplacement and was later awarded a posthumous Victoria Cross. The Australian and New Zealand divisions involved in the attack that day suffered 7000 casualties.

16. Nicholson, *Canadian Expeditionary Force 1914 to 1919,* p. 302.

17. In two weeks of battle, the corps won nine Victoria Crosses.

18.   Edmonds, *Military Operations: France & Belgium 1917*, vol. II, p. 364.

19.   Ibid., p. 362.

20.   The crater was so close to the road that it was possible to walk straight into it from the road. It was formed in July 1915 when the 175th Tunnelling Company blew the largest mine laid by the British to that time.

21.   The 1st Canadian Tunnelling Company was also engaged in similar work to the Australian tunnellers.

22.   Barton et al., *Beneath Flanders Fields*, p. 251.

23.   Bean, *Official History of Australia in the War of 1914–18*, Vol. III, *The AIF in France in 1916*, p. 961.

24.   AWM, 2DRl 123, pp. 40–41.

25.   Edmonds, *Military Operations: France & Belgium 1917*, Vol. II, p. 118.

26.   Private Brame was later badly wounded in the Battle of Poelcappelle during the Third Battle of Ypres when the 66th Division was part of II Anzac.

27.   Lewis, *True World War 1 Stories*, pp. 145–46.

28.   Edmonds, *Military Operations: France & Belgium 1917*, Vol. II, p. 122.

29.   The typed version of the unit history, complied in early 1919 by Victor Morse, has dates extending from 17 to 25 July 1917 when his until commenced operating at locations on the Belgian coast. I believe he meant June, since other British units and tunnelling companies arrived in mid-June 1917 and he writes that work stopped 'on the enemy's advance to the canal'. The German advance on the Yser Canal at Nieuport occurred on 10 July 1917. The cessation of works could not have occurred before the unit was supposed to have arrived at the location.

Chapter 8

1.   A recent geology graduate from Cambridge, William King was commissioned as a second lieutenant in the Royal Welsh Fusiliers in 1914. He went on to serve as a senior geological adviser in World War II at the rank of major and was awarded the Military Cross. He had already been appointed an Officer of the Order of the British Empire in World War I. Following World War II he joined Cambridge University as Professor of Geology. He died in 1963.

2.   'Geological Work on the Western Front', *The Geographical Journal*, Vol. 54, No. 4, 1919, p. 216. Transcript of readings by W.B.R. King, R.H. Harvey and J.E. Edmonds at the meeting of the Royal Geographical Society 19 May 1919.

3.   Ibid., King transcript, p. 202.

4.   They were sometimes referred to as the Hordern boring sets after the Sydney merchant and philanthropist, Sir Samuel Hordern, who paid for the purchase of the sets that left Australia with the Mining Corps.

5.   'Geological Work on the Western Front', King transcript, p. 52.

6.   Royal Engineers, *The Work of the Royal Engineers in the European War, 1914-19, Geological Work on the Western Front*, W. & J. Mackey & Co. Ltd., 1922, p. 37.

7.   Woodward, *The War Story of Oliver Holmes Woodward*, p. 55.

8.   Nine to 16 kilowatts in metric units.

9.   Royal Engineers, *The Work of the Royal Engineers in the European War*, p. 56.

Chapter 9

10. Edmunds, *Military Operations: France & Belgium 1918,* Vol. II, Appendix 10, p. 512.

11. G. Sheffield and J. Bourne (eds), *Douglas Haig – War Diaries and Letters 1914 – 1918,* BCA, Weidenfeld & Nicolson, UK, 2005, p. 405.

12. '"Stand To" on Givenchy Road' in *True World War I Stories – Sixty Personal Narratives of the War,* The Lyons Press, Guilford, Connecticut (date?).

13. Edmonds, *Military Operations: France & Belgium 1918,* Vol. II, p. 359.

14. '"Stand To" on Givenchy Road' in *True World War I Stories – Sixty Personal Narratives of the War.* Lance Corporal Owen survived his wounds at Givenchy, was taken prisoner and spent six months in hospital before being repatriated to England in December 1918.

15. Letter from Robert Stokes to Victor Morse, First Army HQ, dated 7 May 1918.

16. Private letter, Victor Morse to his wife, Aileen, dated 28 April 1918.

17. Ibid., dated 20 May 1918.

18. Ibid., dated 2 June 1918.

19. In what has become known as the Second Battle of the Marne, the French Tenth, Sixth and Fifth armies, which included a number of British and American divisions, turned back the German forces in the huge salient formed over two months of fighting and withdrawal. The battle resulted in an estimated additional 170,000 German casualties.

20. Edmonds, *Military Operations: France & Belgium 1918*, Vol. III, Macmillan, 1939, Reprint IWM/Battery Press,1994, Appendix XX, p. 368.

21. Sheffield and Bourne, *Douglas Haig War Diaries and Letters 1914-1918,* p. 417.

22. Edmonds, *Military Operations: France & Belgium 1918,* Vol. IV, HMSO, London, 1947, Appendix V, p. 532.

23. Ibid., pp. 6–7.

24. Ibid., p. 22.

25. 'jake' was the slang term for 'in good order'.

26. General Sir William Birdwood, GOC Fifth Army.

27. Private letter, Victor Morse to his wife, Aileen, dated 1 September 1918.

28. Ibid., dated 8 September 1918.

29. *The Geographical Journal,* Vol. LIV, No. 4, October 1919, p. 215.

30. Ibid.

31. Private letter, Victor Morse to his wife, Aileen, dated 29 September 1918.

32. Ibid., dated 22 October 1918.

33. Ibid., dated 11 November 1918.

Chapter 10

1. Private letter, Victor Morse to his wife, Aileen, dated 17 November 1918.

2. Quoted in the preface to this volume.

3. Private letter, Victor Morse to his wife, Aileen, dated 25 December 1918.

4. Ibid., dated 14 February 1919

5.   Sir Gerard Moore Heath, KCMG, CB, DSO (1863–1929), arrived in France in May 1915 as a brigadier general and was appointed Chief Engineer II Corps. In November 1915 he was appointed Chief Engineer, First Army, under Haig before becoming Engineer-in-Chief at GHQ from October 1917 until the end of the war. He retired from the army in December 1919.

6.   Private letter, Victor Morse to his wife, Aileen, dated 5 May 1919.

7.   Ibid., dated 20 July 1919.

8.   The Imperial War Graves Commission is now the Commonwealth War Graves Commission with headquarters based in Maidenhead, Berkshire.

9.   Figures taken from *The Work of the Royal Engineers in the European War, 1914-19*, p. viii.

10. Figures taken from *The Geographical Journal*, Vol. LIV, No. 4, 1919, p. 212.

BIBLIOGRAPHY

Official Documents

Department of Defence Headquarters, Circular 495, A.I.F. 143/2/8 – Formation of a Mining Corps – A.I.F., dated 14 October 1915.

AWM Files

AMW4, Series 16, War Diary of the 1st Australian Tunnelling Company.

AWM2, DRL 123, Extracts from 'Letters from the Front' by Major G.I. Adcock, 2nd Australian Tunnelling Company, AWM File No. L/12/11/2112.

AWM 224 MSS79 Part 3, Australian Electrical and Mechanical Mining and Boring Company, War Diary.

AWM 224, MSS 80, Australian Mining Corps, Brief Record.

AWM PR84/272, letters of Sergeant Theodore (Penleigh) Boyd.

Personal Documents

Private letters of Major Richard Victor Morse, DSO, CO Australian Electrical and Mechanical Mining and Boring Company.

The Private War Diary of Sapper Bertie Cleary, unpublished private diary of No. 510 Sapper Bert Cleary.

The Private Diary of Sergeant Edward 'Hughie' Dodd, Australian Electrical and Mechanical Mining and Boring Company, unpublished private diary of No. 4209 Sergeant Edward Dodd.

Books

Barrie, Alexander, *War Underground,* Spellmount, Staplehurst, UK, 1962.

Barthas, Louis, *Poilu, The World War I Notebooks of Corporal Louis Barthas, Barrelmaker 1914-1918* (trans. Robert Cowley), Yale University Press, 2015. Originally published as *Les carners de guerre de Louis Barthas, tonnelier, 1914-1918*, Editions La Découverte, Paris.

Barton, P., Dolye, P. and Vandewalle, J., *Beneath Flanders Fields,* Spellmount Limited, 2004.

Bean, C.E.W., *Official History of Australia in the War of 1914–1918,* Vol. III, *The AIF in France 1916,* Angus & Robertson Ltd, Sydney, 1940.

——, *Official History of Australia in the War of 1914–18,* vol. IV, *The AIF in France 1917*, Angus & Robertson, Sydney, 1941.

Boyd, P., *Salvage,* Australian War Memorial Facsimile Edition, 1983.

Branagan, D., *T.W. Edgeworth David: A Life,* National Library of Australia, Canberra, 2005.

Dunn, Captain J.C., *The War the Infantry Knew*, Abacus, London, 1994 (1938).

Edmonds, J.E., *Military Operations: France & Belgium 1917*, Vol. I, Macmillan, 1932, reprint IWM/Battery Press, 1994.

——, *Military Operations: France & Belgium 1917,* Vol. II, HMSO, 1948, reprint IWM/Battery Press, 1991.

——, *Military Operations: France & Belgium 1918*, Vol. III, Macmillan, 1939, Reprint IWM/Battery Press, 1994.

——, *Military Operations: France & Belgium 1918,* Vol. IV, HMSO, London, 1947.

Farndale, M., *History of the Royal Regiment of Artillery, Western Front 1914-18,* Royal Artillery Institution, Dorset Press, UK, 1986.

Fryer, E.R.M., *Reminiscences of a Grenadier, 1914-1919,* Digby, Long & Co., London, 1921.

Grieve, W. and Newman, B., *Tunnellers – The Story of the Tunnelling Companies, Royal Engineers, During the World War,* Herbert Jenkins Ltd, UK, 1936.

Hills, J.E., *The Fifth Leicestershires,* Echo Press, UK, 1919.

Lewis, J.E., *True World War 1 Stories*, The Lyon Press, London, 2001.

McNicoll, R.R., *The Royal Australian Engineers 1902 to 1919*, Royal Australian Engineers Corps Committee, 1979.

Nicholson, G.W.L., *Canadian Expeditionary Force 1914-1919: Official History of the Canadian Army in the First World War*, R. Duhamel, Queen's Printer and Controller of Stationary, Ottawa, 1962.

Robinson, P. and Cave, N., *The Underground War, Vimy Ridge to Arras*, Pen & Sword, UK, 2011.

Royal Engineers, *The Work of the Royal Engineers in the European War, 1914-19, Geological Work on the Western Front*, W. & J. Mackey & Co. Ltd., UK, 1922.

Scott, Ernest, *Official History of Australia in the War of 1914-1919*, Vol. XI, *Australia during the War*, Angus & Robertson Ltd, Sydney, 1940.

Sheffield, G. and Bourne, J. (eds), *Douglas Haig – War Diaries and Letters 1914 – 1918*, BCA, Weidenfeld & Nicolson, UK, 2005.

Woodward, Oliver Holmes, *The War Story of Oliver Holmes Woodward, Captain, First Australian Tunnelling Company AIF*, MacDougalls Limited, Private Circulation, 1932.

Articles, Pamphlets and Book Chapters

'Geological Work on the Western Front', *The Geographical Journal*, Vol. 54, No. 4, 1919. Transcript of readings by W.B.R. King, R.H. Harvey and J.E. Edmonds at the meeting of the Royal Geographical Society 19 May 1919.

'"Stand To" on Givenchy Road' in *True World War I Stories – Sixty Personal Narratives of the War*, The Lyons Press, Guilford, Connecticut.

Trounce, H.D., 'Mine Rescue Work', Professional Memoir 10, US Army Corps of Engineers, 1918.

Woodward, Oliver Holmes, 'Notes on the Working of an Australian Tunnelling Company in France', Australian Institute of Mining & Metallurgy Proc, new series, No. 37, 1920.

Newspapers

Sunday Times (Perth)

Sydney Morning Herald

INDEX